I was there: The Beatles

by Richard Houghton

Text © Richard Houghton 2016
This first edition © Red Planet Books Ltd 2016

Publisher: Mark Neeter
Editor: Matt Milton

For photo credits see www.redplanetzone.com

ISBN: 978 1 9059 5994 5

Printed in the UK by CPI

I was there: The Beatles

by Richard Houghton

Contents

CONTENTS

CONTENTS

ACKNOWLEDGEMENTS

I could not have written this book without the help of a number of people. I am indebted to the many local and regional newspapers in the UK that kindly featured my initial appeal for people to come forward with their Beatles memories. Several papers were more than happy to run a follow-up piece, knowing that their readerships would volunteer further information and reflecting the great affection with which The Beatles are held to this day by the British public. The same was true in Australia and New Zealand, where I could not have obtained so many personal testimonies without the help of the press. In particular I'd like to thank Terry MacCallum at the *Dundee Courier* and Mike Hill at the *Lancashire Evening Post* for their assistance.

I should like also to thank my many Beatle friends on Facebook who contacted me with memories that I have included, and those that promised stories but weren't able to meet my deadline. I'm sure their stories are on their way as I write. My email address is thebeatlesinthe60s@gmail.com.

The Beatles have been the subject of almost as much analysis in the digital age as they were before the internet became part of our everyday lives. As an online resource I found myself referring to beatlesbible.com in order to check key dates, although a number of the shows described in here had to be verified through other research.

I'd like to thank: Des Henly and Richard Whitehouse, for permission to use an extract from their blog about The Beatles visit to Weston-super-Mare; Beth Kaplan for permission to quote from her book *All My Loving: Coming of Age with Paul McCartney in Paris*; Ray Douglas at Aberdeen Council for the background information about the Beach Ballroom in Aberdeen; David Dills for the Two Red Shoes, Elgin advertisement; the Lancashire Evening Post for permission to reproduce the quotes from Mike Dryland, Mick Garry and Derry Jackson; Norman Scott for permission to reproduce his Beatle photographs and Garth Cawood for permission to reproduce his.

I should also like to thank all of my contributors for taking the time to share their Beatle memories with me and in particular Andi Lothian for his memories of meeting and contract negotiations with Brian Epstein following their unsuccessful first Scottish tour; Fraser Elder, whose cartoon drawing of the group went around the world; Ron Watson, who saw The Beatles many times and who revealed an enthusiasm for and encyclopaedic knowledge of the music of Merseyside in the early 1960s. Ron was also kind enough to introduce me to the music of Kingsize Taylor and the Dominoes and The Big Three.

Finally, I should like to thank: Kate Sullivan for her patience and her willingness to feed me at regular intervals; John Gordon, a jazz guitarist who has made his entire living through music and who didn't rate The Beatles back then and still doesn't rate them now, but who was kind enough to share his memories of sharing a dressing room at The Cavern and set the pre-Beatles music scene in Britain; and my mother, who took me to see The Beatles at the tender age of four. I don't remember anything of it, but others can testify to the fact that – I was there!

Richard Houghton, 2016

The Quarrymen (John Lennon, centre) at St Peter's Church – Mark Fischer is the baby in the audience

EARLY DAYS

John Lennon and Paul McCartney first met at
Woolton Village Fete. John was performing
there with his band, The Quarrymen...

I WAS THERE: MARK FISCHER

ST PETER'S CHURCH

6 JULY 1957, WOOLTON, LIVERPOOL

*The young and
dapper Mark Fischer*

I was three or four when I saw The Quarrymen
at the village fete. I was with my mum. I don't
remember much about it but I do remember
meeting Julia Lennon. Julia was a playful woman
who loved music. She always nurtured the kids.
When I was three-and-a-half I lived with my
father and mother on Newcastle Road, right
across from Julia.

My mother Phyllis and Julia were best friends
and cousins. They would hang out quite
frequently, as my father told it to me. They would

bake together and share each other's recipes such as strawberry cherry pie. They would go out together, taking me with them while my father was at work. They brought me to the first Quarrymen show.

I was too small to remember much but I do remember John holding me after the show when he came to greet his mother. Julia and her friends would sometimes come over for dinner with John. My father and mother adored John over dinner, with his sarcasm and blunt jokes. Julia would often tell John to hush, thinking my mother and father would get offended but they only laughed and enjoyed his company all the more.

Mark Fischer's mother was Julia Lennon's best friend and cousin

ST SILAS SCHOOL

1957, LIVERPOOL

I was in the same class as Richard Starkey (Ringo Starr) at St Silas School. He was just one of my classmates. I remember him because, as a result of a playground scrap we had at the age of about seven, I was smacked on the back of my legs by the head teacher in front of the whole school.

I was a bit of a teacher's pet with the head teacher and it didn't seem fair. After junior school we went our separate ways. although there was a shop at the end of our street which repaired bikes and radios, and which also recharged the large batteries which were used to power the wireless. Richard spent a lot of time in that shop. I don't know whether he was paid or whether he just had an interest in what went on.

I next saw Richard when I was working as an air hostess for a small Liverpool-based airline. 'Love Me Do' was becoming popular and Richard was flying to London. He looked at me and said, in his strong Liverpool accent, 'I know you, don't I? You're...' We spent some time talking about the old days at primary school.

I WAS THERE: GEOFF GRIPTON

LIVERPOOL INSTITUTE

1958, LIVERPOOL

As a pupil at the Liverpool Institute, Geoff Gripton was a schoolmate of Paul McCartney and George Harrison

I was at the Liverpool Institute through the late Fifties and both Paul and George were pupils a couple of years ahead of me. My brother Cliff was in the same form as George and, for a period, we would walk across town in a group from school towards the Hardman Street area, where George and others would get their buses home.

We would then walk on to Skelhorne Street for our bus. I can recall George with his quiff and grey waistcoat and school tie, reversed to be as thin as possible.

I WAS THERE: RICHARD AUSTIN

LIVERPOOL SCHOOL OF ART

LATE 1950s, LIVERPOOL

I passed the 13+ exam and ended up at the Liverpool School of Art in Gambier Terrace, the junior school to the Liverpool College of Art, which was five minutes away. Cynthia Powell [later Cynthia Lennon] was in the year ahead of me. I recall Cynthia as being quite good-looking and very quiet, giving the impression of being aloof since she lived in Hoylake. In her book about her time with John, Cynthia indicates she first met him at the College of Art. But I believe she became acquainted with him during her time at Gambier Terrace, prior to attending the College of Art.

The first time I heard the name Lennon was

> **❛ Fights would start and Lennon would be warned off the school ❜**

Richard Austin (above, second from left) and friends from the Liverpool School of Art; and with special friend, leather jacket and bicycle (left)

when my school friend Tony Campbell, who was in love with Cynthia, said he couldn't understand why she liked John Lennon. I was soon to learn by observation that he was a bit of a Ted. On the occasions Lennon came over to the junior school, I believe to see Cynthia, trouble followed him. He would come accompanied by a group of his hangers-on, who were other Teddy Boys from the College of Art. His companions, although having a very similar disposition, appeared to be in awe of him. Fights would start and he would be warned off the school property by teaching staff.

My cousin David attended Quarry Bank Grammar School at the same time as John Lennon. I asked him about Lennon a couple of times and all David would say was 'oh, *him*!' I then worked in a commercial art studio in Duke Street, close to Ye Cracke pub. Rice Street was a few minutes' walk from the College of Art. I spent a lot of time drinking there – probably too much time. On the odd occasion, Lennon would be there with Cynthia. I'd met him a couple of times but we were just on nodding terms. I always formed the impression that when he was in the pub something would happen. A fight or a fierce argument would erupt. He seemed to have all the trappings of a catalyst. Later, during lunch times I would be at The Cavern where The Beatles, resembling mini Gene Vincents, would put on a tremendous show.

I WAS THERE: IRENE EDWARDS (AGED 13)

ST JOHN'S YOUTH CLUB

1959, ORRELL PARK, LIVERPOOL

Nicky Crouch and Trevor Morals of the St John's Youth Club band, with Faron Ruffley on guitar (centre)

My friend and I knew them in the late Fifties when they used to play opposite our youth club's band at gigs around the dance halls in Liverpool. There was a bloke called Nicky Crouch who was the lead guitarist and a bloke called Eric London who were the early members of this group. Trevor Morals was the drummer. I was very friendly with them until I was about 16, 17.

Then, as it evolved and they got more expensive equipment, Nicky and the drummer joined Faron's Flamingos and then they became The Ravens. It was the time that Pete Best and Stuart Sutcliffe were with Paul and John, before Ringo arrived on the scene. The leader of our youth-club group went to the same school as Paul and John.

In the early days, when no one had any money, the youth club girls would support the group by helping with the transport of the instruments on the Liverpool buses, taking them to the various dance halls. We would help to put the instruments behind the stage and see The Beatles during change over time halfway through the evening.

Nicky and his group would be on from half seven until a quarter to nine. And then The Beatles might be on for the second set. So we'd take equipment back in to the back of the stage and swap over. I don't think I really ever had conversations with them.

But when they started playing we'd be in the front of the stage dancing in front of them and you'd get a nod of recognition out of them. The Beatles were quite frightening really, because they used to dress all in black leather.

IN THE CAVERN

In 1960, The Beatles made their first visit to Hamburg in Germany, where they stayed for more than three months. They began 1961 by playing around the Liverpool area; In February they appeared for the first time at The Cavern Club.

I WAS THERE: JOHN GORDON

CAVERN CLUB

1961, LIVERPOOL

The Cavern was a jazz club. I was in the Clyde Valley Stompers, one of the main Scottish bands touring up and down the country, and I also joined one of the bands in Manchester which was called the Jazz Aces. We used to appear fairly regularly at The Cavern, once every two or three months. Liverpool was like most of the cities in the UK in late 1961, 62. You had two camps of fans. You had the ones who liked rock 'n' roll and the popularity of the *Oh Boy!* show and all the rest of it. But, amazingly, you had this other half which liked traditional jazz. And it was hugely supported, mainly by the student elements throughout all the universities up and down the country – the art schools and so on.

A lot of these little independent clubs up and down the country would feature generally nothing but trad jazz. They very much made an allowance by allowing skiffle groups to appear in jazz clubs. And then it was decided: 'They are popular, these skiffle groups, so we'll make it so that they do an interval spot.'

So that was the general format that you would come across in some of the regional jazz clubs – there'd be an established local skiffle group which was popular and they would share part of the bill with the main bands. They used to use the existing PA which wasn't very good. It consisted of two mics and fairly small speakers that were attached to The Cavern wall itself. It wasn't a sophisticated PA system. It would be very, very basic whatever it was because generally speaking the six-piece jazz bands played acoustic. You only had a microphone at the front and that was for announcements and vocals and maybe the clarinet player, bringing the clarinet nearer to the microphone. That was the only sort of amplification people used.

The Cavern was unlicenced, in as much as you couldn't get a drink in the place. We didn't really stay in the club long enough to get to know The Beatles because we headed out to go and have a drink. And that would be the interval and then they would come on in the interval. I can remember them coming in. We shared the same dressing area, which was located just

John Gordon, the jazzman who had a minor altercation with The Beatles when they didn't get out of the way fast enough at The Cavern

at the side of the small stage of The Cavern. It was only a small room and there'd be nine, ten of us in there. I remember them in the form of a skiffle group heading towards a bluesy type of sound. I can remember times when we played there and they would come on at the interval and the crowd would follow us out to the bars. The audience would just subside down to about maybe 25 people, sitting around chatting and talking. They'd be doing their thing on stage and then we would come back in.

And we usually hung around and gave them the nod that 'after the next number, we'll come on' sort of thing. And then it would be the general melee in the changing room – us trying to grab our instruments, them trying to grab their instruments. One day we did a gig and we didn't have an altercation as such, but they weren't getting out of the way fast enough for us to grab our gear. It was John Lennon and Paul McCartney. We had a bit of a tussle, shoving them out the way while we got our gear because the dressing room was so restricted.

The local Manchester musicians would be all right with them but the Scottish musicians – the type that I was playing with, who were typical Glaswegians – were not very friendly at the best of times. We played at The Cavern roughly 12–15 times when The Beatles were on. We never got to a situation where we as a band thought 'well they're more popular than we are.' The audience had actually come to hear us and not them. So The Beatles were on and the audience accepted that.

It wasn't a particularly big place. It didn't hold a helluva lot of people. And financially it wasn't a particularly good gig. I don't think they got paid much. The appearance that they try to convey in programmes now about that period of time is that, sensationally and overnight, they took the world by storm. To a certain extent it was pretty fast but it wasn't as fast as that. They put in a lot of playing time before they got any recognition.

I WAS THERE: RON WATSON (AGED 16)

CAVERN CLUB

14 JULY 1961, LIVERPOOL

I saw The Beatles play many times, including 12 times at The Cavern between July and December 1961, eight times in Southport and five more at The Cavern in 1962 and in March at the Southport Odeon and May at the Liverpool Empire in 1963. That's 27 times altogether. The band that emerged after Epstein's influence was a different group, but they had to change in order to get the degree of success they wanted. They were a tough bunch but were style-setters both in terms of clothes – like Cuban-heel boots – and indeed in their material, which went right through the R&B and rock 'n' roll era. They put their own stamp on it to great effect. The nearest you get to getting some idea is probably the BBC recordings, because the Hamburg tapes are a bit rough.

I was in The Cavern the first time Brian Epstein came down and remember it well, and also when George Harrison got a black eye after Pete Best was sacked. George would always chat at lunchtime about music and was serious about it, Paul was the ladies man and John was usually disagreeable – whilst Pete was the most popular with the girls. During the same period, 1961–62, Ringo also appeared in Southport at a small club as a member of Rory Storm and the Hurricanes and he was the most experienced member as he was the oldest. And he also had a stage name.

I'm half-Canadian. My mother was Canadian. I went to the local grammar school and then went to work for a company called Canadian Pacific that was in the Royal Liver buildings in Liverpool, on the front. So it was easy to go to The Cavern for the lunchtime sessions. And I was told off by the boss every day because I came back late. They were an interesting phenomenon because the audiences were relatively small – 50 to 100 people. The Cavern lunchtime sessions were very informal. But that was nice because they would talk to you, even people like me. They didn't have any money, so if you bought them a Coke or a hotdog you were a friend for life.

I'd started taking an interest in music when I was 11 years old. My mum bought me a copy of Elvis's 'Hound Dog'. A lot of the stuff that people thought was new I was actually quite familiar with, because it would be B-sides of The Coasters or something like that. I'd had that originally on 78s. So I perhaps had a bit more background knowledge than most. But they'd often come up with stuff I'd never heard of. And I'd immediately rush round to NEMS record shop to try and find the original and get a copy of it. Was George Harrison's version of 'Roll Over Beethoven' as good as Chuck Berry's? No. Was John Lennon's version of 'Twist and Shout' better than the Isley Brothers? Yes it was. They were highly distinctive. If you shut your eyes you knew who they were.

Who was the best band at the time? The Big Three. The other groups would go and see them. When I started to go down, The Cavern had switched from being a jazz club to a rock 'n' roll club. So the way it worked, The Beatles would play two or three lunchtime sessions and Gerry and the Pacemakers would play the other two. And they played from half past twelve to ten past one and half past one to ten past two. That was the schedule, the two sets. But they got two different lots of audiences. We were all doing our one-hour lunch breaks. So you'd get those that came to the first ones, and they then had to get back to work. And people like me that went to the second ones. So the change in The Cavern was pretty profound. It literally was a jazz club and then it completely switched and went on to purely rock 'n' roll. And they brought out quite a lot of innovation.

They'd play one or two original numbers but

A telling-off from the boss was a small price for the young Ron Watson to pay for getting to see The Beatles in his lunch-breaks

❝ I was in The Cavern the first time Brian Epstein came down... and also when George Harrison got a black eye after Pete Best was sacked ❞

Arthur Alexander, the American country-soul singer who sang 'Anna (Go to Him)' and 'Soldier of Love', both covered by The Beatles

essentially they were a covers band. But what they did find was the more obscure American rhythm and blues-type music which was often brought in on the ships from people that worked for Cunard. So Arthur Alexander, Richie Barrett, a whole raft of people. You can hear some of the music on the BBC recordings but you don't get the depth or the fact that they were as loud as they were from recordings like that. But you get some idea.

They were loud in The Cavern, big style, but they weren't the loudest band. The loudest band was the Big Three. Epstein took them on but they didn't get anywhere because they wouldn't do what The Beatles did, which was to conform. There were lots of bands around and often the repertoire was the same. The Beatles had found them out first. So most bands did 'A Shot of Rhythm and Blues'. But The Beatles were the first to do it. The most popular numbers didn't actually make it into the albums.

At lunchtime they weren't under any pressure in terms of appearance. They'd come in in whatever they wanted to come in. So John Lennon turns up one day in a corduroy suit. Well nobody had ever seen a corduroy suit before. 'Where did you get that from?' There was a slight class element in it. The audiences at lunchtime were all basically office and shop workers. They weren't what you might describe, for lack of a better phrase, working-class.

At the evening shows there was more of a mixture of people. But they were still wearing the black leather stuff. And then Epstein took the view that that had to change. He put them in suits and basically they went along with it because they craved success. Or John and Paul did. So they were prepared to compromise. There were quite a few of the Merseyside groups who wouldn't.

And they had the black leather gear, which Astrid Kirchherr had introduced them to. Nobody had ever done that before. The boots that they wore weren't actually the ones that became known as Beatle boots. They bought them when they were over in Germany and they were a different design. First time I saw them I thought 'these are good'. But Liverpool, being Liverpool, at The Cavern somebody shouted out 'What are you doing wearing girls' high-heeled shoes?' which George didn't take too kindly to.

> ❛ John Lennon turns up one day in a corduroy suit. Well nobody had ever seen a corduroy suit before ❜

The Big Three were the loudest of The Cavern acts, according to Ron. From left to right: Johnny Gustafson, Johnny Hutchinson, Brian Griffiths

THE
BIG
THREE

Decca Records

23

There was no discernible Beatlemania, although they had a lot of people there that liked them. You didn't get the screaming and all that sort of stuff. And of course the audience was slightly different because they were people like me who were in what you might call white collar jobs. A lot of the girls worked in the local offices, like Cilla Black. Cilla was a typist but she took my coat and hung it up for me in The Cavern. So the audience was vastly different from the audience at night, because word got round.

The lunchtime sessions were informal. And didn't last that long. They used to play two 30-minute sets. McCartney said they'd never been better than when they did those sessions. When they became very popular, all that was lost. Then you might pay fifteen shillings [75p] to listen to 25 minutes of girls screaming, when I used to pay a shilling [5p] to watch them play for an hour. It was a different product, that's perhaps the best way to put it. They would open their shows with one of three numbers – 'Hippy Hippy Shake', 'A Shot of Rhythm and Blues' or 'Some Other Guy'. On some days seeing them wasn't that big a deal. It was something you could do three times a week. So why would you put it in your diary every single time you went?

John was a troubled character. He would come across as being aggressive, disagreeable. I remember going up to him one lunchtime session in the break and saying 'I really enjoyed that number. Where did it come from?' He just said 'Eff off!' Whereas George Harrison would stop and he would tell you, 'Oh, it's the B-side of so-and-so', and 'It's on this label'. That type of conversation. John rebelled as much as he could. So when they went on stage and started wearing suits he was the always the one who wouldn't do up his tie. Two of them were grammar-school boys. Two weren't. Paul was the PR guy. George was the serious one. He would talk to you about music. He would practise even in the breaks. He bought himself a new Gretsch guitar when they started getting a bit of money and you could really tell it was his pride and joy.

Most of the time I was there, Pete Best was the drummer. It was quite a big issue when Pete was booted out. Ringo had to work pretty hard to get over that. I was there when Ringo stood in for Pete Best for the first time because Pete had a sore throat. But I don't remember it. Pete Best getting the boot – that did not go down at all well. Pete is a really nice guy and he wasn't treated well. He was very popular because he was good-looking and the girls loved him. Whether technically he was a better drummer than Ringo Starr I don't know.

Ringo played on a Sunday afternoon at one of our local places in Southport with Rory Storm and he had his own feature spot. He was actually the most experienced and the oldest. And he had all the gear. But he had to fight hard to gain acceptance and it took quite a while.

I WAS THERE: IRENE EDWARDS

CAVERN CLUB

1961, LIVERPOOL

As our youth-club band became more proficient they joined up with Billy Jones and renamed themselves The Ravens. They would then be on the opposite half of the evening at The Cavern. I went a lot then to the Mardis Gras and to The Cavern. I went with my girlfriend who I went to Queen Mary High School with. I was just going to see whoever performed.

I never went at lunchtime. It was always night time. It was rock 'n' roll. There were other groups in Liverpool whose music I liked better at the time. Cilla Black of course was the cloakroom attendant who then went on to sing with the groups. My Cavern days slowed down in autumn 1961 because I was then studying for A-levels and the amount of homework clipped my wings. It was then only at weekends.

I WAS THERE: RON WATSON

CAVERN CLUB

9 NOVEMBER 1961, LIVERPOOL

I remember when Brian Epstein came down to see them. When you're 16 or 17, the guy who's 24 or 25 who comes down wearing a cravat tends to stand out! I can remember him standing at the back, in what were the arches, looking somewhat bewildered. And I think he had Alistair Taylor (Epstein's personal assistant) with him at the time. And you could tell from the look on Brian's face that he was mesmerised by this. He'd never seen anything like it. But to him they were a bit scruffy, ill-disciplined. So Epstein made them the offer and the rest, as they say, is history.

CIVIL SERVICE CLUB

14 NOVEMBER 1961, LIVERPOOL

Rhona Simon (née Christian), with her husband Bob, back in the Sixties

I grew up on the outskirts of Liverpool and was a teenager in the late Fifties and early Sixties. I became a civil servant and consequently joined the Civil Service Club in the city. It was a club for young people, and many of the groups that became part of the Mersey Sound performed there on a regular basis. Rory Storm and the Hurricanes, The Big Three, Gerry and The Pacemakers, The Four Jays and many other future household names were regulars.

We were located in a little alley called Lower Castle Street, near to Liverpool Town Hall, and were open Tuesday, Thursday and Sunday. I was a committee member and we were responsible for booking the groups. As Tuesday nights were being quite poorly attended, we decided to try and boost the night by booking The Beatles. We paid them £20 per night for four consecutive Tuesdays. They played for the first time on 7 November 1961.

Pete Best was still part of the line-up then. We knew Ringo as Rory Storm's drummer. Pete was the heartthrob of the night – for me at least! I recently came across my diary from that year and the entry for 14 November reads 'Club, Beatles OK. Had good time.' What an understatement that turned out to be! It has always been one of my regrets that I never did go to see them at The Cavern. It certainly was a great era to be a teenager in our great city.

MERSEYSIDE CIVIL SERVICE CLUB

THE FABULOUS BEATLES

On Tuesday, 7th November, 1961

Guest's Ticket 3/-

The member whose name appears on the reverse of this ticket must accompany the bearer and sign the Visitor's Book at the time of admission

I WAS THERE: JIM FINN

CAVERN CLUB

1961–62, LIVERPOOL

I was a teenager in the early Sixties and we used to go to the lunchtime sessions in The Cavern from 12 noon to 2 p.m.. It was two shillings [10p] to get in. The Beatles would be on one day and Gerry and The Pacemakers the next, and it would alternate like that. There was great rivalry between them. One time, when Pete Best was the drummer, The Beatles were belting out a song and Gerry Marsden sneaked

Jim Finn, another Merseyside teenager who was a lunchtime Cavern regular

into The Cavern and worked his way round to the electrical sockets at the back of the stage and pulled them out. He ran out of The Cavern accompanied by some of the foulest language from John Lennon you have ever heard.

One of the elements of The Beatles' popular appeal was the contrast between the two frontmen – John Lennon, the rough and ready type, and Paul McCartney, the ever-polite smoothie. George Harrison sometimes looked as though he had just got out of bed and come straight to The Cavern whereas Pete Best, who I knew at school, was always immaculately turned out.

When we would leave The Cavern, grown-ups – shoppers and office workers – walking past would look disapprovingly at us teenagers, probably because of the very loud music coming from within and spilling out into Matthew Street, which is very narrow and yet, then, was able to accommodate a two-way traffic system.

I WAS THERE: GORDON VALENTINE

CAVERN CLUB

EARLY 1962, LIVERPOOL

We played in a talent competition at The Cavern, a Battle of the Bands type thing. We pulled up outside The Cavern and we loaded our gear in. The walls were dripping.

The place was just smelling of disinfectant that they threw around on the floor. It was a horrendous place. But the acoustics were fantastic. How it got past any fire regulations beats me.

I WAS THERE: FAITH BARTON (AGED 18)

KINGSWAY CLUB

22 JANUARY 1962, SOUTHPORT

I worked in NEMS at the time Brian Epstein became interested in The Beatles [before he became their manager]. Above the shop there was a staff restroom. I was up there one day when the internal phone rang. I was the only person there at the time so I answered it. It was Brian. He wanted to know if I had ever heard of them. Obviously we had a good chat about them. Lots of people were coming into the pop-music department downstairs asking for the record they were on.

Shortly after that he saw them for himself. And the rest, as they say, is history. I used to go to The Cavern most lunchtimes and lots of evenings. It had a unique smell! Before the first time they played at the Kingsway, Brian asked me to organise a coach trip to Southport to support them. This I did with help from a part-time employee, a student who was waiting to join the RAF. It wasn't easy. We really had our work cut out convincing The Cavern Club audience that they wanted to go.

If I remember correctly it cost them five shillings [25p] for transport and entry. Even with the busload there, I don't think the Kingsway was overly full.

I WAS THERE: CHRIS RIMMER

I was on the circuit in the Sixties with lots of bands. My band was Chris and the Quiet Ones. The name came from being asked to turn it down because we were too loud at a local dance. We started playing spots of 20 minutes between

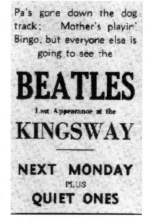

Pa's gone down the dog track; Mother's playin' Bingo, but everyone else is going to see the

BEATLES

Last Appearance at the

KINGSWAY

NEXT MONDAY
PLUS
QUIET ONES

' Brian wanted to know if I had ever heard of The Beatles. Lots of people were asking for the record. Obviously we had a good chat... '

proper dances and we played a lot at the Palace Hotel, Birkdale. We played the YMCA, the Clifton, the Queens and various venues on Lord Street.

But our favourite venue was the Kingsway, run by Mr Ruane. He was an Irishman and a great fella who loved us. He ran the Marine Club on the top floor. Our claim to fame was that we played support group to The Beatles the first four times they appeared in Southport. Pete Best was still playing drums. We talked to Brian Epstein. We had a good rapport with the boys, swapping guitars and all that stuff. George Harrison told our rhythm guitar player, Ray, that one day he might be able to afford a guitar like Ray's pink Fender Strat.

The Beatles photographed in Southport. The former Kingsway Club building finally burnt down and was demolished in 2010

I WAS THERE: KEVIN FINLAYSON

KINGSWAY CLUB

29 JANUARY 1962, SOUTHPORT

The Diplomats played the Kingsway with them. Pete Best was with them. They had a heck of a job to carry their gear upstairs. Three floors you know. They used to have a lot of rock bands up there. They had a good sound. They were just... together! They were nice lads. They weren't big time or anything.

I WAS THERE: RON WATSON

KINGSWAY CLUB

5 FEBRUARY 1962, SOUTHPORT

The Kingsway gigs in particular, where I saw them six times in total, were when The Beatles were at their peak and they were outstanding. In 1962 they really were at their best. Those dates at the Kingsway, where they did slightly longer sets than they would do at The Cavern lunchtimes, that was when they were at their peak as a band and, of course, very few people actually saw that. Those of us that did were lucky.

The set-up at the Kingsway was roughly two 45-minute sets. I well recall helping Pete carry his drums up the stairs; I think on the last date, Ringo stood in for him as he was ill. They were good and they knew it, so there was a slight arrogance about the performance because they knew they could blow everybody else off the stage. They had a wide repertoire. They'd often come up with numbers and you'd think 'Where did they find that from?' The Kingsway ones were in my diary because they were tremendous shows.

If you saw them in that local context, you saw a band that the rest of the world never saw. It was the clothes and the general attitude. Remember: in '61 or '62 people were watching The Shadows doing things in shiny suits, doing funny little steps. And then all of a sudden – bang – this band appears on stage in black leather jeans belting out this very loud music. The contrast was tremendous.

It was Jerry Lee Lewis who said that during that period of time all of America was full of Bobbies – you know, Bobby Rydell, Bobby Vee, all this sort of sanitised stuff. And the one thing The Beatles weren't in those days was sanitised.

I WAS THERE: ROGER BROWN (AGED 19)

SUBSCRIPTION ROOMS

31 MARCH 1962, STROUD

The Beatles came to our local weekly dance at Stroud Sub Rooms before they released their first real hit, 'Love Me Do', so I did not know who they were. They were billed as 'Liverpool's Number One Group', which did not mean as much to us in Gloucestershire as maybe it would in Liverpool. So we did not know them. But we were at a critical age and knew our music, going to Subs each week where different groups played, and buying all the good hits we could afford.

This may seem a strange way to be impressed and become a great fan even before their record was released, but every Saturday night

'Liverpool's Number One group' didn't mean much to Gloucestershire's Roger Brown, but he went to see The Beatles at the Subscription Rooms anyway

before I went out I always watched *Jukebox Jury* on TV. The records would be brand new, some due to be released the following week, and normally played for the first time on the programme. 'Hey! Baby' by Bruce Channel was played on the TV that night and was so good I remembered it. It is a great record and has a wonderful harmonica part in it. That night, John Lennon said he was going to play this new record.

Knowing the quality of the normal Saturday night groups I waited for them to spoil the song and backing – it is not easy to play. Wow – was I surprised! John on the harmonica was really great and their version was better than the original in my opinion. I was a fan from that day.

What a great, never-to-be-forgotten night! I was not surprised at their success. It's funny when the rest of the world likes them too. You almost feel cheated, as you foolishly think you discovered them.

I WAS THERE: JENNIFER FABB (NÉE FARRANT, AGED 18)

My mum, Hazel Farrant, provided refreshments at the Stroud Subscription rooms for various clubs including the Freemasons and the chess club during the week. At the weekends, she provided refreshments for visiting singers and bands on Saturday evenings. I usually helped mum at these functions. I was working at Stroud Shambles Nursery School during the week. I looked forward to Saturdays, when I heard new bands and singers. I remember I was given plastic caps to wear on

The pre-Fabb but very fab Jennifer Farrant

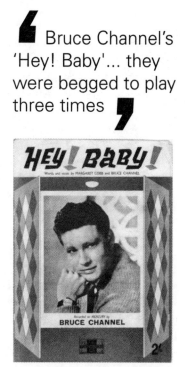

❝ Bruce Channel's 'Hey! Baby'... they were begged to play three times ❞

my stiletto heels to protect the floor at the Subs.

Mum particularly remembers when The Beatles came because Paul asked her for some hot water so he could shave. I am sorry to say I never spoke to any of The Beatles. What a shame!

I WAS THERE: GEORGE LODGE (AGED 22)

The Beatles came as a band to dance to. No chairs were put out. The Subs, as we called them, was a weekly dance. I arrived when the music was in full swing. You just had to pay on the door to get in. I believe it was the Rebel Rousers on stage when I got there. The crowd was already dancing away. Ten minutes after they finished their stint The Beatles took the stage for the dancing to begin again. I remember the dancing slowly stopped as the crowd were all turning towards the stage to watch and listen to the band.

It was soon quite obvious that these young men were something special. I recall two numbers they performed – Leroy Van Dyke's 'Walk On By' and Bruce Channel's 'Hey Baby'. The latter they were begged to play three times. After their time was up they left the stage down the steps. Many of the young people came and crowded round them, shaking their hands. There was no screaming but very warm feelings towards them. I was told later that the boys went for a beer in the Post Office pub opposite.

I WAS THERE: RICHARD AUSTIN

TOWER BALLROOM

29 JUNE 1962, NEW BRIGHTON

I remember being at a dance at the Tower Ballroom, New Brighton, and Lennon yelling and screaming at a heckler who seemed to be having a problem with the band. Lennon had to be restrained by George and Paul from jumping off the stage and getting it on within the crowd.

THE ROCKING

TOWER

BALLROOM, NEW BRIGHTON
LEACH ENTERTAINMENTS
PRESENT

OPERATION BIG BEAT 3

Friday, 29th June, 1962
MERSEYSIDE'S
TOP TEN GROUPS

STARRING PARLOPHONE & E.M.I. RECORDING ARTISTES

THE BEATLES

SUPPORTED BY
★ The Big 3
★ The 4 Jays
★ Kansas City 5
Kingsize Taylor and The Dominoes
★ The Undertakers
★ The Searchers
★ Johnny Templars Hi-Cats
★ Lee Curtis & The Detours
ALSO THE SENSATIONAL LAUNCHING OF A NEW DANCE CRAZE SWEEPING AMERICA

"THE TRANCE"

LICENSED BARS UNTIL
12-15 a.m.
LATE TRANSPORT
Liverpool and all Wirral areas
Coaches leave St. John's Lane, Lime Street, 7-30—8-30 p.m.

TICKETS 6/-
Rushworths, Nems, Strothers, Lewis's and your local record shops.

McILROY'S BALLROOM

17 JULY 1962, SWINDON

I was one of the 160-odd people there with my then girlfriend. We were regulars at the dances and saw quite a few of the rock 'n' roll groups at that time. To be honest, The Beatles were just another group but they did play a lot of the R&B-type music that I liked, plus they played a Buddy Holly and The Crickets number which, as a big fan, put them right up in my estimation!

I was a frustrated guitar player and remember being taken by John Lennon's Rickenbacker, which I had not seen before, and Paul McCartney's Hofner bass. I've got to say there was nothing that made me think that they were shortly going to be the biggest group the world has ever seen, but I would love to be a time traveller and be able to go back to that night knowing what I know now!

BELL HALL

20 JULY 1962, WARRINGTON

I was at the Bell Hall the night The Beatles played. It was on a Friday night and they held music every Friday with a live band – a modern-day disco. Pete Best was the drummer. I was almost 16 and I used to go to keep my brother's girlfriend company as he used to leave us there. She is now my sister-in-law. It was a brilliant night and my eyes were only for Paul. I thought he was brilliant. They were marvellous and it was a great evening. My only regret was that I never got their autographs.

My dad liked music and I told him about the brilliant band I had Sseen and that they were going to be on a programme called *Six Five Special* on what is now Granada. They duly played. What they played I can't remember, but dad said they were rubbish.

But it wasn't long before he changed his mind, possibly because I bought all their records and played them all the time.

I WAS THERE: MIKE RUANE

KINGSWAY CLUB

23 JULY 1962, SOUTHPORT

Mr Joe Ruane (back row, second from right), owner of the Kingsway Club

I didn't actually see The Beatles myself. I was too young. However, my father owned the Kingsway Club in the early Sixties and he employed The Beatles several times. I remember him saying he paid them £8 for their last appearance at the Kingsway.

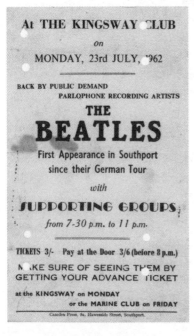

At THE KINGSWAY CLUB

on

MONDAY, 23rd JULY, 1962

BACK BY PUBLIC DEMAND
PARLOPHONE RECORDING ARTISTS

THE

BEATLES

First Appearance in Southport
since their German Tour

with

SUPPORTING GROUPS

from 7-30 p.m. to 11 p.m.

TICKETS 3/-   Pay at the Door 3/6 (before 8 p.m.)

MAKE SURE OF SEEING THEM BY
GETTING YOUR ADVANCE TICKET

at the KINGSWAY on MONDAY
           or the MARINE CLUB on FRIDAY

Camden Press, 9a, Hawesside Street, Southport.

I WAS THERE: GARTH CAWOOD

CAMBRIDGE HALL

26 JULY 1962, SOUTHPORT

I started as a disc jockey. My parents had a ballroom – they were ballroom dancers. I started off with a record-player with a spindle where you put eight records on. But there were horrible pauses in between, so I started to introduce the dances just to fill the pauses up.

I was doing something at The Cavern Club in Liverpool and Joe

❝ I'd like you to meet two protégés of mine. This is Paul Beatle and this is John Beatle ❞

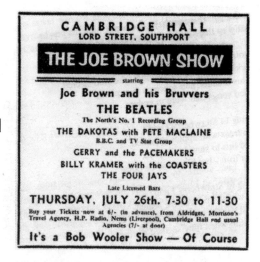

CAMBRIDGE HALL
LORD STREET, SOUTHPORT

THE JOE BROWN SHOW

starring

Joe Brown and his Bruvvers

THE BEATLES
The North's No. 1 Recording Group

THE DAKOTAS with PETE MACLAINE
B.B.C. and TV Star Group

GERRY and the PACEMAKERS

BILLY KRAMER with the COASTERS

THE FOUR JAYS
Late Licensed Bars

THURSDAY, JULY 26th. 7-30 to 11-30

Buy your Tickets now at 6/- (in advance), from Aldridges, Morrison's Travel Agency, H.P. Radio, Nems (Liverpool), Cambridge Hall and usual Agencies (7/- at door)

It's a Bob Wooler Show — Of Course

Brown and His Bruvvers were playing; I knew two of the Bruvvers so I turned up that night, just as a punter really, because I was in Liverpool. And they said, 'We're doing a show for Brian Epstein in Southport. Why don't you come with us?' So I went with them.

Joe was top of the bill because 'A Picture of You' was number one and the supporting bands were all Brian Epstein's bands. I was sat with the Bruvvers in the dressing room and we were all sat with our backs to the mirrors. And Brian came in. I had met him at The Cavern and spoken to him before. He came in and he said, 'Joe, I'd like you to meet two protégés of mine. This is Paul Beatle and this is John Beatle.' He always called them John and Paul 'Beatle' at that time.

Later on I spoke to him. I said, 'Look Brian, I've got these clubs and these ballrooms in Yorkshire and I'd like to bring a couple of the bands over. I asked, 'Will they travel?' He said 'Yes'. So I said, 'Can you give me some clues as to the prices?' So he took a business card out, a NEMS Enterprises business card, and he wrote on the back: 'Beatles, £35; Gerry and the Pacemakers, £18; Billy J Kramer and the Coasters, as it was then, £15; and The Big Three, £11.'

So I went back to my friend I was working a couple of these places with and we said, 'Let's take it steady.' So we booked the Big Three for three nights at £11 a night. And they drove back to Liverpool each night and there were no motorways then of course. And I got to know The Beatles very well.

**I WAS THERE:
ALAN WRIGHT**

MARINE HALL

25 AUGUST 1962,
FLEETWOOD

I was a member of a well-known and very popular Fleetwood band called The Trespassers. I stood in the wings watching The Beatles literally die on stage that night. We played the Marine Hall quite a few times before and after and had a loyal following in the area. A number of people have claimed to have played at

The Trespassers: they watched from the side of the stage while The Beatles 'died' on stage

the Marine Hall on that night and, over the years, more than a few have approached me to confirm that they made the story up.

Having done our set we were approached by an associate of The Beatles who offered a 'well done, lads' and then told us that if we were interested he could arrange for us to get work in Hamburg. I often wonder how different our lives might have been if we had taken up the offer.

I WAS THERE: JENNY MASKELL

CAVERN CLUB

MID-1962, LIVERPOOL

We just turned up and paid on the door. When I used to go, it was just like ordinary blokes. John Lennon was sarcastic. Very sarcastic. I didn't really like him very much because I was so young. I couldn't cope with his sarcastic attitude. I'm sure some of the older girls could. But I used to love George. George was lovely. He used to treat everybody the same. And Paul was the same. We all loved George and Paul. But John was very sort of sarcastic all the time. You felt as though you couldn't just have a chat with him. But the others seemed to appreciate the fact that they had the fans there and they used to give you photographs and sign things. George and Paul were my favourite Beatles. I used to like John Lennon's music. I used to like his vocals. In fact I preferred them to the other two really. But personality-wise it was definitely George and Paul.

It was very small. It was just like a tunnel really. There was no alcohol at The Cavern. It was great because my parents were happy with that. Because I was underage, obviously. The licensing age was 21 in those days. I was only about 14, 15. And they used to just come on and do the odd set in-between other people. I went with older people from Huddersfield, who were about 18 or 19. Nobody checked your age. But obviously there wasn't any drinking.

They didn't play in long sections. I didn't care who else was playing. So we just used to hope there were a few sets played while we were there. At the beginning they were very accessible people. And then they started bringing their LPs out and then they became untouchable for us really quite quickly.

We went over to Liverpool once and we went to George Harrison's mother's house for tea. She invited us in, which was quite odd really. And I was only about 15. But also it would sound strange to a parent now, allowing your 15-year-old to do that – people seemed a bit safer in those days. And that's why we were able to go around on the train or the bus and go to these places. Our parents thought we were quite safe.

I WAS THERE: JAN BOUNDEN (NÉE BIRD)

CAVERN CLUB

AUGUST 1962, LIVERPOOL

I'd gone up to Liverpool to meet a school friend who had a cousin there and we went to The Cavern. That raised my interest in The Beatles. I didn't see The Beatles in The Cavern but I did experience the atmosphere you get with The Cavern Club. And I do remember quite distinctly the look of it – the steaminess you used to get. Because you went underground to the old Cavern. And I remember doing something called the Liverpool Stomp.

I WAS THERE: ALAN LAVERY

TOWN HALL, LYDNEY

31 AUGUST 1962, LYDNEY

I was in a band called The Rebel Rousers. We were a local band based in Cirencester and we supported a lot of the groups. We supported Gene Vincent, The Barron Knights, people like that. Most of the top people in those days, because we were on the circuit playing Forest of Dean, Lydney, Birmingham, Bristol.

I played lead guitar. We played rock. We had a contract to do all the American bases. On a Saturday night, if you were playing, it was for squaddies. But when you did a Sunday night in the officers mess, you had to play waltzes and things like that. We did a lot of country and western. We could play most things. I supported them when they played in Stroud, and in Lydney the night before. When we got that first booking for The Beatles they weren't known round here. Obviously that's why all the posters said 'The Sensational Beatles' and that, because they were more known up in Liverpool.

Town Hall, Lydney

Both places were packed. They had good PR in Epstein. He sort of got the word about. They were in suits. Just ordinary suits. We just sat in the dressing room and talked like you do with most other groups. They said to us, 'What do you do between the gigs?', because we went on for three-quarters of an hour and they went on for three-quarters of an hour. In between that we sat and chatted. 'What do you do now?' 'Oh, we go over the pub now.' So they said, 'Well, that's what we'll do then.'

And then at the end of the evening we just sat down and chatted like you normally do with most groups. Chatted about who you'd played with and things like this. They were on the way up then. We didn't get a sense that they were going to be anything big. We played with most bands and some of them were brilliant, but you never got the same sort of vibe with The Beatles. Sounds Incorporated. We played with them a lot. They used to back a lot of bands as well. Musically, they were much better really. They were brilliant.

I can't remember what we got paid, but it wasn't a lot in those days. We used to practise on a Tuesday and Thursday because we always aimed to get two new numbers out a week. Those days there were so many different bands, so many different styles, and that's what we used to try and do so we could be kept up with everything. I had a day job. I was a mechanic. Cozy Powell used to come and listen to our practices. Our drummer taught him to play. He's dead now. I'm the last one standing in The Rebel Rousers.

The Fab Four in early September, 1962

I WAS THERE: TONY MARTIN

SUBSCRIPTION ROOMS

1 SEPTEMBER 1962, STROUD

I was at this dance. I was jiving with a few friends right in front of the stage all night and so was very well aware of what went on. I didn't think they were very good. I'm not saying they were bad, but they weren't very good. Their performance was absolutely nothing like their subsequent performances and recordings. These weekly Saturday night dances had been going on for years and we were used to hearing a lot of really tight bands. That was our benchmark and yardstick. By comparison The Beatles didn't make a great impression.

There were probably many mitigating factors for this. I remember Jock (the Subscription Rooms manager) telling us that they'd driven all the way down from Liverpool (few motorways in those days) and had arrived exhausted, penniless and hungry. He took them to the local fish-and-chip shop and bought them a meal. Not a good start. Their repertoire was all standards. This may have been at the suggestion or insistence of the promoters. There was certainly no sign of what was to come.

If they'd given any hint of 'Love Me Do', 'Please Please Me' or 'I Saw Her Standing There', it would have been unforgettable. They didn't, and it wasn't. We also have to remember that Stroud does not compare in any way to Liverpool or Hamburg. I don't recall the hall being empty – I would say it was comfortably full.

I WAS THERE: TONY NEWSON

BRS BALLROOM

27 SEPTEMBER 1962, BIRMINGHAM

Tony Newson, having a jive on the dance-floor, in August 1962

It was in Ward End. Sadly they knocked it down a couple of years ago. The Charles Russell Hall was the actual British Road Services social club the rest of the week. That's where they went to have their sandwiches during the day. It had a stage at the one end and it wasn't too big a size. It was just the job for how they were then. I think it was run by Reg Calvert, an agent from Rugby way. He was the promoter for it and I think he was the one who brought them down. The dance was called the Teen Beat. It was there for a few years. It went through from pre-Beatles, through the Joe Browns and people like that. They were in their leathers. We loved them. They were great. They looked a

Tony Newson, whose Beatle haircut was why his wife first fell for him

bit rougher than what we were used to. We were used to the likes of Joe Brown in his smart suit and tie. And then you got the scruffy-looking Beatles. At that time we all dressed smart as well. We all had suits and ties on. So they were a bit of a revelation.

But it was the music that did it. The music stood out for me. And the picture of The Beatles at that period, with Pete Best slumping over his drums looking very insolent, that was just how they were. They did have that rebellious outlook – but it was the music that sold it. Pete Best was still drumming for them the first time I saw them. My ex-wife, who I met down there, has got that photo. I'm sure if Ringo was with them then, they wouldn't have been giving those pictures out. I remember them announcing on stage that they were about to issue their first single. And I remember they played 'Love Me Do'.

I was a service engineer then and I used to get about quite a bit. Once, I was on my way back from Stoke-on-Trent and we went into a cafe. 'Love Me Do' was on in there and I recall thinking, 'Wow, I remember them singing that on stage'. It felt like I was a part of it. Of course, I was mainly there for the girls in those days.

I WAS THERE: VAL DINGLEY (AGED 15)

It was at the BRS in Bromford. My friend Linda and I, we were groupies in those days. We went every Thursday to see groups. It was before they'd done the first record so they weren't really famous. They came on

Val Dingley and her friend Linda Stokes: Linda got to snog Paul while Val had to settle for John

and we were really impressed with them. They were still in leathers then. They were rock 'n' roll. They did announce that they'd made a record. And we followed them out to their tour van, stalking them. As you do.

As they went to get in the van we asked if we could have the autographs. So they gave us pictures of them with the autographs and we got chatting. And then had a bit of a snog! But I wasn't really pleased because I liked Paul. We both liked Paul, you see. And unfortunately I got John. And she got Paul. And then they invited us into the tour van, with the beds and everything, and then I think we got a bit frightened.

Did we have a drink? No, I don't think we had a drink. We just had a little chat. They signed the autographs and that was about it. And then we saw them at the Plaza in Handsworth. I think they were in the suits and they'd had the hit record. So when we saw them in '63 they were all smartened up. I've got Paul McCartney's autograph and I've got John Lennon's autograph on a picture of Pete Best. I'haven't got Pete's autograph. I've got a picture of Pete Best but he wasn't actually with the group then. I was gonna sell it, but my daughter Anna's such a Beatles fan

I had it framed and gave it to her because she wanted it.

I was more of a Stones fan myself. I saw the Stones at the Plaza. I can't remember too much about it. That's where all the big acts in Handsworth were at the time. We saw a lot of the early groups up there. We were groupies. We used to hang about, you know? Shane Fenton. Screaming Lord Sutch – I had a little snog with him. I was terrible! I've never kept all the autographs. I should have done.

My husband had the round collar and the Beatle haircut then and that's why I first liked him. Because he looked like one of The Beatles!

Author's note: The Beatles' first single, 'Love Me Do', was released on 5 October 1962

I WAS THERE: TONY CAMPBELL

CO-OP HALL

5 OCTOBER 1962, NUNEATON

I was in a band called The Mighty Avengers and I worked with The Beatles at Nuneaton Co-op Hall on the Friday that their first single, 'Love Me Do', was released. George and I had a Chet Atkins jam in the dressing room.

CO-OPERATIVE BALLROOM, NUNEATON

TEEN BEAT
TONIGHT
BUDDY BRITTAIN
AND THE REGENTS

AND FOR THE FIRST TIME IN NUNEATON, THE
FABULOUS NEW RECORDING GROUP

THE BEATLES

SUPPORTED BY THE AVENGERS

THE BIGGEST-BEAT SHOW EVER!

7.45 to 11 pm. Admission: 5/-

Above: advert for the Buddy Brittain/Beatles gig, supported by The Mighty Avengers (below), for whom Tony Campbell sang and played lead guitar

THE MIGHTY
AVENGERS

Decca Records

COPYRIGHT

Above: The Mighty Avengers, featuring our contributor Tony Campbell. Managed by Andrew Loog Oldham, the group had a hit with 'So Much in Love'. Below: the Co-Op Hall, where they supported The Beatles

TOWER BALLROOM

12 OCTOBER 1962, NEW BRIGHTON

I managed to see The Beatles perform three times. The first time was at the New Brighton Tower Ballroom when, along with a multitude of other groups, they supported Little Richard. I thought that The Beatles that night were phenomenal. 'Love Me Do' had just been released and they had a charismatic energy about them that was just irresistible.

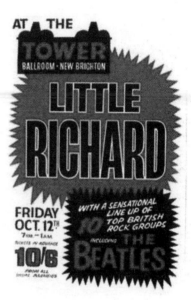

AT THE TOWER BALLROOM · NEW BRIGHTON

LITTLE RICHARD

FRIDAY OCT. 12TH
7PM — 1AM
TICKETS IN ADVANCE
10/6

WITH A SENSATIONAL LINE UP OF TOP BRITISH ROCK GROUPS INCLUDING THE BEATLES

They looked so very different for a start. Most group members still had Teddy Boy hairstyles back then, Ringo included. They had better gear than the other groups and a great raw driving sound with wonderful harmonies to match.

The fact that they had three front-line vocalists also set them apart. Most of the other groups on that night were good, notably the Big Three and Lee Curtis and the All Stars (with Pete Best on drums). But The Beatles put them all in the shade, and Little Richard too in my opinion.

> 'Love Me Do' had just been released and they had a charismatic energy about them that was just irresistible

PUBLIC HALL, PRESTON

26 OCTOBER 1962

I was at both the Preston gigs. At the first one, only about a hundred people were there. We went backstage at the interval because we recognised the drummer, who was at Butlins with Rory Storm and The Hurricanes. Of course that was Ringo. And my cheeky mate said, 'Remember us from Butlins?'. To which he said, 'Yes'. I'm not sure he did.

I WAS THERE: PETE MORRIS

The second time I saw them, exactly two weeks after the first, was at Preston Public Hall. That night remains one of the greatest memories of my teenage years and is still fresh in my mind now, even after 54 years. The Beatles were second on the bill to Mike Berry and The Outlaws, who had recently been in the hit parade and were supplemented by a local dance band, The Syd Munson Orchestra.

All these assorted musicians shared a large communal dressing room to the right of and behind the stage at the Public Hall. There was no need for any security at all because nobody was actually famous at this time, so you could freely wander in and out of the backstage area without anybody questioning you. Only being 14, I wasn't interested in drinking in the bars, so I spent the whole evening either watching the groups on stage or hanging out in the dressing room and so I managed to observe The Beatles at close quarters.

To me as a young teenager, it seemed that they had arrived from another planet. I had never met anybody remotely like them. They looked so different from everybody else, they sounded different in conversation and they had a really wacky *Goon Show* humour between them that was unique.

That night I think they played three sets of about two hours in total. I remember leaning up against the front of the stage when they played their first spot and the dance floor was almost empty. I remember John Lennon holding his hand over his eyes, looking out and saying 'Good evening, everybody, wherever you are.'

They started playing and sounded so good, despite the lack of atmosphere and no lighting on the stage whatsoever, apart from the normal houselights. It's hard to imagine now, with all the great music they produced in the following years, that they were a covers band in 1962. I remember them playing some Chuck Berry, Elvis, 'Sheila' by Tommy Roe and songs like 'Mr Moonlight' and 'A Taste of Honey', which made it on to albums later. As the night went on, the hall became full and The Beatles rocked the place.

Other things I recall from the dressing room are standing next to George Harrison and Paul McCartney and one of The Outlaws, who were all sitting down playing big semi-acoustic guitars doing some Chet Atkins-style country picking. The Outlaw was, I think, Ritchie Blackmore of Deep Purple fame and the bass player was Chas Hodges from Chas and Dave.

I remember John Lennon being asleep at one point on a long table in a corner of the room. George was mainly quiet and just having conversations with one or two people. Paul and Ringo, however, were very lively. Paul was very chatty and Ringo was quite loud and funny. Every time someone offered Ringo a ciggie, he would take the whole packet off them and offer everyone else one.

I remember sitting on a table next to Paul while he was writing out a setlist and inviting suggestions from others about what songs to sing. There were no other Beatles involved in this,

Pete Morris (middle) saw The Beatles in Preston in 1962 and recalls John Lennon being asleep on a table

though. Somebody said 'A Picture of You' by Joe Brown but Paul dismissed it, saying it had become old hat.

I can also remember standing on the steps at the side of the stage with Paul and my older brother, watching Mike Berry and The Outlaws on stage. How I wish I had a camera with me that night to capture some of those moments. At least I managed to get all their autographs, which I still have to this day.

I WAS THERE: GORDON VALENTINE

ST JAMES' CHURCH HALL

23 NOVEMBER 1962, GLOUCESTER TERRACE, LONDON

I met them twice. One time we applied to the BBC for an audition. There was a show coming up for talent new to television. The audition was on Friday. It was at St James' Church Hall in Gloucester Terrace. We went by train. We put the amps and guitars in the guard's van and rode down by train. It was very pleasant. And on the way down I was reading the *New Musical Express* and I was reading about this funny-looking group called The Beatles. I'd heard 'Love Me Do' and it was different.

We got two London cabs to put all the gear in and set off to Gloucester Terrace, and when we pulled up Epstein's big white Jag was outside. Although we didn't know it was his at the time. We walked in and ten feet away from us The Beatles were playing a Chuck Berry tune. Then they played 'Love Me Do'. I'd been playing guitar from about 1959, playing in all sorts of groups, and ended up with The Johnny Taylor Five.

We'd seen groups come and go, so it was no big deal to see The Beatles, who were

The Johnny Taylor Five, with Gordon Valentine far right

going to be famous, there. We had a chat with them and we put our gear on the floor and set up. We did the audition and we got the show. And The Beatles didn't. It was a programme called *The 625 Show* from Bristol, a national programme, and the compere was Jimmy Young. I think we had about 12 million viewers.

I WAS THERE: ALAN VAUGHAN

Alan Vaughan and friends: Vaughan auditioned for the same BBC TV show as The Beatles

During 1962 a colleague and I, both from Stroud, attempted to break into the popular music business, having written a number of songs and performed for some years.

We attended the same BBC TV audition as The Beatles. We were auditioned directly after The Beatles and chatted to them. We loaned George our Vox amplifier when his packed up.

I WAS THERE: KEVIN FINLAYSON

CLUB DJANGO

6 DECEMBER 1962, QUEEN'S HOTEL, SOUTHPORT

The name of our band was The Diplomats. We were a Southport band and we specialised in the Buddy Holly stuff, though we used to do Beatles stuff and general rock 'n' roll. We used to do a lot in Southport, and travel around a lot – we actually played with Freddie and The Dreamers, Billy J Kramer, Gerry and The Pacemakers and Sounds Incorporated. We were busy, out five or six nights a week. That's all we did for five or six years.

On Monday nights, we used to play at Belle Vue. Jimmy Savile was the DJ. He used to have pink hair. We played with The Beatles at the Queen's Django Club on a Thursday night, before they had any hits or anything. And Paul's amp had gone off, his bass amp. He and Ringo came over. Ringo came over to look at my kit. I had an American kit, a Ludwig kit, you know. And I said, 'Of course you can borrow the amp.' And we had a little natter and Ringo said he liked that kit and I said they'd go a long way and he said, 'Well I don't know about that.' So I was right, wasn't I? Because he's worth £190 million – approximately!

I wonder if he remembers that? I obviously influenced him because a few months after, I think they were on *Scene at 6.30*, and he had the drum kit there, the same kit.

I WAS THERE: RON WATSON
CAVERN CLUB

7 DECEMBER 1962, LIVERPOOL

There was another club in Liverpool called the Iron Door, which is where The Searchers made their name. The Cavern was the principal venue, but they played all over Merseyside as they got more popular and more well-known. And Epstein wanted to move them around a bit. They started playing on the outskirts. And then they did their first nationwide tour and then basically that was it. They essentially left Liverpool. At that stage, for people like me, that was almost the end of the era. They were never the same. And when they started putting on those round-collar suits and had those rather silly photographs sipping out of Coke bottles, this was not The Beatles we knew. But it was probably necessary for a commercial and acceptance point of view.

We were very fortunate. You saw them develop. You saw them change, particularly after Epstein took over. But you also saw them as a rock 'n' roll band that were literally unbeatable. There were lots of bands on Merseyside who were extremely good. But The Beatles wiped the floor with most of them – with probably one exception, The Big Three. When The Beatles came back from Hamburg they were more professional, they were more distinctive. They learnt a lot out there. People were pleased they were doing as well as they did, but we all knew they'd gone. They were just not the same sort of band. You had all these thousands of people screaming and you think 'What is all this about?'

**MEMBERSHIP CARD
1962 SEASON**

Ending 31st December, 1962

I was over in the States a few years ago and I did a radio phone-in which went across Michigan, Ohio and all these places. And this lady rang and said she'd seen The Beatles at Shea Stadium in New York in 1965. And I said, 'Well actually you didn't.' If you saw Elvis in Las Vegas in 1976, it wasn't the same Elvis that was on the Louisiana Hayride in 1955 or '56. It was a different product. Unless you saw them at the Star Club in Hamburg or The Cavern in Liverpool or other venues in '61, '62, you never really saw them as a band.

Kingsize Taylor and The Dominoes made an album out in Hamburg for Polydor. It was the best album of the era by a Merseybeat group. And The Beatles' tracks were recorded by Kingsize Taylor. The quality's poor and the performance is pretty sloppy because it was New Year's Eve and I think they were blind drunk. There's no recording that captures what it was like to be there during that period and I think it's a great shame.

TARTAN BEATLES

In January 1963, The Beatles embarked on a short tour of Scotland.

I WAS THERE: ARTHUR MCKERRON

TWO RED SHOES

3 JANUARY 1963, ELGIN

Rugby-loving Arthur didn't really go for the mop-top look

I was a rugby player. I played hooker. We used to go there every night after rugby, after the game or after training, and have a meal. It would have been a Thursday. The back café was part of the Two Red Shoes. You entered it from the front side, looking down towards the old library. We were sitting in the dining area downstairs, next to the kitchen. Mrs Bonici was there, the wife of the owner at the time.

And they owned the Two Red Shoes. And I said, 'Who's that playing upstairs tonight?' 'Oh,' she says, 'it's some group called The Beatles.' And I said, 'Oh, do you mind if I go upstairs?' Because you could go upstairs and through to the dance hall. 'Can I come and see who's up the stairs there?' And she said 'Aye, up you go.' And I went up and there was just these four boys on the stand, on the platform.

The place was deserted. One couple were more or less just walking or jiving around the hall and three or four couples were at a wee higher level where they had seating and tables. And about two of the tables had folks sitting at them. And that was all that was in the place at that time. And that would have been somewhere in the region of 9 o'clock at night because we had just finished our meal. The place was dead. At that time nobody recognised them.

I WAS THERE: ADELINE REID

In the Sixties I was a student nurse training at Dr Gray's Hospital in Elgin. Along with another student I lived in a boarding house not far from the Two Red Shoes ballroom. The landlady was very genteel, a companion to a Lady before getting married. She was aloof and did not tolerate bad manners. We were her girls and she was very protective of us. All boyfriends were given the once-over for approval or not.

Next door was another boarding house whose owners were friends of Albert Bonici, the owner of the Two Red Shoes. All of the artists who appeared at the ballroom stayed there and, as you can imagine, it was an exciting time

A cheeky John Lennon leaned out the window and asked student nurse Adeline to take his pulse

for us next door to meet with some of them.

However, along came The Beatles and seemingly their appearance at the Two Red Shoes did not go down too well. My friend Joan and I were unable to get tickets and, if I remember rightly, the cost was 4/6 [23p], quite an expense for us in those days. Regardless, next day when I was about to go to hospital for duty,

THE ELGIN FOLK MUSIC CLUB
Presents

The "Love Me Do" Boys
THE BEATLES
plus

The Alex. Sutherland Sextet
in

THE TWO RED SHOES
on

THURSDAY, 3rd JANUARY

9 p.m. - 1 a.m.   Admission 6/-.

Buses return to Buckie, Forres, Coast, Lossiemouth, etc.

The Beatles were hanging out of the window next door. I could have reached out and touched them.

Their personalities were cheeky and outrageous, and not what we were used to. I thought they were fun. Wearing a hideous outdoor nurse's uniform, they shouted comments at me. John Lennon asked me to take his pulse. My face went the colour of a tomato. At the house door appeared our landlady, who proceeded to reprimand them for their cheek. She did not approve of them talking to her girls in such a shocking manner! You can imagine the chat at the hospital – especially a week later, when The Beatles became famous.

I WAS THERE: FRASER GOW (AGED 18)

TOWN HALL, DINGWALL

4 JANUARY 1963

I worked for the Milk Marketing Board. I had another two mates with me that day. One was James Burgess. He had muscular dystrophy and he was in a wheelchair. And the other was James Gordon. The hall that was used wasn't used that often. The venue was the local town hall in Dingwall itself. It was one of the halls that was donated by Carnegie. He donated it to the town. There's an upstairs and a downstairs. You could probably get a couple of hundred into it if they were dancing. It would be now and again that a special band would come up.

We always went up the road to what they called the Pavilion in Strathpeffer, where they held dances every Friday and Saturday night. That was the in place for going dancing but we thought, 'Well we'll go and see what these guys are like.' I reckon there was about 20 of us there in total in a great big hall. It was just pretty empty. They were quite a loud band and in an empty hall it was probably making it worse. More echo than anything else, you know? Because there wasn't the crowd to dull the noise. They were a bit of a rock band. We thought, 'Och no, we can't be arsed with this.' So the three of us went away up to the local dance further up the road. The other venue used to run free buses to their venue, so we went off to see the local band which was The Melotones.

I think they cut their losses and stopped playing. I think the ones behind us got their money back. And about three weeks later they were the in thing! And they were off and running.

I WAS THERE: DOREEN DOUGLAS (AGED 18)

I was a dance-mad teenager and along with my late sister and friends decided we would go to Dingwall to see for ourselves what all the fuss was about concerning this new pop group. I was never a fan of The Beatles and it took a lot to give up Strathpeffer Ballroom and The Melotones but after some thought we decided we would give it a try. Along with the Melotones I think there was also one of the Irish showbands, which was really fab. There was no contest.

The Town Hall was almost empty and the few that were there, including my crowd, all shared a taxi and headed to the Strath. The Beatles were getting pennies thrown at them along with the jeers. Someone told me later that The Beatles had been seen in the bar at Strathpeffer Ballroom sussing it out.

I WAS THERE: SARAH PURCHASE (AGED 18)

I clearly remember them. It was a bit of a disaster as just a handful turned up. Myself and my friends were not impressed with them and left for Strathpeffer to see the group at the Pavilion. I can remember Ringo Starr was not there and the rest just sat around the stage making conversation with us, and feeling disappointed by the turnout.

I WAS THERE: BILLY SHANKS (AGED 17)

They weren't very well known at that time. The word on the street was they were four lads from Liverpool. I didn't know anything about them. It didn't register that they had recorded 'Love Me Do'. And the funny thing is that when I went in the door to go in and go upstairs, the doorman said, 'Before you pay, go up and have a listen.' They actually played that song, 'Love Me Do', when I looked in the door and I thought, 'No, no, it's not my type of music.'

I walked out and went to the local village hall five miles away to hear The

The Town Hall in Dingwall, where hardly anybody turned up to see The Beatles

Melotones. I'm afraid I wasn't a very good judge of the music, because about six weeks later they were top of the charts and three months later they were worldwide and they changed the face of music. They were dressed very smart, all in black suits. Long hair, obviously, which hadn't hit the Highlands of Scotland by that time. We were still in short-back-and-sides. I suppose some of the locals would say they looked scruffy. But they were tidy. A lot of the locals who came to the door decided 'no, that's not my style of music' and went to Strathpeffer.

The 19 that did stay talk about it to this day. One lad told me 'I pulled up outside the hall. I saw this green Volkswagen Beetle van with black beetles painted on the side and thought they were gypsies or tinkers or something.' And he thought, 'They can't be up to much. We're not going in there.' So they didn't even go into the hall, because they saw The Beatles' van. The band was booked for £42 and the charge at the door was two shillings [10p] so they made quite a loss on the night. At the Caird Hall in Dundee later that year half the people couldn't get into the hall. Unfortunately Dingwall didn't look at it that way.

I WAS THERE: MARGARET PATERSON (AGED 17)

I was almost 18 when I attended the Beatles dance in Dingwall. It was my first date with my late husband Tommy and I thought he had stood me up. The dance was almost over when the friend Tommy had given a message to remembered to tell me to go to the Strathpeffer gig and that Tommy would meet me there.

I sat on the stage all night chatting to The Beatles, and Paul in particular, who told me not to be upset as there were more fish in the sea than ever came out of it. He was lovely! They said, 'Where is everybody? This town is dead!' And I replied, 'Oh, no offence boys, but there is a great band on at the Strath and everybody is there and I'm going there soon. Why don't you come?' I am certain I saw them there but I met Tommy when I got there. I was married to my Tommy for over 30 years but he sadly died 19 years ago in a fishing accident. The Beatles were great. I organised the gig in Dingwall for the reunion of the 19 people who attended the Beatles performance and plaques were installed by Highland Council. One was placed at the stage and the second plaque was placed at the front door of the town hall. Many people come to have their photograph taken with that plaque.

THE BEATLES PLAYED HERE 4TH JANUARY 1963

I WAS THERE: HUGH PHILLIPS

I was in a group called Beat Unlimited. It was a five-piece band. We'd been playing in the Hamilton area for a few years so we were quite well-known in central Scotland at that point. We were playing up in Strathpeffer in the north of Scotland at the Spa Pavilion. It's quite a big, 600-person venue. And down the road The Beatles were playing in Dingwall just as they were coming back from Germany.

They played in Dingwall Town Hall two or three miles away and the story was that no one had gone to see them because nobody knew them. They all came to Strathpeffer Pavilion where we were playing.

I WAS THERE: ANDI LOTHIAN

MUSEUM HALL

5 JANUARY 1963, BRIDGE OF ALLAN

I had The Beatles in tandem with another promoter from the north of Scotland, a man called Albert Bonici, in January 1963. And that was just for town-hall dances, which wasn't successful. They played in the north of Scotland. Elgin Two Red Shoes ballroom was one. The Town Hall in Dingle, where there was only 16 people and they

THE MUSEUM HALL,
BRIDGE OF ALLAN
SATURDAY, 5th JANUARY

THE "LOVE ME DO" BOYS
THE BEATLES
also ROY PURDON and the
TELSTARS
8.30 p.m. to 11.45 p.m. Late Transport
Admission, Five Shillings
Tickets from Preston Travel Service
Next week—Top Recording Star—
EDEN KANE

all left and went up to Strathpeffer for a competition at the time to hear the local band The Merry Macs was another.

And I ran the last night, which was a Saturday night in a place called Bridge of Allan near Stirling. There was a hundred people there – 96 drunk young farmers and 4 women. So the place was just a rammie. I had only one doorman with me so I was doing a lot of the bouncing as well.

The Beatles went on, did their stint and a penny hit Paul's guitar and chipped it. I was quite despondent about it because we had lost money on the event. It was the only time that a dance promoter had got the use of the Bridge of Allan borough museum hall, which was reserved for weddings and funerals and young farmers events. And I had got it on the premise that there was no damage and a lovely chandelier in the middle of the ballroom was almost wrecked so I think it was probably the one and only public dance that occurred in that era in the hall and it was The Beatles. They still talk about that.

They stayed in the Royal just up the road in the Bridge of Allan and about five years ago, my wife and I just happened to pop in for lunch. Unbeknown, the waiter asked, 'Do you know who stayed in this hotel?'. And we replied, 'No'. And he said 'The Beatles.' We said 'Nooo!' So it was a big event!

I had heard 'Love Me Do' when it was released in November and really thought that it would be a big hit. But it only got to 18, so there was no interest in The Beatles at that point. For the last quarter-of-an-hour of the dance I went up and sat in the balcony and they announced that they were going to play three numbers, all of which had been recorded and were likely to be their next releases. And I was sitting up there quite despondent but the music just shattered. 'She loves you, yeah yeah yeah...' It just hit me like no other music had. I'm a musician. 'I wanna hold your hand...' I

THE BEATLES
PARLOPHONE RECORDS

just realised the significance of the music.

Outside of The Beatles and George Martin, I was one of the first people to hear those songs they had recorded. On the Sunday I phoned Albert and said, 'You know Albert, although we've lost money we need to get these guys back. They're going to be fantastic.' And he said, 'Well, I quite like them too.' And I said 'No, I mean we really have to get them back. We have to get them back before any of these songs come out because they're all going to be huge.'

The autographs of all four Beatles (above), signed in Aberdeen on the back of a publicity photo (opposite)

I WAS THERE: HAMY HARWOOD

BEACH BALLROOM

6 JANUARY 1963, ABERDEEN

I played in local group The Strollers from 1959 to 1965. We were the supporting band at the Beach Ballroom for Dusty Springfield, Joe Brown and other bands at various towns across the northeast of Scotland. The main music shop where all the groups in Aberdeen went was Forbes in George Street, managed by Harry Lord. I went to Forbes to meet the rest of our band and they were talking to some guys in the shop. I asked who they were and George, my rhythm guitarist, said they were The Beatles and were playing the Beach Ballroom the next day.

I got talking to them and George Harrison was playing one of the guitars in the shop. George had a problem with his guitar and I think someone lent him a guitar for the following night. I always remember how dirty his fingernails were.

I WAS THERE: NORMAN SHEARER

My friends and I, who were in a local band called The Facells, saw these four scruffy looking individuals falling out of their van the afternoon of the concert. I remember being surprised, as I had heard 'Love Me Do' on Radio Luxembourg and thought it might be a girl group.

The concert was terrific though, but not for all of the audience. There are still silly rumours that they were booed off the stage but that is palpable nonsense. They were well received by the bulk of the audience and I still have a very clear picture in my mind of John Lennon standing on the stage with his guitar slung square across his body belting out 'Johnny B Goode' and 'Roll Over Beethoven'. My impression was that they were great and six weeks or so later I was proved correct, as they took off with 'Please Please Me'.

My mate Ian was also there, sitting with his girlfriend near the front. He remembers that they finished with 'Love Me Do' and that the curtains were supposed to close. They didn't, and they repeated the song whilst Paul was urging the technician to close the curtains. They finished and still the curtains didn't close so they sang it again

The fabulous Facells: Norman Shearer is sitting on the amplifier. Norman heard 'Love Me Do' and thought The Beatles might have been a girl group

The Facells again: Norman in the centre

and this time – success! That concert was an extraordinary night which I will never ever forget.

I WAS THERE: LIZ WILSON

Liz Wilson thought The Beatles were 'scruffy' with 'funny accents' – but she loved listening to them

My friends and I were regulars at the wonderful Beach Ballroom concerts for years, arriving early to queue and always managing to get a front-row seat. I remember it being a freezing night, and my friends and I huddling in the entrance waiting for the doors to open.

Whilst queueing, four scruffy-looking guys approached us to enter. Of course the door was locked. Artists always use the back door to enter. Chatting to them, explaining the situation, they were really nice. I loved listening to their funny accents. I'm sure they thought ours the same. We spoke to them while waiting for the attendants to unlock the door, finding out they were the act for the evening. Once they gained entry, we chatted excitedly about meeting the guys who were to perform, wondering if they were going to be any good. Little did we know what we were about to witness. When they came on stage – wow, what a transformation! Gone were the four scruffy guys and there stood The Beatles wearing cute suits, with their identical Beatle haircuts.

I cannot remember the opening number but the sound and their vocals was something I will never forget. A wonderful memory to have. I met The Beatles! Wish I had got their autographs!

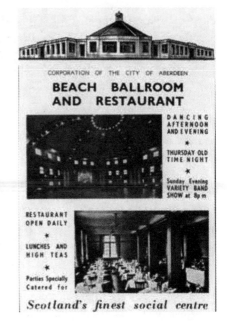

CORPORATION OF THE CITY OF ABERDEEN

BEACH BALLROOM AND RESTAURANT

DANCING AFTERNOON AND EVENING

THURSDAY OLD TIME NIGHT

Sunday Evening VARIETY BAND SHOW at 8p m

RESTAURANT OPEN DAILY

LUNCHES AND HIGH TEAS

Parties Specially Catered for

Scotland's finest social centre

I WAS THERE: MALCOLM STRACHAN

We'd formed a band in Aberdeen called The Playboys and we went to see quite a few gigs at the Beach Ballroom and they always chatted, these bands that came and played. But really they were nowhere near these guys when they arrived. They were totally different. There was a definite aura about them. I'd seen them on a Granada TV special one teatime and they were doing 'Love Me Do' and I remember seeing them then and thinking, 'They look really different'. The fact that they all sang, and McCartney had his left-handed bass. And we saw they were coming to Aberdeen and we thought, 'We'll definitely go and see them.'

They were totally different. Before that you relied on singers with backing groups. Shane Fenton and The Fentones. Mike Berry and The Outlaws. Johnny Kidd and The Pirates. Joe Brown and The Bruvvers. And they were all good, but The Beatles were just very different. And the stuff they did as well. Their own stuff and also Chuck Berry stuff, The Crickets. Paul McCartney did 'Til There Was You'. It was really very, very good indeed. It wasn't a dance as such. It was a concert. Aberdeen

City Council owned the Beach Ballroom and in those days on a Sunday evening you couldn't have a dance. It wasn't allowed. And there was no alcohol licence either. It was a very good dance floor. They laid a tarpaulin out on the floor and just laid seats out, so you were actually sitting at a concert. When we arrived we just went strolling in and there was a coffee bar upstairs so we went upstairs and there was hardly anybody there. And the four of them were just sitting there, having a cigarette and having a coffee. We stood and chatted and chatted for ages. It was good fun.

Paul McCartney was definitely the leader-cum-PR chap. He did most of the talking. He was very interested to know the kind of stuff that we liked, and tell us the kind of stuff that they liked. They offered us cigarettes. I didn't smoke, but they offered us cigarettes. They never stopped smoking. As they finished one they lit another one, especially Ringo Starr and George Harrison. They just smoked all the time. I talked to John Lennon about the Star Club in Hamburg and how hard they'd worked, because they'd work from nine in the evening until three in the morning. And I said, 'What was it like in the Star Club?' And he went, 'It was just a converted gas chamber.' It went right over the top of my head and they all started laughing.

They were in suits but it wasn't the round-necked ones. It was the ones with the ties and the proper collars. They were very smart. There's been a load of urban myths that when they actually played here they got the raspberry, that they got booed. That definitely did not happen. They went down very well. They really did. They did two sets. When they finished, they played 'Please Please Me'. John Lennon said, 'We're gonna play our new single 'Please Please Me'. It's out in a couple of weeks time. Please go out and buy it.' And that was the final number. And they shot into that and we thought, 'This sounds really good!' Sitting chatting to those guys you definitely knew they were going to make it. They just had so much confidence. It was a fantastic evening. And so great to have actually met them.

I WAS THERE: BRIAN BEATTIE

It was a Sunday. I remember going with my mates. I'm sorry to say they didn't make much of an impression on us. And if I remember right they didn't make much of an impression on the crowd either.

I'm just disappointed I don't have my ticket or any other memorabilia. They would be worth a fortune!

I WAS THERE: BILL COWIE (AGED 15)

The Beehive Youth Club had a Wurlitzer jukebox and on it was an exciting new record, 'Love Me Do' by The Beatles, which I played all the time when I was at the club. When I saw the advert in the *Evening Express* for the concert featuring the Johnny Scott Orchestra with special guest band The Beatles I just had to go and see this new band I really liked. Tickets were three shillings [15p] and it was an all-seated concert. I went with my brother Mike. The support band was the Johnny Scott Orchestra, the regular band. Their gear was all at the back of the stage so The Beatles had all theirs at the front. They were right in the front of the stage.

As we arrived early, we had an opportunity to chat with The Beatles before the show about music, Hamburg and the Liverpool scene. We knocked on the stage door and were invited in to meet them. Because back in those days there wasn't security. It didn't exist then. If you were invited in, then fine. They were tuning their guitars and discussing their playlist.

Being a musician myself I was interested in their guitars. John played a Rickenbacker bought from a GI in Hamburg, George was using a Gretsch Country Gent on loan from Hessy's guitar shop in Liverpool as his own was in for repair, and Paul handed me his Höfner bass. I noticed their playlist, taped to Paul's guitar, only included two Lennon/McCartney songs – 'Love Me Do' and 'Please Please Me'. The rest were all classic rock 'n' roll. I requested Chuck Berry's 'Sweet Little Sixteen' as it was a favourite with my band.

The Beatles played two 45-minute sets. In the first section they did a great selection of rock classics and 'Love Me Do'. John dedicated the Chuck Berry song especially for the 'lads in the front row' – me and my brother! I could see how talented and destined for stardom they were. After the first set we went back into the dressing room and talked about their favourite groups and singers. Tea and biscuits were served by a waitress in her old-style black-and-white council uniform and Paul offered us a cup of tea. John asked where in Aberdeen he could buy a guitar case. I suggested JT Forbes as they had a good selection of secondhand equipment and I knew Harry Lloyd the manager would be helpful. I drew a map for them to go to the shop the following day.

During the second half of the show they announced their new single 'Please Please Me'. The audience were enjoying their music very much by their applause and reaction. I could hear every song as there was no screaming. They were absolutely great. They were very polished and a great bunch of guys. And the crowd loved them. They were really good. It was obvious to me that they were something special. I got that gut feeling.

I knew that this band was going to go far. They just had that style, professionalism and charisma about them. I've seen a lot of good bands live. They were definitely the best.

There was a rumour that circulated about The Beatles being booed. That's not true. It never ever happened. They ran a bus service to the Beach Ballroom. The local Corporation bus transport did what they called a late bus on a Sunday down to the ballroom and there were several buses waiting outside. The timing of the concert and when it finished meant you were a bit touch-and-go to catch a bus. So some people got up and went to get on to catch the bus. There was a bit of confusion then as to what was happening, why these people were leaving. There certainly was no booing. During the break, when they went off after their first set, everybody thought that that's all they were getting – 45 minutes. And there was a sort of sigh of disappointment. But then the Johnny Scott Orchestra, when they came on, said The Beatles will be back on again. There was definitely no booing. Just a bit of confusion with the crowd.

Apparently Brian Epstein asked them to break up their set, to do it in two halves instead of doing it all in one. As I was leaving I asked Tucker Donald, the resident Johnny Scott band singer, what he thought of them. He said 'they were okay' but he was not that impressed. Six months later my band The Falcons was booked by dance promoter Gordon Hardie. The Falcons appeared at the ballroom on the same stage as The Beatles. I'm the luckiest guy in Scotland. To actually have The Beatles play a personal request for me.

I WAS THERE: KATHLEEN DONALD (AGED 15)

My friend Pat Masson and I went to the concert that they used to have at the Beach Ballroom every Sunday. On a Saturday night there was the dance. It was brilliant for dancing on a Saturday. But on a Sunday they had these concerts. They put chairs out because dancing wasn't allowed on a Sunday. You were just there to watch the concert. So I saw a few of the groups there that came up. Joe Brown and The Bruvvers, Shane Fenton.

The Beatles? They were terrific. They were really good. We stayed behind and went to their dressing room. There was quite a few folk there. But I knocked on the door and Paul answered it and we just asked if we could get their autographs. 'No problem.' They all came to the door and just signed a piece of paper. So it was quite exciting at the time. John was my favourite. And Paul was Pat's favourite. When I got married and left my parents' home, my mother had a clear-out and threw away the Beatles autographs. Can you imagine? When I tackled her about it, she said 'Oh, it was just a few names on a bit of paper.'

I WAS THERE: GAIL LAING (NÉE FRASER, AGED 15)

Gail Laing kept her Beatle autographs until her mum threw them out

❝ I talked more to George because I thought he was nice-looking ❞

At the interval, I and others talked to them at the side of the stage where I got their individual autographs. I talked more to George Harrison because I thought he was nice-looking.

I kept those autographs until I got married in October 1967 and left the family home. A few years later my mum moved house and unfortunately she must have thrown the autograph book out. She probably thought that it was rubbish. I wish I still had them, knowing the value of them. A lot of people didn't like them, but I personally did. I still have some 45s and EPs.

I WAS THERE: ALICE McKAY (AGED 16)

I first heard The Beatles singing 'Love Me Do' on Radio Luxembourg and was immediately captivated by them. When I read in our local newspaper that they were coming to Aberdeen and appearing at the Beach Ballroom, myself and three of my friends went to see them. Now the Beach Ballroom in Aberdeen was a very popular dance hall and on Sunday nights they ran concerts. Many other Sixties stars appeared there – Joe Brown, Gerry and The Pacemakers, Eden Kane, Dusty Springfield and others.

When I told my friends about The Beatles and I'd heard them on the radio and thought they were brilliant, three of my friends agreed to come with me to see what I was raving about. The fourth friend said, 'Yeugh! A name like The Beatles, that's too much like creepy crawlies. I'm not going!' So off we went, the three of us.

Boy, they were brilliant! If my memory serves me correctly, they took the place by storm. We went backstage and met the boys and spoke to them and got their autographs, which I still have. They were just normal young lads then, very thick Liverpool accents and so down to earth. George Harrison was my idol! My friend who didn't come has certainly rued the day she didn't.

I WAS THERE: LOUISE SIMPSON (AGED 17)

The Beach Ballroom held many concerts there on a Sunday and we were able to see many groups. I remember enjoying it. It was well received, and there were no boos as has been rumoured since.

My friend and I were surprised to see Ringo Starr as we had seen him at Skegness Butlins holiday camp that summer. He was the drummer in the band there.

I WAS THERE: ALLAN SMART (AGED 18)

I thought their performance was outstanding and to a large degree groundbreaking, but a proportion of the audience were not particularly impressed. In subsequent years I had the privilege of attending two further concerts – at the ABC in Blackpool in 1963 – when the reception they received was unbelievable. Knowing The Beatles were performing there was the deciding factor in choosing to go on holiday to Blackpool. Seeing the Fab Four performing live on stage three times will always remain as being one of my happiest memories as a teenager.

I WAS THERE: JAMES STRACHAN

On 5 January 1963, my late friend Hughie Sutherland and I were at the Beach Ballroom for the dancing. During the band's break, Johnny Scott made an announcement that the Sunday night concert – on the following night – would be featuring an exciting group called The Beatles. He stated that the group had been getting rave plaudits during their time in Hamburg. After a bit of debating, we decided we would go to the concert.

During the evening we asked a number of people if they knew anything about The Beatles. The consistent answer was 'Never heard of them!' We were unsure if The Beatles were a local group. In the early Sixties Aberdeen had many local groups appearing in clubs and dance halls. The Beatles did not play on the main stage. They played on the dance floor to the left of the stage. They certainly played music you would have loved to dance to.

John Lennon came across as the lead man. The audience sat on chairs on the left side of the dance floor, taking up about a third of the floor area. Early on in the concert, Hughie and I were convinced that the left-handed guitar player went to Old Aberdeen School. We almost convinced ourselves it was a guy called Billy from Merkland Road. Twice, when they were singing, the three guitarists turned round and pointed their guitars at Ringo, bringing a smile. Ringo looked a dour kind of guy. The audience cheered and applauded him smiling.

At one point John Lennon said that the next song they were about to sing would be released very soon. It was 'Please Please Me'. After 10p.m. John Lennon asked the audience to request any song they had

The teenage James Strachan was convinced Paul McCartney was a lad from a local school

played. The late Donnie (Brian) Fraser requested 'A Shot of Rhythm and Blues', which they duly sang. At approximately 10.10p.m. a number of girls left their seats to go and collect their coats. When he noticed the girls leaving their seats, John Lennon said over the microphone that he did not think they were that bad. The girls came back and stood at the back of the hall, making ready for a quick exit to catch the bus the council provided.

Unknown to the band, the majority of the audience were getting ready to leave as soon as the concert was finished to catch the public bus home because the council laid on buses for both Saturday and Sunday – taking the passengers to Garthdee, Mastrick/Northfield and the Bridge of Don. You missed your bus at your peril, as the drivers did not hang around and money to pay for a taxi was almost unthinkable.

At the finish The Beatles were given a warm cheer for their performance. Hughie and I only had just over a mile to walk home. We finally agreed the left-handed guitarist could not have been Billy. We were not even sure Billy was a musician. How were we to know that the left-handed guitarist was to become Sir Paul McCartney? Several weeks later I met Hughie, who told me that group we had watched called The Beatles were No.1 in the pop charts. It still gives me pleasure telling people that I saw them live at the Beach Ballroom – to my wife's annoyance!

I WAS THERE: ELIZABETH WALKER

Elizabeth Walker and friend: she confirms that The Beatles were most definitely not booed off

I was there that night with a friend. A group appeared every Sunday night so it was just another group. Rumour has it that they were booed off, but I can't remember that. It was a great night.

Of course, 'Love Me Do' had come out in October 1962 and my husband remembered it was played on *Juke Box Jury* on BBC TV on Saturday night. It was voted a miss three-to-one by the *Jury* panellists. One said 'The Beatles? What kind of name is that?'

I WAS THERE: ROBERT WILSON

I am told that the compere was Mr Alfred Wood. When it came to introducing the not-yet-so-famous four, the story goes that he invited those present to welcome not 'The Bee-tles' but 'the Bee-attles.' This account was given to me by two different people who, like me, were his work colleagues. Being much younger than Alfie Wood, as he was known to many, I never had the courage to ask him to confirm this blunder.

I WAS THERE: ANDI LOTHIAN

BRIAN EPSTEIN'S OFFICE

7 JANUARY 1963, LONDON

We flew down unannounced to meet Brian Epstein on the Monday morning and we arrived at lunchtime, turned up in his office in London and he sat at his desk and he said 'So you think they're going to do well then?'

'Well, Brian, it's a bit more like we want to help you,' I replied. 'The guys are really good and the weather was bad and so we'll take them back.' And he said 'Oh you will?' And we were paying them forty pounds a night. Remember it was 1963.

'And I said, 'The only thing is, Brian, we can't pay them forty pounds a night.' 'Oh you can't?' 'No, we can't,' I said, 'We can pay them thirty pounds a night.' And he said, 'Oh, you can?' And I said, 'Yes we can.' He said, 'Well, I tell you what. I know why you're here. I know, like you know, they're gonna be huge. So despite the Bridge of Allan Borough Museum Hall, despite that and everything else, they quite enjoyed their wee stint in Scotland. So you can have them back but there's three conditions.'

'Oh. What are the three conditions?' 'Well, first of all, he said, 'it's

Before he began promoting acts such as The Beatles, Andi Lothian played in several Scottish jazz bands

Andi Lothian moved from making music – jazz – to booking rock acts when he realised the writing was on the wall

none of your wee dance halls. You can have them back in October.'
And I'm thinking, 'October! Well, all these three numbers will be out,
they'll probably all be number one and they're going to be huge!'
So we're getting a bit excited. 'Condition number one is it's going to
have to be late in October just before they go to America. Condition
number two is, because they're doing concerts in America, I'd like
them to do concerts with you and with other promoters around
that autumn period. So it's going to be concerts.' Well, we'd never
promoted a concert at that point...

And he said 'The third condition is it's not your thirty pounds a night.'
'It's not?' 'No.' 'It's not forty pounds a night?' 'No.' And he held up four
fingers and a thumb. And I said 'Fifty pounds a night?' He said 'Five
hundred pounds a night.' Which is probably equivalent to ten grand
a night now. And he said, 'OK, I'm going to leave the room for three
minutes and I need your decision when I come back one way or the other.'
And he just left the room.

And Albert was flabbergasted. He said 'Well, that's that then.' And I said
'Albert, we've got to have them. We've got to pay this.' It wasn't much of

a risk for me because I didn't have much money. Albert had the money. We came back and, much to Albert's chagrin at the time, we booked them. We got three nights in October.

I had left school when I was 17 and formed a jazz band. When I was 19, I was Scottish jazz band champion, so my background was as a musician. One of the odd things about The Beatles was that boy bands came in and replaced traditional jazz and we found ourselves supporting these kids instead of being the main attraction, and I saw the writing on the wall.

> **I'm going to leave the room for three minutes and I need your decision when I come back, one way or the other...**
>
> *Brian Epstein*

And so I went into promoting dances locally at the age of 20. I was coming back late at night from dances and listening to Radio Luxembourg and I began to realise that in order to make a success of this I had to endeavour to predict which releases were going to make it and which weren't. Because the managers wanted the bands exposed, but obviously they would endeavour to double the money, even if the record was not a hit.

I realised very quickly that I soon had a gift for picking those ones that were likely to be in the top ten at the time they were coming to Scotland. That was always my goal, if I could book them one month, two months, three months, four months ahead, judging how long it would take for that release to climb to its highest point. And it was either good luck or some bit of intuition, perhaps.

But I would say that, from my perspective, the fact that these two numbers hit me as being so brilliant was what made us take this huge risk of booking a completely unknown band at money way beyond what they would have earned if the records hadn't done anything. But I was so certain they were going to be huge.

They had two number one hits by the time they got to us. The third one had just been released and was going to go straight to number one. I put the tickets on sale in June and we sold out in Glasgow in a morning. It was pandemonium.

ABERDEEN

7 JANUARY 1963

After school the next day [after the gig] I went into JT Forbes and asked Harry if The Beatles had been in the shop. He said, 'Who? Those long-haired scruffy Liverpudlians?'

He did sell John a case. The following year, as their fame spread, he changed his attitude and put up a banner declaring 'The Beatles shopped here!'

'PLEASE PLEASE ME'

The Beatles' second single, 'Please Please Me',
was released in the UK on 11 January 1963.

EL RIO CLUB

26 JANUARY 1963, MACCLESFIELD

I was waiting outside for my friend. A car stopped alongside me and a
broad Liverpudlian voice asked, 'Is this the El Rio, love?' Little did I
know then that this was Paul actually speaking to me.

When I recall this to my friends, most of them think I made it up.
Very few people now remember the El Rio, although I had wonderful
times there seeing lots of groups of the time.

I WAS THERE: DAVE JACKSON

The El Rio was in the Brocklehurst Memorial Hall. The main entrance
was up a short flight of steps at the narrow end of the building. There
was a lengthy delay to the expected start time. They had to travel from
Stoke after an appearance at the King's Hall.

I was waiting with a friend who had to be home by 10.30, so she had
to leave before the show started. The performance was something extra
special – a very tight and perfectly performed set. There was a fantastic
buzz in the hall, well worth the ticket price of five shillings. My daughter
Lucy was born in 1974 and she and her friends are impressed that I saw
The Beatles live.

I WAS THERE: KEN HOOPER (AGED 26)

I used to go to the El Rio and one of the doormen used to let me in
because he knew that I'd done a bit of boxing, because in the army I
was a boxer. He was leaving and he said, 'Can you help us out?' And

that's how I stepped in to do the job. I worked the door on the El Rio every week for a year or two. We had all sorts of groups every week. It was well supported, the El Rio. I was just doing a job because I was getting paid and I wanted extra money. I was paid £2 or £3. I worked at the Parkside Hospital in the engineer shop.

I was on the door when The Beatles came up the steps at the front. They had made a record but it hadn't been played just before they came to the El Rio. It was ready to be released. I think they had come from Stoke to Macclesfield and they were going on to Manchester, like three places. They were just getting known, you see.

There were people who couldn't get in – they were queuing up down to the Waters Green pub. The boss, a Jewish bloke called Betesh, told us to keep letting them in. You couldn't move. You couldn't dance or anything like that. They were swinging on the rafters at the top. If you could get 200 people in there, there must have been 500. That's how bad it was. It was unsafe. You'd have never got away with it today.

I WAS THERE: BRENDA CLARKE

My recollections of that night are quite sketchy, probably because I was one of the very few people who weren't actually that keen on The Beatles. My main memory is what a mess the room was at the end of the night. Part of the décor of the El Rio was ropes hung across the ceiling. Because so many people came that night, a lot ended up standing on tables and chairs to get a better view. Some of them hung onto the ropes, as they were on the floor, and some of the tables and chairs were missing legs.

I WAS THERE: TONY CLARKE

Brenda and I met at the El Rio. I took an extra job there to help save for an engagement ring. There were usually three of us on the door, two of us were local and one from Manchester. The El Rio only served soft drinks, so early doors was mainly girls, with the lads not coming until the pubs closed. Then the place would be quite busy: 200–300 people. On the night The Beatles came the numbers doubled and it was very busy right from the doors opening.

Brenda and Tony Clarke actually met at the El Rio, where The Beatles played on 26 January 1963

They had brought in an extra doorman from Manchester so I was assigned to look after the group, showing them to the dressing room which was in the basement and – after they finished playing – taking down the fans three at a time to get autographs. The lads were very personable, chatty and modest, bearing in mind the effect they had just had on the audience! The music really was fabulous and everyone there that night knew that this group was very special.

As a thank you for looking after them they gave me three lots of autographs, each signed by all of them. I gave two of them to really keen fans and put the other one somewhere safe. We've never seen it since and Brenda and I, who have now been married for 53 years, think it must have got lost in one of our many house moves.

I WASN'T THERE: ALAN LINGARD

I remember it well. My wife and I used to run a youth club at a Macclesfield church and the members had been asking us to organise a dance for them. They assured us that they would all be there and bring a load of mates. We went ahead and booked a local hall and laid on some music. Hardly anybody turned up. Where were they all? You've guessed it. Down at the El Rio listening to this band from Liverpool that we had never heard of.

ISLE OF MAN

FEBRUARY 1963

The Beatles never performed on the Isle of Man but I well remember my
father, who did all the bookings for the concerts on the island in the Sixties
for the now-defunct Palace and Derby Castle Company, asking me what
I and my friends thought about a group called The Beatles, who had had
success with a record called 'Love Me Do'. I told dad they were great and
that he had to book them.

He had been offered them for one night for £250 during the 1963 summer
season and had to get permission from the board of the company to book
them. The board told him – and he then told me – that they thought The
Beatles were a one-record wonder and they wouldn't be around by the time of
the 1963 summer season. And that anyway, they were too
dear at £250. The rest is history!

PRINCESS THEATRE

FEBRUARY 1963, CLACTON

I was a school boy at Clacton Secondary Modern in the
Sixties and a story which was part of local folklore was
that the notorious entertainments manager who ran
the Princess Theatre, owned by Clacton Urban District
Council, turned down the chance of having The Beatles
perform the week before their first record hit the charts
on the basis that they would be of 'little or any interest'.
The CUDC was abolished and replaced by Tendring in
the early Seventies. They owned a good music venue in
the Princess Theatre – I recall watching Hawkwind
there circa 1970 and possibly Quintessence. But
they missed a trick with The Beatles.

*Steve Bassam in his
Sunday best, early 1960s*

I WAS THERE: BRIAN COOK (AGED 20)

MANEY HALL

1 FEBRUARY 1963, SUTTON COLDFIELD

I saw The Beatles concert at Maney Hall, Sutton Coldfield. A young lady where I worked told me about the show, saying this group is just making the charts. I went with my pal Brian Trow. As we did not drive then, we got there by two buses. The problem was no buses ran in the area after 10 p.m. Consequently we had to walk home some ten miles.

I WAS THERE: KEITH PADLEY (AGED 17)

I attended Maney Hall dance on the night The Beatles were there. I travelled on my Lambretta scooter which I had just bought at the time and which I have still got.

I met up with my pals there. I used to go with a couple of mates. I

Keith Padley (on guitar, second from right) and his band The Casual 5

was in a small group called The Casual 5. We thought The Beatles were just another group at the time. I remember I had to get up to go to work next morning as a television engineer.

I WAS THERE: PAT BROWN

I saw The Beatles there. I can't remember too much about it, only that they were great and we were all a bit screamy! I went with my friend Elizabeth and shortly afterwards we went to London and saw them at the Odeon. We went down on a coach that was arranged by a youth club in Merc Green.

Keith Padley and Todge (Anthony Rogers) were at Maney Hall together the night The Beatles came to Sutton Coldfield. Keith was on his Lambretta and Todge was all Brylcreemed up. Mods vs Rockers didn't kick off that night

I WAS THERE: SHEILA BOLTON (AGED 16)

My friend Janet and I saw The Beatles at Maney Hall. We were both 16. It was an arranged visit as we had not been to Maney Hall before but we were very aware of The Beatles at that time. We liked their single 'Love Me Do' better than 'Please Please Me'.

I remember them singing 'I Saw Her Standing There'. I don't recollect Maney Hall being very crowded as we could get right up to the stage and had plenty of room to dance. The Beatles seemed ordinary guys and very approachable. We saw them again at the Plaza Handsworth and it was a very different story – it was packed and we said to ourselves how lucky we were to have seem them before they were very famous.

It was a very vibrant time to be a teenager and we regulary went to pubs where live bands played. We saw Carl Wayne and The Vikings (The Move), Denny Laine and The Diplomats and many more. I also have the Rolling Stones' autographs as my friend was performing on the show *Ready Steady Go*. She was miming 'All I Want for Christmas is a Beatle'!

I WAS THERE: ANTHONY (TODGE) ROGERS

I was in a rock band called Tony Brent and The Dakotas. I was the vocalist. I was also in a skiffle group with Chris Boughton and Allan Smith. Allan and I grew up together and bought our first guitars with our paper-round money.

The night The Beatles came to Maney Hall, I was there with Allan Smith and we were ready for the girls, with hair greased down with Brylcreem and quiff pushed up in the front. We could have touched George Harrison. Both being in rock bands ourselves, we were more interested than most.

Anthony Rogers, a.k.a. Todge. A man of many names, he was also vocalist for Tony Brent and The Dakotas

Paul stood next to George and then, of course, the great John Lennon.

We were particularly interested in the small guitars they were playing. How could such a fantastic sound come out of such small guitars looking more like violins than the big heavy Burns and Fender guitars we were used to playing? We knew these kids had got something. And, of course, not long after that they were known the four corners of the world with their fabulous music.

HELEN SHAPIRO GIGS

On 2 February 1963, The Beatles embarked
upon a UK tour on a bill headed by Helen
Shapiro, a female singer with two No.1
singles to her name.

GAUMONT THEATRE

2 FEBRUARY 1963, BRADFORD

*'Package tours'
were very common
in the early Sixties,
and this variety-
show-style line-up
was no exception*

I was booked to see Helen Shapiro at Bradford Alhambra (aka Gaumont)
and didn't even know that The Beatles were on the bill. They performed
a few songs and then announced that they had just recorded this song
and that folk would be able to buy it in a couple of weeks. They played
this particular song, 'Love Me Do', and all the girls in the audience went
wild. The audience didn't scream for Helen but The Beatles brought
something different to the stage and the audience began shouting and then

screamed and screamed for more at the end of their act.

My friend Trevor and I looked at each other in amazement. 'What's happening?' he asked me. I was as clueless as him. We had never seen anything like it before. The excitement was overwhelming. Now we know it as the beginnings of Beatlemania.

> ❮ 'What's happening?' We had never seen anything like it before. The excitement was overwhelming ❯

I WAS THERE: ALAN LIGHTOWLERS (AGED 19)

Myself and four friends were present when The Beatles appeared with Helen Shapiro and others. We had tickets for the stalls and sat about six rows from the stage. All of us were members of a local youth club and had a real interest in pop music and the charts. We attended a number of concerts at the Gaumont around this time. The Beatles had become known to us from their appearances on Granada TV's *People and Places*, ABC TV's *Thank Your Lucky Stars* and BBC Radio's *Saturday Club*. We attended the concert specifically to see The Beatles and were not disappointed. The Beatles appeared in the first half of the show and opened to a rapturous reception with the audience on their feet. Around six numbers were played and they closed with 'Please Please Me', which sent the audience wild. I can still picture in my mind Paul McCartney with his baby face and left-handed guitar.

For the rest of the show people were chanting for The Beatles to reappear, which of course they didn't do. It was obvious to all of us that we had witnessed something very special and we all came away as firm Beatles fans. Inspired by seeing The Beatles at the Gaumont and also by the film *Summer Holiday* featuring Cliff Richard and The Shadows, we decided to form our own group, which we subsequently named The Atlantics. Four of us purchased guitars, amplifiers and drums and embarked on music lessons in Bradford. Once we had learned the basics, we commenced hours of practise to put together a portfolio of instrumentals. At a later date we added a singer, but the problem was he would only perform Buddy Holly songs. Nevertheless we began to play at our local youth club dance nights, other youth clubs and some local pubs.

For this we were normally paid £5 per night between the five of us, which paid for a couple of pints, a fish-and-chip supper and a contribution towards our hire purchase commitments on the equipment. It wasn't a lot of money but the group gave us access to girls and we were living the dream!

I WAS THERE: CHRISTINE McCABE

We enjoyed The Beatles when they came to the Gaumont. I remember they weren't yet at the height of their fame then. But we still stood on our seats.

I WAS THERE: MIKE DUNKERLEY (AGED 18)

ASTORIA BALLROOM

12 FEBRUARY 1963, OLDHAM

My father owned a manufacturing business in the centre of Oldham and I started work in the office there in early 1962. In September of that year I started studying on a day release basis for the Ordinary National Certificate in business studies at Oldham College of Commerce on Brunswick Street, which was later demolished to make way for the Oldham bypass. My classmates and I soon became friends – and more, in some cases – with the girls who were there full-time doing shorthand/typing courses.

It was the beginning of the Swinging Sixties. The Astoria Ballroom had just opened and most of us were regular attendees at their Saturday Palais Nights. Discos had not been thought of in those days. A suit and tie were the required male dress and nobody was allowed in after 10p.m. It was our high spot of the week. The building had housed the Gaumont Cinema until it closed in about 1961. The owners then undertook a lot of refurbishment with the top half of the building becoming a bowling alley and the bottom half being the Astoria Ballroom. When the grand reopening took place in November 1962, free tickets were given to businesses around the Star Inn, which was the pub opposite, with the result that my father received one and gave it to me. So I was there on the opening night.

With so many pop groups being formed in those days, Tuesday nights became 'Teenbeat Special' group night, where groups from all round the country would appear. I cannot claim to have seen them all, but I remember seeing Gerry And The Pacemakers, Freddie Starr And The Midnighters, a Liverpool harmony group I really liked called The Chants and, of course The Beatles.

The Beatles live on-stage at the Astoria Ballroom, Oldham, February 1963

That night, dozens of us from the college aimed to meet up at the Astoria, but when I arrived on the Number 9 bus from Royton there was a queue stretching right down King Street towards the Duke of Edinburgh pub, which was another landmark road junction. No tickets had been issued as all-ticket events were very rare in those days. My then girlfriend was almost at the front of the queue and had saved me a place so I just jumped in and we were amongst the first into the building. I was keen on this young lady, and enjoyed a brief romance with her. So keen that... I cannot remember her name! Only that she lived on Walker Road in Chadderton.

> ❝ There was just a mass of humanity, mainly girls, screaming at the group ❞

Half-an-hour later there was pandemonium outside as the doors were shut, thus denying access to hundreds who were waiting to get in and couldn't. Helen Shapiro was on the bill, but when The Beatles were on stage there was no chance of any dancing on the floor. There was just a mass of humanity, mainly girls, screaming at the group. To hear what The Beatles were singing was extremely difficult, but I do recall hearing snatches of all the songs they tried to sing amongst the noise.

What did impress me was how smart they looked. Whilst I never had a Beatles jacket, I went on to own, and still have, a number of tab-collar button-down shirts and knitted ties. When the show finished there was just time for a quick kiss and cuddle with my girlfriend before we rushed off to catch the last bus to our respective homes. I wonder what happened to my girlfriend from Walker Road and if she remembers witnessing this event?

I WAS THERE: ROY POTTS

I remember going to see The Beatles at the Astoria on the corner of King Street and Union Street. The queue was long, going down King Street as far as the Duke of Edinburgh public house. Metal barriers were in place to keep the queues orderly. I was going with my mates Fred Winterbottom, David Wostenholme and Roy Eccles. I arrived late and, as my mates were already in the queue, I jumped the barrier and joined them. We all gained admission to a packed crowd and a memorable performance.

I WAS THERE: NEIL REYNOLDS

THE RITZ

15 FEBRUARY 1963, KINGS HEATH, BIRMINGHAM

The Ritz, as it was back in 1963

I saw The Beatles live three times. I was knocked out by 'Love Me Do', so went to see them the first opportunity I got. 'Love Me Do' had only been released three to four months previously and it was before they became really, really huge. There were a few of us from school went, including my best male mates and at least one girl, Sandra Oakley.

The Ritz, Kings Heath and the Plaza at Old Hill were owned by the same woman, Ma Regan. The acts would do an early show at one of the ballrooms and dash over to another and perform a second show while the group who was on there first travelled in the opposite direction to swap over. The Ritz gig was the best because it was more intimate. There wasn't all the screaming that drowned them out at later gigs and some watched them while others danced. I saw them again in October. By that time you couldn't hear anything. Only girls screaming!

I WAS THERE: TONY LEE

One of our friends had the job of ferrying the turns, including the Rolling Stones and The Beatles, in his voluminous Humber Hawk between the Plaza in Handsworth and The Ritz in Kings Heath, which were both converted Birmingham cinemas. We were greatly

The Beatles photographed around the back of The Ritz, 1963

impressed by his good fortune, particularly as he had never passed his driving test or obtained vehicle insurance. Consequently, we always refused to travel with him. He didn't have a ticket to ride!

I WAS THERE: NEIL ROBINSON

CARFAX ASSEMBLY ROOMS

16 FEBRUARY 1963, OXFORD

We were the support band to The Beatles at Carfax Assembly Rooms. Admission was six shillings [30p]. Unusually, we were asked to set up in the afternoon. Guitarist Will Jarvis, myself and our roadie took all the equipment to Carfax and unloaded and set up. There at the time were John Lennon and Paul McCartney. We set up our gear and actually

The Madisons: they supported The Beatles at Carfax Assembly Rooms

played a few rock 'n' roll songs with the two of them. They asked us if there was anywhere nearby where they could eat and the four of us walked from the hall together. Originally Will suggested Browns in the covered market but it was decided to go to a Chinese in Ship Street.

For some reason, and looking back on it I have no idea why, I said I needed to go home and turned down the chance to eat with them. So Will, John and Paul went there to eat without me. A personal and rather unpleasant memory of the day is that after we had changed for the evening gig, we left our possessions in the changing rooms at the back of the hall. The only people in there were ourselves, The Beatles and their road manager. On returning after the gig my jacket and wallet containing £17 (which was a lot of money in 1963) were missing. This was reported to the police. The jacket, minus wallet, was found the next day by the police by the side of the road leading into Basingstoke which, by coincidence, was where The Beatles played next.

I WAS THERE: PAUL WEAVER (AKA PAUL FANE)

I was the drummer with the Madisons. I used to work in a men's outfitters in Queen Street and didn't finish work until about 5 p.m. So I had a routine of having a shave and getting myself ready when I got to the venue, in the hope that the rest of the group would set my equipment up. On this particular evening I had taken delivery of a brand new Ajax drum kit and the lads took the drums to the dance hall and set them up. I arrived and went to the Ladies, which was the only place there was any hot water. As I was shaving, I could hear all this drumming going on. A heck of a lot of pounding and

Paul Weaver (middle) was the drummer in The Madisons. He heard a Beatles drum duet and shouted at Paul McCartney to stop thumping his brand new drumkit

drumming. I thought, 'This sounds a bit odd.' So, covered in shaving cream, I came out of the Ladies and walked into the dance hall to see Ringo Starr banging away on his drum kit and Paul McCartney banging away on mine! Now there was an unwritten understanding between musicians that you didn't interfere with each other's equipment. So I saw red and shouted at Paul McCartney to get off my drum kit. I don't know whether anyone had ever shouted at him in that way before. I think he was a bit taken aback. I was annoyed because I hadn't played the kit myself. It was a brand new set and, had he taken the trouble to look, he would have seen that all the drum skins were completely pristine and had never been played. Bellowing at Paul McCartney and telling him to get off my drum kit wasn't one of my finest hours.

A couple of years later I saw the interview with John Lennon where he responded to the question 'Is Ringo Starr the best drummer in the world?' with 'He's not even the best drummer in The Beatles.' And I thought, 'That's quite true, actually.' Because Paul was a good drummer. It's just that he happened to be hammering away on my brand new kit!

I WAS THERE: KATE DRAKES

GRANADA THEATRE

23 FEBRUARY 1963, MANSFIELD

I was one of the lucky people to see The Beatles at the Granada way before they were famous. Top of the bill should have been Johnny

Kidd and The Pirates, but they had an accident on the way to Mansfield and never turned up. Consequently, The Beatles played way more than they were going to – and we were hooked. They looked so different in their smart black collarless jackets and pudding-basin haircuts. I don't remember screaming but they certainly gave me goosebumps.

While waiting outside for my friend Carole, a lady of the night came up behind me and said, 'Get off my patch, bitch!' I had no idea what she meant but moved very quickly! I wonder now – what was I wearing?

Kate Drakes' evening watching the Fabs ended with a run-in with a lady of the night

I WAS THERE: COLIN KIRK (AGED 19)

I was at that show and have still got the programme, with Helen Shapiro top of a bill which also included The Red Price Band, The Honeys, Dave Allen, Danny Williams, The Kestrels and Kenny Lynch. The stalls cost 6 shillings and sixpence [33p], which was a lot of money for us then and they did shows at 6.30 and 8.30 p.m.

I went with my workmates who were all in the building trade – myself, Malcolm and Lynne were plumbers working at the same firm, Malc's brother Colin was a bricklayer and Lynne's brother Brent was a plasterer. We went to the 8.30 p.m. show, which gave us time to get home from work, get ready and meet at 6.30 p.m. for a couple of pints in the Eclipse, the pub opposite the Granada in Westgate. It was very crowded outside the cinema, with people waiting to get in for the second show. And also a lot of people who did not get tickets, who were just there to soak up the atmosphere.

When the audience from the first show came out it got very busy indeed. Watching The Beatles you could hardly hear them singing with the girls screaming their heads off, but it was a great performance and we all agreed after that they would go far. The rest, as they say, is history.

It was a great period in music and they wrote such an amazing amount of songs, which even today will get people up dancing, remembering the words. They shaped the music world that we have today. It was great to be there.

The very dapper young Colin Kirk (right), sporting a smart-casual get-up that he presumably didn't wear on plumbing jobs

I WAS THERE: DES TURNER

I remember seeing The Beatles at the Granada cinema in Mansfield – converted to a stage – on two occasions in 1963 when I was, or should have been, studying for my O-Levels.

The first occasion was in February '63, the very early days of 'Love Me Do' and 'Please Please Me' and, as I recall, The Beatles at that time had only been booked as a support act to Helen Shapiro. Even so, their performance was rapturous and the crowd noise deafening.

I WAS THERE: BOB WILSON

The top turn was Helen Shapiro, but as for any details, well, the mists of time have done a lot of fogging. As a teenager I used to go to most of the Granada shows with pals and they were always enjoyable and memorable. I would always go to the live groups and then see many of them later on *Top of the Pops*.

Off the top of my head, I remember seeing The Beatles, The Rolling Stones, The Shadows, Manfred Mann, Tommy Roe, Bruce Channel, Del Shannon, The Kinks, Johnny Kidd, Joe Brown, Gene Vincent, Peter Jay, Billy Fury, Chris Montez, Dusty Springfield, Helen Shapiro, Frank Ifield – and a lot more!

GAUMONT THEATRE

26 FEBRUARY 1963, TAUNTON

Geoff Cross, an adopter of the Chelsea boots and greasy quiff rocker look

I was at the Gaumont Theatre – now the Mecca Bingo – and I had stalls tickets. They were not top of the bill. I'm sure that was Joe Brown, but I might be wrong. I was lucky because their second release had just hit the No.1 spot that week and when they came on the girls went mad. I can remember just hearing something but not that much, which was a pity because I was a big fan. I do remember that the amplifiers were tiny compared with today and the PA was minimal.

Author's note: Danny Williams topped the bill, replacing Helen Shapiro, who had a heavy cold.

ODEON THEATRE

1 MARCH 1963, SOUTHPORT

I could not believe the screams. My father said, 'How can they hear? They can't hear what they're singing.' My dad managed the Gaumont. We were from 1956 right the way through. My father put on all sorts of shows. He was such a showman. I'll give him his due. He used to promote and do whatever he could to fill the place. And he used to fill the place. The Gaumont's capacity was around 2,000 people. And dad used to fill it every Saturday night.

I think it was the first time, when they were supporting Helen Shapiro, that I met them, because my father brought me backstage. And obviously they hadn't hit the big time then. John Lennon had his glasses on, which were so thick you could probably see the moon with them. And Ringo Starr had his arm in plaster and my sister Valerie sat having a good old chat with him. She sat on Ringo Starr's knee. He was really nice.

John Lennon was smoking. They were all smoking. He was quite a nice sort of bloke, but he wasn't particularly interested in us. He was obviously thinking about the show, where they went wrong. I think he was just having a bit of a post-mortem after the gig, to see what they could improve on.

Paul McCartney was preening. I didn't get on with him. I thought he was a bit egotistical. He was the pretty-boy 'look at me' one, which didn't go down well with my father. George Harrison was the nicest of the lot. He was lovely. Really interested. He certainly made the effort. I was talking with them and I said to George Harrison, 'I've got to get into this. What's the best advice you can give a young lad who wants to pick up a guitar and play?' And he looked around the dressing room, which wasn't great quality. They weren't built for pop stars. They had the bare necessities, with mirrors with lamps round it. And it was cold and damp. And George looked around the dressing room and he said, 'Well, if I were you I wouldn't bother!'

I WAS THERE: BARBARA SYKES

CITY HALL

2 MARCH 1963, SHEFFIELD

My dad used to be a commissionaire at Sheffield City Hall. We used to go to all the concerts. We used to go from school, me and our Carol. Sometimes we'd be in school uniform. Carol was the sensible one, even though she was the younger one. She was the one who said, 'Don't scream. Dad told us not to scream!' and I said, 'All right, Carol, I won't.' And then she'd be screaming alongside us. And when we went in the back I always got a kiss from them, or a photograph. But I never got a photograph with The Beatles.

Barbara Sykes: she covered her arm with a plastic bag so as not to erase all The Beatles' autographs on it

It'd always be, 'Come on girls, they're due to go back on stage.' But there was always one that was hanging back, that was the last one out, and I'd be going, 'Oh come here, let's give you a kiss. Let me put my arm around you!' And Carol would be going, 'Come on Barbara, we'll get in trouble!'

I had The Beatles' autographs on my arm. And I covered it in a plastic bag when I went in the bath so I didn't get my arm wet. Because I wanted to go to school the next day and show everyone at school 'oh I've met The Beatles.' Plus I got their autographs in my autograph book as well which, sadly, I sold not long ago. But we did meet them. I remember John Lennon asked my dad could he take me out? And my dad said, 'No you can't! Come on, girls. Get their autographs. Come on. Let's have you out of here.' Because they'd sing. Then they'd have a break and we'd go in in the interval to go and meet them and get their autographs. Then we'd go back out.

At the City Hall they used to have seats on the stage. And my dad said, 'If you girls are sitting on the front you've got to behave yourselves. No screaming. No running to touch 'em. We'll put you there so that everybody else behaves.' But of course we screamed. And they'd turn round and sing to us so we were actually sat on the seats on the stage when The Beatles were playing, so that was quite exciting. It was lovely.

I remember that we used to go in the stage door at City Hall. And what we used to do when we got to the stage door was that we used to knock on the door and say 'Dad, it's me' and he'd let us in. And as we got there this time there were crowds of girls around the door and we eventually did get to the door – banged on the door – 'Dad! Dad! Dad! It's me!' Then all the girls were banging on the door – 'dad! dad! It's me!' As they were shutting the door, they shut the door on Paul McCartney and they opened the door again and dragged him in. But the girls didn't realise it was one of The Beatles. They thought it was the police holding them back. They used to hold them back and we used to walk through. We were pretty lucky girls, I'll tell ya! It was absolutely fantastic.

When you came out your ears would be ringing. You couldn't hear what they were singing because they were all screaming. It were wonderful. We were lucky to have a dad that got us in. We used to catch the bus into Sheffield city centre, 'town' as we'd call it. We'd come out of school, get on the bus and we'd start on the bus. 'Crikey, I wonder what it's going to be like?' You'd get all giddy and excited. And I think that's what it was. And it built up and built up. And then they came on.

They always had somebody else on besides The Beatles. It was Helen Shapiro. And the person compering the show would be going 'We're gonna have The Beatles on in a bit. Who'd you like best?' And they'd say their names and we'd all scream at the ones we liked. And I think it built up from there. 'Who's coming on next? Who do you like best? Do you like George?' And he'd say each name and all the girls would scream at which one they liked best.

When we were sat there on the stage it was so difficult not to get giddy and scream, and especially when they turned round and they looked at you. 'Oh God, he's looking at me.' Somebody had made a beetle, like a kid's crawling beetle, and they threw it on the stage to them.

And one of The Beatles picked it up, brought it over and gave it to me. That was quite exciting. I've still got it in the loft somewhere. Next day, going to school with The Beatles' autographs on my arm? Well, it were all right, that.

I WAS THERE: WENDY DRIFFIELD (NÉE FROST, AGED 15)

ROYAL HALL

8 MARCH 1963, HARROGATE

My cousin Trevor Stannard was there. He was 19 years old. He went backstage afterwards and there were a few guys trying to hold back the girl fans fighting to get into The Beatles' dressing room. So he helped the guys push the girls back and was invited to meet the group.

Paul and John greeted him but were busy working on a song but George and Ringo chatted to him for a while. He asked them what they thought of Harrogate and they said it was OK, but there were too many old ladies and tea shops!

He knew I would want their autographs and George tore a piece of cardboard off a box in the room and they all wrote their names.

I've still got it and I never collected any other autographs – it would have been downhill after that! We

Above: Wendy Driffield. Below: poster and programme for the Royal Hall, Harrogate, where there were 'too many tea shops' for The Beatles

went together to see them perform in York not long after. My cousin was Beatle mad: he had the hair, the jackets and the boots! Great times.

I WAS THERE: DUNCAN CURRY (AGED 17)

RIALTO THEATRE

13 MARCH 1963, YORK

Paul McCartney signing autographs outside the Rialto, York

I saw them in March 1963 and then again in November 1963. The first time John Lennon didn't turn up – he had a throat infection. So there was just three of them. I'd been used to watching Cliff Richard and The Shadows and Elvis Presley and all that. It was about the time that we formed a band out Easingwold way. We were in a band for about three or four years called The Pandas.

It's a little market town about eleven miles north of York. There's a town hall bang in the centre of the market place and they used to have dances there in the Sixties. I worked in the printers downstairs. We were in this band and it was our third gig. We were supporting a dance band called Charles Hutchinson and his Band. And I was terrified I might break a string. Chris Montez and Tommy Roe were flavour of the month in those

Duncan Curry (right) on bass guitar, playing in his band, The Pandas

days. Chris Montez and Tommy Roe were top of the bill.

Groups playing and singing were something new. Before that it was singers with their own backing groups, like Cliff Richard and The Shadows. The Beatles closed the first half of the first show. They were dressed in black with the Beatle collars. I didn't know much about them.

And I went along that night and McCartney sang that song from *The Music Man*, 'Till There Was You'. And I thought, 'What on earth was that? I've never heard anything like that before.' It was fantastic. We'd just gone to see Chris Montez and Tommy Roe. And the three of them came on and it was instant impact. Everyone knew how good they were.

About two weeks later they were on television and everybody in the world knew about them. Well, all England knew about them. They were on a Bill Grundy show called *People and Places* just after that. And then they got a show on the radio called *Pop Go The Beatles*. That was on Monday nights. So they just kept getting more and more publicity.

Although there was only the three of them they got through it perfectly well. I knew they were going to be big. I certainly knew they were going to be big by the time I saw them in November.

I WAS THERE: JOHN PAUL ROBERTS (AGED 15)

I always used to go with my friend Ron. I had only just left school. The firm that I worked for at the time was a chartered accountants and we used to do the accounts for the Rialto and the Clifton Bingo at the time, when Mr Prendergast had it. And the chap used to go quite regularly there to do all the cashing-up and the ticket sales and everything.

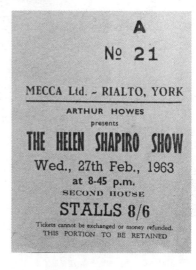

It was about 9/6 to get in, in them days. I remember seeing them twice – the four of them. I also saw the show where George was missing. There was only three once because George Harrison didn't come – he had a bad cold or throat. I don't know whether somebody actually stood in to play the guitar.

Author's note: John Lennon was absent for the March 1963 show in York.

I WAS THERE: PETER HALL (AGED 15)

EMBASSY THEATRE

17 MARCH 1963, PETERBOROUGH

I saw The Beatles perform at the Embassy. The concert I saw featured Chris Montez and Tommy Roe. The evening was opened by a local band called The Dynatones whose bass player, Colin Hodgkinson, still lives locally. I went alone, although I later discovered that my future wife was also there.

The Embassy Theatre, Peterborough

They played 'Love Me Do' and finished with 'Twist and Shout' and I still have a copy of the tour programme.

I WAS THERE: DEE BESLEY

ABC CINEMA

20 MARCH 1963, ROMFORD

I was there with my best friend Sheila to see Chris Montez and couldn't understand what all the screaming was for. I found it a bit embarrassing. The Beatles were playing second fiddle to Tommy Roe and Chris Montez. I had not heard of The Beatles. It must have been shortly before the group's popularity skyrocketed as the Liverpudlian foursome performed a little-known concert at a cinema in South Street, Romford. I've always said it is my claim to fame that I saw The Beatles before they were famous!

I WAS THERE: MALCOLM PAUL (AGED 16)

I first heard the sound of The Beatles at a party at Heaton Way youth club in Romford, Essex, on the Saturday immediately before Christmas in 1962. I had not previously heard of them but the record being played, 'Love Me Do', sounded very distinctive and quite different from anything else I had heard. It immediately aroused my interest and some days later I bought 'Love Me Do' / 'P.S. I Love You' at Wells Music Stores in Romford with one of those record tokens which were very much favoured as Christmas presents at that time.

I was born in October 1946 and had therefore only recently turned 16 years of age. That said, my interest in pop music was already well established, although access to recorded music on the radio in those days was very much restricted by the Musicians' Union and the record companies who feared its impact on their members and their profits.

I very much favoured American music. 'All Shook Up' by Elvis Presley was my first ever purchase and others such as The Everly Brothers, Ricky Nelson, Del Shannon, Brenda Lee, Roy Orbison and, most notably, Buddy Holly – still a lifelong favourite – were played unremittingly on my Dansette Major record player. This was all to change over the early months and the big freeze of 1963.

'Love Me Do' was only modestly successful in the UK charts, but sufficiently so as to provide a platform for the group on radio and television, particularly the former, during which the powerful individual personalities within the group began to emerge to an increasingly wide audience. The first time I was able to see them live was in March 1963 at the ABC cinema in Romford. They were on a tour headlined by Tommy Roe and Chris Montez, two Americans who had had huge UK hits with 'Sheila' and 'Let's Dance' , respectively, the previous autumn. The Beatles had been signed up as a supporting act prior to their increasing success and popularity, not least enhanced by their release of 'Please Please Me' at the beginning of the tour.

A group of friends, perhaps six of us, took the bus into Romford for the 9 p.m. performance clutching our 12/6 tickets, all of us already big fans of the group from their radio performances of many of the numbers that were to appear within days on their first LP, *Please Please Me*. The Beatles did not disappoint and performed most of the tracks that were to become so familiar, culminating in 'Twist and Shout', with John Lennon at his loudest and best. They generated great excitement and it was the first time that I sensed, not least from the audience reaction, that they were going to be something more than a short-term phenomenon.

Sadly, signed as a supporting act, their performance closed the first half of the show and created somewhat of an anti-climax for the audience and the two Americans that shared the second half. As we went home on top of the bus I recall quite clearly an ongoing discussion amongst us about which one was Lennon and which one was McCartney (I got it wrong on that occasion!), suggesting that their songwriting talents were already registering with people. The release of the *Please Please Me* album finally marked their arrival as a remarkable new talent.

Even my parents and those of my friends took to their music and their humour and personalities as they became regulars on radio and television. Everybody seemed to buy the album – not a cheap purchase at 32 shillings for most people in those days.

I WAS THERE: ALAN SNOWSELL

I saw The Beatles at the ABC Romford. They were supporting the Tommy Roe/Chris Montez tour together with The Viscounts, Debbie Lee, Tony Marsh and The Terry Young Six. They had released 'Love Me Do' to reasonable reviews but were not top of the bill. The thing I remember about them was that they were very professional, but not necessarily going to be listened to in 2016!

I WAS THERE: JULIE CRUICKSHANK

My parents and neighbours in George Street, Romford – where we lived – told me that Ringo's step-grandmother lived in George Street and that The Beatles stayed at her house after the concert.

THE FIRST ALBUM

The Beatles' first album, *Please Please Me*, was released on 22 March 1963.

I WAS THERE: BARRY ANCILL

GRANADA THEATRE

26 MARCH 1963, MANSFIELD

Approximately two weeks after The Beatles appeared in Mansfield at the Granada on the Helen Shapiro package they were back as part of the Chris Montez/Tommy Roe tour, and on a cold Tuesday night myself and an old mate of mine, Donald Walker, were there. The bill, if my mind serves me right, also included Bill Black's

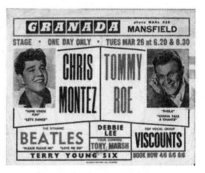

Combo, a band who worked with Elvis. The Beatles on that cold night were third on the bill to the two American stars but they totally upstaged them, making them look third-rate with the crowd going wild. What a night!

It was also rumoured that, with The Beatles not being able to get out of the theatre, a certain Mansfield lad called Shane Fenton (alias Alvin Stardust) bought them fish and chips. A night I will never forget. About three months later, Donald and I were travelling to London in the middle of the night. It was mid-week and we used to help my brother-in-law in his removals business. He pulled into Watford Gap services southbound on the M1 and said he was going to have a sleep.

We jumped out of the wagon and somebody shouted 'The Beatles are in the Grill and Griddle northbound!' We legged it over and –

sure enough – there they were, sat at the bar and returning from recording *Pop Go The Beatles*, which I had listened to the previous teatime before we set off. Us, and the world, were to hear much more from them.

I WAS THERE: JUNE FREEMAN (AGED 18)

I remember seeing The Beatles very well. I went with my friend Anita. We went to most of the shows at the Granada in Mansfield. We were 18 and had gone to see Chris Montez and Tommy Roe. I had never heard of The Beatles but, boy, when they came on I knew they were going to make a big impact on the music world. They were the last act on the first half. They were fantastic.

Girls were screaming and shouting. We didn't want them to leave the stage. The second half was an anti-climax really and although I enjoyed the rest of the show I fell for The Beatles that night and especially Paul, although he didn't replace Cliff Richard in my affections! I still have the programme from that night. We saw a lot of the top acts at the Granada. I remember

Above: Shane Fenton, later to be better known as Alvin Stardust. Did he buy The Beatles fish and chips?
Below: June Freeman fell for Paul so badly he almost (but not quite) replaced Cliff in her affections

' Girls were screaming and shouting. We didn't want them to leave the stage '

one concert when Gene Vincent was in the audience and, because he hadn't got a work permit to perform on stage, he sang from there. Those were the days.

I WAS THERE: DES TURNER

The second occasion was a month later, in March '63. This time they were supporting Chris Montez, and I think Tommy Roe was also on the bill. By now they were hugely popular and the audience noise was even louder, so much so that I couldn't hear all the words of the songs, but could only pick it out by the rhythm of the drums and guitars. On both occasions well worth seeing – pity I couldn't hear it!

Even in those early days, the freshness of their music and their charisma shone through, and it's something I will always remember, and be pleased to tell the grandchildren about – who is Olly Murs anyway? Who could have imagined the global phenomenon they would become?

I WAS THERE: ELAINE SMITH

We were at the show when they were a support act to Helen Shapiro. We heard everything and thoroughly enjoyed the show. But The Beatles were at the Granada again as support act to Chris Montez, and due to their popularity Chris Montez exchanged with The Beatles and gave them top billing. There was screaming and shouting but we still enjoyed it, as did my younger sister who we took with us. We thoroughly enjoyed that show as well and we are both so very proud to be able to say that we saw the Fab Four live in Mansfield – twice!

I WAS THERE: JULIE CAUSEBROOK (AGED 14)

ABC THEATRE

27 MARCH 1963, NORTHAMPTON

For a short time, like most people of my age, I had a frenzy over The Beatles. Paul McCartney was my favourite. I was at school in 1963 – Spencer Secondary Modern School for Girls – and can remember that the first time The Beatles came to Northampton I couldn't get a ticket to get in to see them. This was mainly due to not being prepared, and I hadn't saved up enough pocket money for a ticket – they were like gold dust and went very quickly.

But my best friend Glennis Blenco and I went down to the Savoy cinema to try to see them arrive. The word was that they would be arriving by helicopter and everyone was excited and on the lookout for something to happen. A crowd mingled outside the cinema but we saw nothing.

We were all told later that they were smuggled in the back way to the cinema through one of the factories in St Michael's Road. Although we were on the lookout, unfortunately we didn't see them, but I did have a run-in with Tommy Roe. I was walking up Abington Street towards the cinema when a guy ran into me outside the Wedgewood restaurant/cake shop. He was being chased by a horde of girls and was running down Abington Street from the cinema; he knocked into me and grabbed me by the shoulders to stop me falling over.

He apologised for nearly knocking me down, said he had to go and then ran into the Wedgewood to escape the horde of screaming girls chasing him. I then realised it was Tommy Roe. Meeting him briefly somehow made up for not seeing Paul McCartney on that occasion. My brief impression of Tommy Roe was that he was a really lovely guy and so polite. He must have escaped because I never read anything in the *Chronicle & Echo* to say different.

I WAS THERE: ROGER FRISBY

For the first Beatles visit in March, a mate had a spare ticket because he had finished with his girl and I went instead. It was on a Thursday night and we went for a drink before the show in the Bantam Cock next to the cinema. In early 1963 people were aware of the group but not the individuals, and unknown to us they we drinking in the back room, so when we left we were mobbed by girls asking which Beatle we were. We had to say that we were not John or Paul. I think we missed a great chance to enjoy ourselves but no matter!

We had seats in the balcony and I had the records they had already released so their set was familiar, but live they were better than anything we had ever seen. They could sing for a start and harmonise as well. Groups didn't do that. They were after Chris Montez and before Tommy Roe, who were good. I suspect that most people went to see Tommy Roe, who had a current hit with 'The Folk Singer', rather than The Beatles. But they must have been impressed with them.

The year before, we used to run dances in our youth club and were looking for different groups other than the Northampton groups so we went to see a local chap who booked acts for mainly working men's clubs. He gave us a list of groups he was currently booking. They were London-based generally, Nero and The Gladiators and Neil Christian and The Crusaders, each at around £125 each.

We asked if there was anyone cheaper. We were advised that groups from Liverpool were becoming popular and also

Roger Frisby: he was once asked, in a pub, which one of The Beatles he was

cheaper – The Searchers, Gerry and The Pacemakers. And a group called The Beatles could be had for about £50. We normally paid about £5 to £7 and thought we would lose a fortune on these unknown groups, so we declined!

I WAS THERE: JOHN HARRIS

I was there with friends from Northampton Technical College, all aged 17 or 18, for the 'Please Please Me' tour. As far as I was concerned, 'Love Me Do', although not a number one in the charts, represented the breakthrough in British pop in the same way that 'Hound Dog' had marked the start of the rock 'n' roll era seven years earlier. The music of The Beatles and subsequently the other Mersey and Brit groups expressed the new optimism of the post-war years. We were happy because we believed we could change the world.

We could hardly hear The Beatles because of the predominance of 13- and 14-year old girls in the audience who screamed throughout their performance but the material was so familiar that it didn't matter. It was Chris Montez who left the biggest impression, with his all-action performance.

My parents, being in their 60s then, were indifferent to my musical tastes, but most parents didn't think it would last. Having said that, those with a passion for music in general seemed impressed and interested in The Beatles' music and I think many parents were at least fascinated.

I WAS THERE: PETE SPENCER (AGED 13)

I went to both concerts with my sister Diane, who was 16. I wasn't too bothered about going – I was just getting interested in folk and blues music, Bob Dylan in particular. But my mother's friend owned a shop in Weston Favell, Northampton, and she'd been given two tickets in return for putting up a poster in the shop window and passed them on to my mother to give to us.

It was the first pop concert I'd been to, apart from seeing Tommy Steele at Skegness a few years earlier. As far as I remember, the first show was more about Chris Montez, who had had a hit with 'Let's Dance', with a few screams when The Beatles played.

The Beatles were the first-ever gig for 13-year-old Pete Spencer

I WAS THERE: CAROL NEEDHAM (AGED 16)

I got the tickets the day they were released, but didn't queue. I just went in and got them about midday. My friend and I were in the front row. The Beatles were the last act before the interval. I wasn't impressed. George, I think, had black teeth and I was much more interested in seeing Tommy Roe, who headed the bill. In all honesty I don't remember Chris Montez. Tommy Roe caught my eye and winked at me – that was the highlight of the show as far as I was concerned.

When The Beatles returned later in the year, people queued outside the ABC all night to get tickets. I didn't bother with this performance but did go to many other live concerts at the ABC over the next few years, much to my parents' disgust. We would often walk the four miles home so that we could calm down, although this often made matters worse as it made us much later home than if we had caught a bus.

I WAS THERE: DI NEWBERRY (NÉE BENSON, AGED 13)

I was lucky enough to be at both concerts at the ABC in Northampton. The first one I went primarily to see Chris Montez and Tommy Roe but was well impressed with The Beatles then. I even managed to get Paul and George's autographs after the show at the stage door.

Autographs from George and Paul, which Di Newberry managed to nab after the Northampton ABC gig

I WAS THERE: GISELA OAKES (AGED 14)

I attended Notre Dame High School in Abington Street, Northampton, and was due to go on a school Mediterranean cruise in March of 1963. When we heard The Beatles were coming to town on 27 March, I cancelled my place on the cruise and my friend Christine and I bought tickets for the first performance at 6.30 p.m.

We played truant from school and spent the day waiting at the stage door behind the ABC cinema, hoping for a glimpse of The Beatles, who were supporting Chris Montez and Tommy Roe – but to no avail during the day time. The Beatles weren't as popular then as they became a few months later, so we very much enjoyed their short time on the stage as there wasn't too much screaming as far as I can remember. But it was over far too quickly as there were other acts to appear (seven in total) and two performances per night.

After the concert Christine and I again took up our positions at the stage door. Our waiting was rewarded when George Harrison – my favourite! – and Paul McCartney emerged and we walked down Abington Street with them as far as the Gayway Nightclub, which was down a short

The Beatles signing autographs after the show at the ABC

alleyway at the top of Abington Street, opposite what is now the Radio Northampton building.

As you can imagine, it was very surreal and, being only 14 years old (nearly 15), we were incredibly embarrassed and tongue-tied. I had a pack of Maltesers and offered them to George and Paul and we all shared the pack. I kept the wrapper – which was white then – and the pen they used to write their autographs until I sold my Beatles and Stones memorabilia at Bonhams in 2009.

Unfortunately there was no sign of John and Ringo. I think John had a girlfriend from Northampton at the time so he was meeting her. We did know her name at one time but I cannot recollect it now. Knowing someone from Northampton probably explains how they were familiar with the Gayway Nightclub. They seemed to know where they were heading as if they had been there before.

Friends and I also went to see The Beatles seven months later at their 6.30 p.m. performance at the ABC on 6 November, but they had become so popular by then it was difficult to hear the music above the screaming. Happy days!

Gisela Oakes: George was her favourite

Pauline Lever (far right) had to sit next to her mum at the Northampton Beatles gig

I WAS THERE: PAULINE LEVER (AGED 12)

In 1963, I went to see The Beatles in Northampton. At that time I emulated everything my sister did – or tried to – so I became a fan because my sister liked them. I liked George because my sister did, although I really did think he was the cutest.

I had to sit next to my mum. I think I spent a lot of time just watching the fans, and they fascinated me. My sister, always the more ladylike of the two of us, was horrified by the screaming. They sang 'A Taste of Honey', which I really liked, 'Please Mr Postman' and others, of course. I remember 'Please Please Me' because The Beatles shook their heads through it. At the end my mum grabbed my hand and led me back to the coach. My sister took her own time getting back to the bus.

I WAS THERE: KEITH SHURVILLE (AGED 14)

I was getting into the music scene and liked Tommy Roe's 'The Folk Singer' and obviously had heard Chris Montez's 'Lets Dance' and The Beatles' 'Love Me Do'. On seeing that they were all appearing in Northampton I persuaded my parents to let me and a friend go to the ABC and purchase tickets. It was after I bought the tickets that 'Please Please Me' was released and so I was the envy of my friends when I disclosed that I had tickets to see The Beatles.

I travelled from home in Earls Barton with a friend, I cannot remember who, and the experience was unbelievable, with screaming girls only intent on the seeing The Beatles. It's funny but my main lasting memory of the whole event was Chris Montez singing 'You're the One'.

I WAS THERE: DIANE STRATFORD (AGED 11)

I went to the show with my seven-year-old brother and my grandma and granddad. The tickets had been given to my granddad as he knew the manager at the theatre and they hadn't sold them all! I remember thinking they were certainly different to anything I had ever seen before and, lo and behold, several months later they were a household name.

How I have wished over the years I had stopped to speak and get their autographs. I have been a lifelong fan. Grandma and granddad thought they were too loud.

I WAS THERE: JOHN KIGHTLEY

For many years I worked with the touring producer Owen Price, who always seemed to give me the job of controlling the mic leads – no remotes then – for the scores of stars that performed there over the years, something one couldn't do for the groups because they all played with mic stands and the mass of amplifiers either side of the stage. There was always good behaviour from the groups. They spent much time at the back of the stage strumming guitars and, contrary to many rumours at the time, the girl fans were not allowed backstage. Can you imagine the chaos if they had? There was a lot of screaming and shouting that greeted the lads just before the interval.

I WAS THERE: CHRIS GALE

ABC CINEMA

28 MARCH 1963, EXETER

They were supporting Chris Montez and Tommy Roe and I got their autographs. I thought, 'They'll probably go places.' They came to the stage door, which they used to do at the ABC in those days. I had The Beatles autographs and I had a few others in a book.

I married young. I was about 19, 20. And when we got a flat and I moved out, I left all this stuff in my bedroom along with a lot of old records. When I eventually got a house, I said to my mother, 'I'll take all that stuff away that's in my bedroom.' She said, 'What stuff's that?' I said 'all the old records and books and everything.' She said, 'Oh, I ditched that old stuff.' I said, 'Mother, that's my youth you've just thrown away!' She just binned it. So whether the bin men realised what it was and they got lucky or it just went to the tip I don't know. I think it's in landfill now.

Above: backstage at the ABC cinema, Exeter, 28 March, 1963. Below: the blunt Mr Brunt

**I WAS THERE:
SUSAN HUTCHINSON
(NÉE BRUNT, AGED 21)**

PAVILION GARDENS BALLROOM

6 APRIL 1963, BUXTON

I was living in the Grove Hotel. My parents were the managers. On one of the occasions when The Beatles came to perform at the Pavilion Gardens they wanted to stay at the Grove Hotel overnight. However, having booked in at around 4 p.m. and

❝ I don't care if you are the bloody Cockroaches – get out! ❞

used all the facilities in the rooms, they decided to go back to Liverpool after their performance. My father, who was not a meek and mild man, said they must pay for the use of the rooms as they would need cleaning before they could be re-let.

So John Lennon said to my father, 'Don't you know who we are? We are The Beatles.' To which my father answered, 'I don't care if you are the bloody Cockroaches – get out!' Needless to say, no one knew how famous they would become – what a pity I didn't get an autograph. Bed and breakfast at the time was £1 5s [£1.25]. Perhaps they couldn't afford it.

LEYTON SUPER BATHS

8 APRIL 1963, LONDON

Norman Scott, in the middle of the Fab Four

I was quite a successful DJ for a good number of years. I started off in my local youth club in Chingford, Essex. I saw an advert one day in the *New Musical Express* that a guy was looking for DJs for clubs and, as it turned out, the guy actually lived in Chingford. His name was Ron King and he owned an entertainment agency called Galaxy Entertainments. I think the biggest group he had signed to him was Amen Corner. I went for an audition and got a job as a DJ. And what this guy used to do was find church halls that you could hire, and he hired the same halls the same day every week. And he had about five or six different halls all over the place

Needs must: if no beer glasses are available, tea cups will do

and we'd go along and we had to set up all the DJ equipment.

One of the halls Ron King hired was a place called Leyton Super Baths. It was an indoor swimming pool but they only used it as a swimming pool in the summer period. In the winter they boarded the swimming pool area over and it was a dance hall. It had a big stage and I deejayed there, and every so often we'd have bands on. The Beatles had their first two records – 'Love Me Do' and 'Please Please Me' – out, and they were moving on to bigger venues like theatres. But Brian Epstein kept them to their contracts to finish off doing the few remaining dance halls that they'd been booked for and one of those was the Leyton Baths.

I wasn't DJing that particular night, it was just a bands night, but because I worked there I just walked anywhere I liked. And of course The Beatles weren't as big then as they became but nevertheless it was a sell-out. It was packed out. So I went round to see them and they said they'd like a drink. I can't remember if the Baths sold alcohol, but there wasn't a bar behind the backstage so I went across to the pub opposite and I brought back four bottles of beer for them. And then we found out we'd got no glasses so they drank the beers out of the cups. I've got a picture of them with cups in their hand but it's not got tea in them. It's beer.

We got on really, really well because they liked the same music as I did. I was a big rock 'n' roll fan in those days. Bill Haley and Little Richard and Jerry Lee Lewis, and they were into those. Then it was almost time for them to go on stage and I asked them if I could take a photo of them. So John Lennon said, 'Yes, that's no problem. I'll line the guys up. Once we line up, I'll count to three and you take the photo.' So that's what he arranged. But Paul McCartney had been about to clean his teeth and he'd still got the tube of toothpaste in his hand. So John Lennon counted to three but John, being the fool that he was, went 'one – two – THREE!'

Well we all jumped including Paul McCartney and, as he jumped, Paul squeezed the toothpaste tube and a whole stream of toothpaste shot out and went all down his trouser leg. He wiped the toothpaste off but there was a big white stain on his trousers and Ringo Starr said, 'You'd better cover that up, Paul, because nobody will believe it's toothpaste.' And off they went. They did a whole set of cover versions and obviously 'Love Me Do' and 'Please Please Me'. And I think it was the very first time they played 'From Me to You', because they announced it was their new single.

'FROM ME TO YOU'

'From Me to You', the third Beatles single, was
released on 11 April 1963.

BRIDGE HOTEL

15 APRIL 1963, TENBURY WELLS

*The Fab Four on the street
outside The Bridge Hotel,
Tenbury Wells*

At that time my late wife was living in the town and I was in lodgings
there. My late father-in-law was one of the organising committee and
Maureen always claimed that it was her idea that they were booked. She
got the autographs at the time. I am hanging on to her autograph book for
the kids' inheritance!

MAJESTIC BALLROOM

17 APRIL 1963, LUTON

At the time Elvis and Cliff Richard records were more popular in
the charts. In a side street in the town suddenly appeared posters

Beatles postcard, signed by the group at the Majestic Ballroom, Luton

advertising 'One night spectacular featuring The Beatles.' I remember friends saying, 'What a funny name for a group. They can't be great if they're in a small cinema.'

We'd just been to see The Tremeloes playing live at St Albans in a big theatre. They couldn't compare with The Beatles. The opinion was they were a band for the girls. None of the boys that I knew liked them.

I WAS THERE: CHRISTINE BALDWIN (NÉE WHITTAKER, AGED 17)

IMPERIAL THEATRE

11 MAY 1963, NELSON

I saw them at Nelson Imp in 1963. I was working at the Borough Building Society on Parker Lane, Burnley, the building now occupied by Contact Burnley. My friend Pam's boyfriend, David, had a cousin called Bill who was playing in a supporting group. Bill showed me around backstage but there was nobody about.

I knocked on the dressing room door and Paul McCartney answered. He took my autograph book into the dressing room where all four Beatles signed it. I still have the autographs.

Paul McCartney heard Christine Baldwin's knock

I WAS THERE: JAN BOUNDEN (NÉE BIRD, AGED 14)

GROSVENOR ROOMS

17 MAY 1963, NORWICH

I remember walking there. I don't remember walking home. I got their autographs as well. I went with school friends. I went to school with a girl called Jenny and the other girl was her friend. I can't remember what her name was but I think she got the tickets. The tickets were 7/6 [38p]. We might even have got them on the door. I still have my ticket and the flyer. And the flyer's got their autographs on the back. I actually got Paul and John and George's autographs addressed specially to me. It was a place called the Grosvenor, which doesn't exist anymore, on Prince of Wales Road, quite near Thorpe station. They used to have lots of groups there but that was the only time I ever went.

At the time everybody seemed to like The Rolling Stones or Elvis Presley or Cliff Richard. And I didn't really like any of those. I liked Billy Fury. And then along came The Beatles and I did like their music. The three of us were standing right against the stage and I can remember the wooden stage not being particularly tall. I think it came up to my knees

Jan Bounden lured The Beatles out of their white van

as we stood there. We were actually right against the stage, with The Beatles on the stage. I was to the left of the stage and George Harrison was near me. He used to stand on the left so I was near George Harrison and then Paul.

You wouldn't have known they were going to become as famous as what they did. *The Daily Mail* published a photograph of the four of them walking down Oxford Street and I wrote to the *Daily Mail* and they sent me the photograph. I took that to the Grosvenor and after the performance I went round to the side gate.

There were some very tall iron gates but you could see through these gates and there was a white van which is what The Beatles had come in. And they were in the van and I remember calling their names and eventually John and George and Paul came out of the van. But not Ringo. And those three signed this photograph I'd got. And it says, 'To Jan love from John, George and Paul.' But on the flyer I've got all four signatures.

So the photograph is addressed to me but I haven't got Ringo's. Paul actually signed on my wrist and then I went home and covered it with cellophane and then when I went to school on the Monday, because the concert was on a Friday, I was quite famous. So on Monday I went to school with my signature of Paul still wrapped up. And I didn't wash it for about a fortnight. I wouldn't ever sell the autographs because it's just memories. My memories.

I WAS THERE: SANDRA HAWES (AGED 16)

I went with a girlfriend from school. Her name was Lorna Hannant. Her uncle was the manager of the Grosvenor. It was done through her. He asked her would she like to go and she asked me would I like to go? A night out! So she took me with her. And that's how we came to see them. And the thing of it was, on the night he asked, 'Did we want to go backstage and get to meet them and get their autographs? And we said no. We didn't think we wanted to do that. I don't think we were really that struck, to be quite honest. We liked them and it was nice to see them. I can remember it was only a little stage they were on. And we stood right in front of them. I think we both liked George at the time. So we missed out on the autographs because we said 'no' to going backstage. I'd have been thousands in now!

ROY ORBISON GIGS

The Beatles embarked on a further UK tour headlined by Roy Orbison, but audience reaction was such that the 'Big O' was soon demoted to second place.

EMPIRE THEATRE

26 MAY 1963, LIVERPOOL

❛ From 1963 onwards they were a totally different band ❜

Roy Orbison was the headliner at the Empire show and they did a short 30-minute set. They were OK and that was a bit quieter than the Southport Odeon show. But from 1963 onwards they were a different band.

Don't get me wrong. It was after that that their huge ability as songwriters came to the fore. There was never evidence of that in the early years. The songwriting side of it was not evident in those early days.

When you started listening to the albums, and the songwriting talent came out, you started appreciating the hidden treasure.

I WAS THERE: SUE INNIS (NÉE ROBINSON, AGED 18)

GAUMONT CINEMA

28 MAY 1963, WORCESTER

I went with a girlfriend who was a year older. I cannot recall her name. I had heard of The Beatles on Radio Luxembourg, whilst I was away nursing in Northampton. I kept telling everyone how good they were but they did not seem to know anything about them. It was the winter of 1962. So I congratulate myself on being the first to spot their potential.

However, not long after when they had their first hit, everyone wanted the record. All the lads wanted the Beatle jackets and the longer hair, which parents objected to. It was manic. I was sitting in the second row from the front of the stage.

I was disappointed however, as I could not hear them for the screaming. Several young girls were escorted out because they were overcome and felt faint. However, the little I did manage to hear was

Sue Innis (above) was the first among her crowd to discover the Fab Four

great. They made a great sound and played all their hits. I did not join the throng to see them leave the theatre as it was mayhem. But it was very memorable.

I WAS THERE: SANDRA LONGMIRE (AGED 14)

Having first read about The Beatles in some teenage magazine, it was decided that Paul McCartney was the most beautiful boy in the world! There was

Gaumont Theatre
WORCESTER
THE BEATLES /
ROY ORBISON
1st Performance 6-15
TUESDAY
MAY 28
CIRCLE
L38 7/6
No Tickets exchanged nor
ney refunded
TO BE RETAINED

Sandra Longmire managed to get front-row seats to watch the Fab Four at her local Gaumont

great excitement when we found out that The Beatles were appearing at our local Gaumont. My friend Mary's mum went and queued to get us tickets on the front row for 12/6 [63p]. There were two performances in those days and we went to the first house, as it was called then. We had decided not to scream, as Paul would then notice us. The naivety of being only 14 years old!

After the show, where Roy Orbison was actually top of the bill, we waited outside for autographs. They were by then becoming quite famous and it would not have been safe for them to come out and face the mob. We handed our autograph books in and they came out duly signed, but to this day I am never sure if they are genuine as I believe both Neil Aspinall and Mal Evans, who worked for The Beatles, were very good at faking their signatures.

They did however talk to us through the dressing room windows. It was quite a pleasant evening as I recall. I remember George just gazing out of the window at all

❜ One of the girls who lived close by went home and got George a hard-boiled egg ❜

the crowd. He must have felt trapped. One of the girls who lived close by went home and got him a hard-boiled egg. I wonder if she remembers that?

Paul was also using a cine camera at the time and he was filming us all screaming. I often wonder what happened to that piece of footage. To conclude the evening I remember my mother and little brother appearing, not to take me home but to join in! Much to my embarrassment, my mum started shouting for Ringo!

I WAS THERE: JOHN PAUL ROBERTS (AGED 15)

RIALTO THEATRE

29 MAY 1963, YORK

They used to do two sessions. They did the half-past-six and half-past-eight shows. Roy Orbison was the main one on. They finished the first half. And when we knew they were on, I used to get the front seats. I used to get the front seats within the first half-an-hour for most of the groups that were there – The Beatles, Gerry and The Pacemakers, Little Richard, Gene Vincent and all those.

No 7 N

MECCA Ltd. – RIALTO, YORK

KENNEDY STREET ENTERPRISES & TITO BURNS present

ROY ORBISON

AND

THE BEATLES

Wed., 29th May, 1963

at 6-40 p.m.

FIRST HOUSE

STALLS 8/6

Tickets cannot be exchanged or money refunded. THIS PORTION TO BE RETAINED

All the groups in the Sixties like. I've got all of the programmes for them. I liked the late Fifties – Little Richard, Gene Vincent. Jerry Lee Lewis. And then it was the American groups like Tommy Roe, Chris Montez and all those lot.

The Beatles stood out. It was a different sound. I was in the first two or three rows. The audience was screaming, going mad. We were at the front so you could hear them a bit. We always went to the second show. After everyone else went round to the back door to try and get autographs.

We went up to the stage and stood just in front of the stage and the roadies came on and were taking all the equipment down and they were just there talking and walking about.

GRANADA THEATRE

1 JUNE 1963, TOOTING

I saw them on a package show at the Tooting Granada. They opened with 'Please Please Me' and John did not play the harmonica but picked out the intro on guitar instead. I next saw them at *The Beatles Christmas Show* at what was then Finsbury Park Astoria, which was a variety show and good enough for me to go again the following year.

> There was the usual barrage of screaming but I could always hear the music and it was excellent

At all three shows there was the usual barrage of screaming but I could always hear the music and it was excellent, which was not surprising given their apprenticeship in Hamburg. They were a very special talent, but I think all their good stuff petered out in 1964. In my honest opinion their best album was the first. *Please Please Me* was recorded in 12 hours when they all had streaming colds. They asked to postpone the recording and were refused. Perhaps for this reason it has all the best aspects of a live performance.

HIPPODROME

2 JUNE 1963, BRIGHTON

I saw them a few times, but one concert in 1963 sticks out. We knew tickets would go fast and they went on sale on a school day. It didn't occur to us to skip school – we wouldn't have dared. We were at grammar school and terrified of getting told off. Parents didn't approve of The Beatles then. They thought they were scruffy and also distracting us from school work – so they were correct there! So they refused to get tickets for us, although after a year or two they changed their minds a bit as they thought the Rolling Stones were appalling so The Beatles were quite preferable!

Anyway, my grandma, bless her, went and queued for tickets for myself and my three closest friends as a surprise. We were so thrilled. So off we went, four young teenagers, by ourselves on the bus and so excited. We didn't hear a thing of course as we just screamed and screamed. I'm not even sure why. Funny that in those days parents didn't mind you going somewhere by yourself so long as you were home on time by the 10.30 p.m. curfew and didn't get run over or make them stay up late.

Roy Orbison was on the bill. We had front-row seats for that show but we didn't want to see poor Roy. He came on with his trademark sunglasses. We thought he was blind and I'm ashamed to say we sat poking our tongues out, making funny faces as we thought 'Get off! You're boring and you can't see us anyway!' There's nothing quite so insensitive as a group of 14-year-olds, and it was only years later we found out that he had sensitivity to the light and wasn't blind. By then we were old enough to know better and I confess to feeling a little ashamed.

I WAS THERE: JACK STRUTT (AGED 20)

Jack and Pam Strutt – both big fans of the 'Big O'

Together with my future wife Pam, I saw them at Brighton Hippodrome when they first appeared in the town. The tour had started out with the 'Big O', Roy Orbison, topping the bill after huge success with songs such as 'Only the Lonely', 'Crying', 'In Dreams' and 'Falling'.

However, by the time the tour reached Brighton, what became known as Beatlemania was taking hold and the boys effectively topped the bill. Also on the bill that night were Gerry and The Pacemakers, balladeer David Macbeth, one-hit wonder Louise Cordet and Tony Marsh, acting as compere. Pam was 17, so this was one of our early dates. It would be back to work next day, but this was too good an opportunity to miss.

We had booked to see the show not because The Beatles were in town but primarily to see Roy Orbison, who was – and still is – my favourite male pop singer. His songs never date. When we arrived in Middle Street for the second house it was bedlam. The teenage girls who had come to see The Beatles were already in a state of high excitement and it promised to be a memorable evening.

I imagine Roy may have been somewhat apprehensive before going on stage, given that the vast majority of the audience were there to see The Beatles. But any fears he may have had were soon dispelled – he had a walkover. He just stood at the microphone with his black guitar and dark glasses without hardly moving, except to pull out his harmonica for 'Candy Man'. I don't know how long his act was scheduled to last but my memory is of sustained cheering at Roy's performance and I'm sure he carried on for a long encore.

At this stage of the tour The Beatles were closing the show and, as elsewhere, the Hippodrome audience went berserk. I don't recall hearing too much of the music because of the screaming girls. The atmosphere was something I had never experienced before at a pop concert and I'm so glad I didn't miss it. My only regret is that I didn't retain the tickets or programme for the show.

I WAS THERE: ROGER GRIGG

BIRMINGHAM TOWN HALL

4 JUNE 1963, BIRMINGHAM

In my early 20s, I used to see most of the big acts when they came to Birmingham. I saw The Beatles at Birmingham Town Hall. When we bought the tickets for the show, Roy Orbison was headlining and it was he who we'd booked to see. The Beatles were only a support act and were just becoming really popular.

By the time we went to see the show, The Beatles were huge. Roy Orbison stood down to become the support act to The Beatles, going on stage before them. After the performance we could understand why.

As soon as The Beatles came on stage the audience exploded. The

Roger Grigg: another Roy Orbison fan who got more than he bargained for, but wasn't disappointed

teenage girls in the audience screamed throughout the performance. Although we could barely hear The Beatles above the audience noise, it was a fantastic experience and one I'll never forget.

I WAS THERE: TONY NEWSON

Roy Orbison was the big name then. And The Beatles were put on as top of the bill. Roy Orbison was dropped down the order to come on before The Beatles. But he was so great. I can't remember The Beatles very much but I can remember Roy Orbison. They were all screaming for The Beatles all the way through until Roy Orbison came on. And he shut them up and then they were all screaming for him to stay on. Even knowing that The Beatles were going to follow him. That's how good Roy Orbison was.

I knew what to expect from The Beatles but it was the one and only time I saw Roy Orbison and I'd been a fan going back to 'Only the Lonely' from the time I was leaving school. He definitely lived up to expectations. He was great. Of course they were the scrubbed-up Beatles when they were at the Town Hall.

I WAS THERE: NEIL REYNOLDS

I saw them supporting Roy Orbison. I was there and still have the programme. He'd got such a great voice. The audience were totally respectful so you could hear every note. That wasn't the only contrast – the Big O had a great voice but no stage presence and hardly moved. The Beatles were the complete opposite, jumping about and very animated.

I WAS THERE: SUE FLANAGAN

The show at the Town Hall was quite tame compared to the others I saw. I saw Roy Orbison too, but The Beatles were all everyone wanted to see. I had already bought 'Please Please Me'. In my diary I wrote 'Saw Beatles at Town Hall. Absolutely great, fab and all the rest. Love them all. JL especially.'

Sue Flanagan's teenage diary: a testament to her love of The Beatles

I WAS THERE: SUSAN BROWN

ODEON THEATRE

5 JUNE 1963, LEEDS

I managed to see The Beatles twice at the Odeon in Leeds. The first time was The Beatles/Roy Orbison concert in 1963. It was just when The Beatles were rising to the top. My friend and I got seats for the early performance but were a couple of rows from the back in the stalls. We were there almost as soon as the doors were opened and had only been seated for a short time when we heard a few 'murmurings' and turned round only to see Ringo walking along the back row just behind us, having nipped out to a local sweet shop. Paul was walking down the aisle at the far side. They both then disappeared through the door next to the stage (oh, that I'd thought to get autographs).

In the programme, which I still have, both Roy Orbison and The Beatles were due to play in the second half, Gerry and The Pacemakers closing the first half but, from memory, Roy closed the first half. It was just a brilliant concert with nothing untoward happening as far as I remember (unlike my second concert).

I WAS THERE: JENNY MASKELL

When we saw them the first time in Leeds, Roy Orbison was top of the bill and they were supporting him, and then the second time they went very quickly from appearing first on television to being a phenomenon.

How long did it take? Six months. A year, maybe. I think it was because they were so different

❜ They were so different from anything that had come before... and it was at the right time as well ❜

from anything that had come before and because it was at the right time as well. People had been watching Cliff Richard, Billy Fury and there was just something different about them. It was just their clothes, their hair. Just everything about them, really.

I WAS THERE: ERNIE ROBINSON (AGED 19)

KING GEORGE'S HALL

9 JUNE 1963, BLACKBURN

I saw them at King George's Hall. It was before we were married. We booked tickets to go and see Roy Orbison and not The Beatles. He was top of the bill. I think Gerry and The Pacemakers were on

King George's Hall, Blackburn

the same bill. Margaret seems to think Cilla Black was as well but I don't think she was. So when we booked, The Beatles were just a support act. I wanted to see Roy Orbison. But everybody was more excited about The Beatles than Roy Orbison.

Now I really didn't know anything about them. They were just a name as far as we were concerned. But obviously other members of the audience on the night we went must have heard about them or something because people were stood on the chairs and screaming. We were surprised at the number of screaming girls and people standing on their chairs. We were looking at one another and thinking, 'What's all this about?'

After all the enthusiasm, the screaming, the standing on chairs and the clapping, Roy Orbison seemed an anti-climax. So we saw them before they were really, really famous. Or they might have been famous and it passed us by, because we were thinking we were going to see Roy Orbison!

I WAS THERE: MARGARET ROBINSON (AGED 18)

I can't remember how we got the tickets but they were a supporting act. They weren't the main act that night. They were the supporting act for Roy Orbison and all the girls were getting carried out. Fainting. It was a really good show.

THE PAVILION

10 JUNE 1963, BATH

Llyn Harrington (crouching at the front and, below, in the centre): pictorial proof that he and his crowd preferred booze to bands

My crowd never went to see them, preferring to spend our cash on booze! Later that evening, at kicking-out time, a group of northern blokes asked us for directions and we spent some time taking the piss out of one another's accents. The next day we were surprised to see in the local paper a photo of these blokes, who were in fact The Beatles and friends!

CITY HALL

15 JUNE 1963, SALISBURY

I went to the concert with the lady who became my wife in September 1963. We took with us our three bridesmaids, who were in Salisbury for the purpose of having their dress fittings. If I recall, John Lennon had appeared on *Juke Box Jury* earlier in the evening and was flown to Old Sarum airfield to appear at the gig. My wife and I have been married for 52 years now.

I WAS THERE: JEAN DEVINE (AGED 14)

I saw them in '63 when they were in concert in Salisbury at the City Hall and couldn't here a thing basically. It was just screaming – screaming, screaming, screaming all the way through from the audience so you didn't hear them at all playing. And I think that was general actually over the course of all of their concerts. I think I must have gone with a school friend but I really can't remember which one it was. It was my very first concert. And what a great way to start!

The Beatles at Salisbury City Hall was Jean Devine's first ever gig

I WASN'T THERE: MALCOLM MOSLEY (AGED 12)

ODEON CINEMA

16 JUNE 1963, ROMFORD

A mean and moody-looking Malcolm Mosley: sadly too young at the time to do any more than gaze at the big Beatles billboard

I was in the first year of the senior school and developing a great love of pop music. I used to catch the 252 bus from Romford to my school in Collier Row. On my way home I used to sit upstairs at the front on the right-hand side with my friends. The bus travelled down South Street towards Romford station and the Romford Odeon was about 50 yards on the right-hand side before the station. As the Odeon came into view we could see advertised The Beatles' name in big letters and I used to wish to be able to see them. To this day I still regret not having seen The Beatles perform.

I WAS THERE: DENISE BENNETT (AGED 14)

My friend Marilyn and I went. My mother bought the tickets. I was wearing a Beatle jacket with no collar that my mum had made me in dark brown corduroy. dad dropped us off. We had front-row seats in the wings. There were four girls who sat behind us and they had made Paul a 21st birthday card as it was his birthday that week and I believe they got to go backstage after the show to hand it to him. We all screamed throughout the whole performance. After the show my friend and I – along with many others – went around to the back door and screamed at anyone who poked their heads out of an upper window!

I WAS THERE: ALAN SNOWSELL

By the time I saw The Beatles in June they were stars and topping the bill at the Romford Odeon. It was quite a line-up as it also featured Gerry and The Pacemakers and Billy J Kramer and The Dakotas, with the Viscounts as support. After a long forgotten argument with my dad, he did not give me the money for the gig in advance, so on the day I simply turned up at the theatre for the early show in the hope of getting a spare cheap ticket. I remember seeing a green Ford Classic arrive at the side of the theatre and Paul McCartney climbing out and rushing into the side entrance, pursued by screaming fans. I wandered into the theatre more in hope than anything and was surprised to be able to purchase a standing ticket for four shillings and sixpence [23p]. This actually afforded me a better view as I was raised above the seated audience and it also cut out a lot of the screaming. I should have kept the ticket! I am still a huge fan of The Beatles, who can do no wrong as far as I am concerned. They were a great innovative group of down-to-earth lads who deserved their acclaim.

I WAS THERE: JILL SNOWSELL (NÉE GOODALE)

Jill and Paul Snowsell: though they did not meet until four years later, both of them were at the same Beatles gigs in Romford

I went to the ABC in Romford in March 1963 to see the Tommy Roe and Chris Montez tour but have no recollection of The Beatles at all. I then went to the Odeon in Romford with my friend Christine Chetland in June and remember an incredible evening. I got off the bus, met up with Christine and, as I passed Romford station, my abiding memory is of a girl standing there having been to the earlier performance and talking to friends with an expression of wonderment on her face, with a finger demonstrating the round collars on The Beatles' suit jackets, and about their hair!

The *Romford Times* published an article on the front page with a photograph showing The Beatles all looking out from a narrow brick balcony at the side of the Odeon and down at the fans before the first performance began. I still have the first Beatles LP I bought. I wrote all over the back: 'Paul is fab, smash, smart, cracking, gear.' 'Paul is fabulous, swinging, marv.' 'Paul is great.' 'The Beatles are gear, fantab.' My husband-to-be was at both these concerts but we didn't meet each other until about four years later.

I WAS THERE: HAZEL BARHAM (AGED 14)

I was lucky enough to be in the audience. We did nothing but scream the whole way through and I wonder now if we ever really heard them singing. I can remember also being hauled off The Beatles' car, screaming, by a policeman.

I WASN'T THERE: RICHARD TOLBART

I didn't see The Beatles because I was too young to go but I remember seeing an article in the *Romford Recorder* about how they stopped in Chadwell Heath High Street to buy cigarettes!

I was disappointed I hadn't been there to meet them because that's where I lived and it's amazing such a small moment in time would make the local paper.

I WAS THERE: MALCOLM PAUL

They seemed to tour relentlessly. Having seen them in March, it was a welcome diversion to see them again in June as I was in the midst of taking my GCE O-levels. This time they topped the bill and closed the show, but with some very adequate supporting acts in the form of Gerry and The Pacemakers and Billy J Kramer and The Dakotas, all of whom had emerged from Merseyside on the coattails of The Beatles – and their songwriting skills.

I WAS THERE: JEAN JONES (AGED 26)

ODEON CINEMA

21 JUNE 1963, GUILDFORD

I was lucky enough to get hold of two tickets to see The Beatles with my best friend Mary Davies. We were, ironically, both married to men from the northenmost part of North Wales, a mere spitting distance from the wonderful Liverpool, but they weren't interested in a night of screaming women when the snooker hall and beer beckoned. And obviously they were quite right. I recall there being other artists on the bill that night but we were not remotely interested in them. We were both in love with The Beatles and that was all.

My favourite Beatle then (and now) was Paul. Such a cheeky face on him. Mary was smitten with John. They were all so smartly dressed in beautiful dark fitted suits. What I most recall about that evening was John – with the greatest of humour – picking up several pairs of women's undies from the stage and thanking the ladies most profusely for their generous gifts.

Fortunately, we were sat just too far from the front to make it worth the risk of throwing a pair of our best bloomers. I'll never forget the ringing in my ears from all the screaming, which lasted until the next day. We felt we were too old to scream at 26 – we had a bit of a squeak though, and clapped a lot. A fab night, one I'll never forget, and I feel so privileged to have seen them.

I WAS THERE: AVELINE JAMES

TOWN HALL, ABERGAVENNY

22 JUNE 1963, ABERGAVENNY

I was fortunate enough to see The Beatles in Abergavenny Town Hall. I saw them before they were famous really. I think they were just on the brink of it then. At the time we didn't realise it was any big thing. We were just all excited. There was a promoter chap called Eddie Tattersall and we saw Lulu and The Dave Clark Five. We were very fortunate to see as many people as we did. Several of my friends were not permitted to go as parents were quite strict in those days. One friend I was in school with – her parents wouldn't hear of her going. I think The Beatles were pretty squeaky clean myself and I think my parents thought the same. It might have been a different story if I'd wanted to go and see The Rolling Stones.

The tickets sold out fairly quickly. An old boyfriend of mine keeps telling me that he was the one who bought me the ticket but I don't know. We had been to the football ground in the afternoon to see John Lennon arrive in a helicopter, much to my mother's delight. I think John Lennon had some other event that he had to attend and then had to get here for the evening. The helicopter landed at the Thursdays

The Fabulour Fortunes (back row) were the local support band for The Beatles at Abergavenny

football ground and my mother had my younger brother and my niece in a pram and she was more excited I think than some of the teenagers to go and see this helicopter landing. It was mayhem there! There were quite a lot of males in the audience but I think it was the women, the girls, that were the screaming fans there. It was absolutely jam-packed. The evening went in a blur of joy – and screaming!

I'm in a photograph taken at the Town Hall. You can see me stood right in front of Paul McCartney. A chap I was at school with many years ago was a big railway fanatic and when one of the photographers in town died he went to the auction and bought a lot of his memorabilia and a lot of his old films. He just happened to find these photographs of The Beatles that he'd taken on the night at the Town Hall. So he had them printed off and lots of people bought them. It was just strange how they came to life again.

My father had the Esso garage on the Hereford Road at the time and the following day they just happened to pull into the garage for petrol. So, to my surprise, dad came to tell me that Paul and John had come in for petrol so I had the great pleasure of meeting them briefly and getting their autographs, which I later gave to my young brother to take to school and show his friends some years later. Unfortunately they did not get back home with him and to this day I do not know who took them. I still don't know what happened to those autographs. My brother now has to live that down every time we get together.

Still – good memories! My favourite was and always will be Paul McCartney.

I WAS THERE: KEITH COLLETT

I was there that night. It was electric. Eddie Tattersall was the main man that brought them and many other groups like The Hollies to the Town Hall.

I had suits made to measure at the local Burtons shop for The Beatles and The Hollies. They were great. I would like to go back to those days!

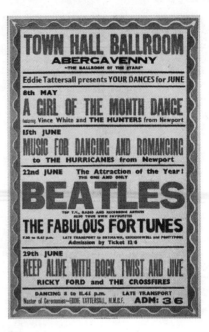

I WAS THERE: GORDON VALENTINE

ASTORIA BALLROOM

25 JUNE 1963, MIDDLESBROUGH

They were getting bigger and bigger. We heard they were coming to the Astoria Ballroom in Wilson Street in Middlesbrough. So we went along and saw the manager and asked if they needed a support band. And he said yes. And so we turned up and on the afternoon a few of us were there carrying the Vox amps in and the drums and all that. And The Beatles came in – just walked in – and we talked to them and they were incredibly scruffy. Ringo Starr had a jumper on with big holes in the elbows.

I asked Paul McCartney, 'Are you getting enough work?' and he said 'Yes'. Any time I see any of the boys from the group now, they always take the mickey out of me for saying that! They came on and you couldn't hear them for screaming. But they were just very nice blokes, very pleasant fellas. We thought, 'Just another band...' My God, they changed the world.

I WAS THERE: GARTH CAWOOD

QUEENS HALL

28 JUNE 1963, LEEDS

Garth Cawood, compere for the night at Leeds

I was booked to do a compering job. This was with The Beatles and Acker Bilk. Acker Bilk was top of the bill. But The Beatles had just broke and they then had to reverse the running order.

Acker still went down an absolute bomb but he didn't close the show. The Beatles had to close the show. I met them a few times. The picture of me with The Beatles was taken in Leeds at the Acker Bilk show.

I WAS THERE: JENNY MASKELL

I was about 14, 15, 16 when it was all going on. My mother was only 18 years older than me and she was interested in them as well. She came with me. We did it as a family. They were on a television programme called *Calendar* in 1962 and I went to an all-girls school and all the girls were talking about seeing them. And we found out that they were based at The Cavern in Liverpool. It was before they went to Germany, I think, and then we heard that they were supporting Acker Bilk in Leeds. I remember this tram shed place. Acker Bilk was playing there and The Beatles were the supporting act. There were no seats. Everybody was stood around. I could have touched The Beatles from where I was standing.

And Acker Bilk's 'Stranger on the Shore' was top of the pops at that time so he was obviously the starring act. It was a mixed audience. Jazz fans who'd gone to see Acker Bilk. We'd gone to see The Beatles. We did stay and watch Acker Bilk because obviously he was on at the end. We actually went into The Beatles' dressing room. They were fairly accessible at that time. They were still walking about. In fact, Paul McCartney and Ringo Starr walked out when we were just sort of hovering about before we actually went in and the friend I was with asked Paul McCartney for his autograph. I don't know whether she's still got that.

I WAS THERE: PAULINE PORTER (AGED 15)

REGAL THEATRE

30 JUNE 1963,
GREAT YARMOUTH

It was totally amazing. It's so far back I just can't remember. They were top of the bill. I went with girlfriends from school. I was living in Gorleston. You're totally star-struck. I don't think I heard any of the music at all, because there was so much noise going on. The theatre? You wouldn't have got another person in there. It was absolutely packed. And you never heard any of the music. It was just permanent screaming. Paul was my favourite. It was a big deal at the time. Oh my God. I did see The Beatles!

I WAS THERE: SUE FLANAGAN (AGED 17)

THE RITZ

5 JULY 1963, BIRMINGHAM

My friend and I worked in Birmingham town centre. I had no time to get home and back so went straight from work. I asked someone what bus to catch and found the stop and got chatting to another girl in the bus queue. I asked her where the Ritz was in Kings Heath and she said, 'Are you going to see The Beatles?' 'Yes we are,' we replied. 'Are you a member?' 'No,' we said. 'Well you won't get in, but if you save me and my friend a place in the queue we will sign you in.' Deal done. The queue wasn't too bad but we were early. The girl from the bus queue arrived, we let them in and into the dance hall we ran. The stage was just a raised wooden platform and I sat on the left end and waited.

On they came and guess who

Above: page from Sue Flanagan's diary, July 1963.
Below: Sue and friend, Birmingham, 1963

was at the feet of Paul McCartney? Yes – me! He smiled at me and I very gently reached out and held his foot, encased in a Beatle boot. And my hand stayed there for a little while. And Paul sang I don't know what song. I was in heaven. The Redcaps played next, and as Ringo's drums were being taken to the door they caught up in the dress I was wearing. What a night. Only Dave Walker, the singer from The Redcaps, said to me, 'You do know John is married, don't you?' Well, I was devastated.

I WAS THERE: MAGGIE BELL

THE PLAZA

5 JULY 1963, HANDSWORTH, BIRMINGHAM

The Plaza was situated in Rookery Road, Handsworth, and, along with another venue called The Ritz, belonged to Ma and Pa Ryan. My husband Michael was employed there as a barman and told me about all the groups that played there. When I asked him about The Beatles, he said he 'thought they were quite good'.

WINTER GARDENS GIGS

The Beatles appeared at the Winter Gardens
in the seaside resort of Margate, Kent, playing
two houses a night for six consecutive nights.

WINTER GARDENS

8–13 JULY 1963, MARGATE

My father was Jack Green, the entertainments manager of the Winter
Gardens, and it was he who was responsible for booking The Beatles for
the week from 8 July, 1963 – twice nightly! He had the foresight to make
the booking in January of that year just before they really took off. I was
born and raised in Margate until sadly my parents divorced and I moved
to London with my mother. However I was allowed to take some time off
school and take two friends from school to see The Beatles. I suddenly
became very popular! My father arranged seats for us quite near the
front and we screamed ourselves hoarse. It seems a shame now that we
didn't listen to them singing. At the interval my father took the three of

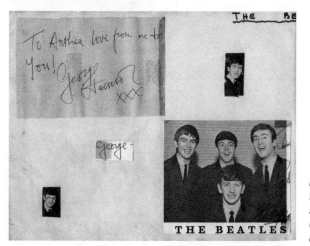

Beatles memorabilia
from Anthea Craig's
scrapbook, with
George's autograph
on the left

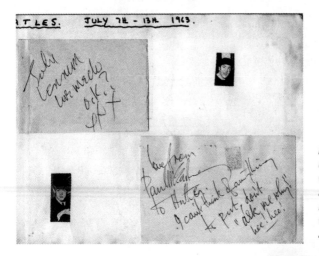

More from Anthea Craig's scrapbook, with George's autograph on the left. Below: Anthea with her father Jack Green

us backstage to meet The Beatles and get their autographs. I asked them to use a name of one of their songs in the autograph. George was my favourite and I so hoped he would use 'with love from me to you' – which he did. John and Paul were also happy to comply, but Ringo was rather grumpy and did not.

At that time it was rumoured that John was married so I asked him straight out if he was married. He looked a bit nonplussed but he said yes. It was a wonderful experience that I often look back on. Incidentally, I took a set of autographs back to a school friend who could not attend and she got about £3,500 for them about ten years ago. I could never sell mine!

I WAS THERE: JENNY WILKIN (AGED 13)

I emigrated to Canada in 1974 but grew up in Margate from 1960 to 1967 and attended one of their concerts in 1963. My father was the Deputy town clerk of Margate and died of a massive heart attack at the age of 49 in 1963, leaving my mother (then aged 39) and three daughters. My older sister had already moved out on her own to Sussex, leaving me and my nine-year-old sister Trish in Margate with my mother. As a kind gesture, Jack Green, entertainment manager for the Winter Gardens and a colleague of my father, gave front-row tickets to my sister and me, together with backstage passes to meet The Beatles at intermission.

Above: the programme for The Beatles gig on Monday, 8 July. Below: Jenny Wilkin and her sister, who had front-row tickets and backstage passes

The concert in itself was an overwhelming experience with hundreds of fans screaming and crying hysterically from start to finish. At intermission my sister and I were collected and ushered backstage, to the rage of devoted fans in the audience! We were taken to The Beatles' dressing room. We were greeted by Paul McCartney who was very friendly and welcoming. George was friendly but shy and did not interact much. Ringo was quite sullen and basically ignored us and John sat with a towel over his head the whole time so we could not even see his face! I am sure they were not thrilled to have to accommodate two "children" during their break but they were not rude to us.

We left after our 15 minutes with them with autographs in our autograph books and signed photos – all of which were lost over the years – and boasting rites with our peers.

I WAS THERE: ROZANNE DUNCAN (AGED 17)

At the time I was working in my first job at David Greig supermarket, Westbrook. I was engaged to be married and took a part-time job as a programme seller at the Winter Gardens so when I was asked by the supervisor how many shifts I would work I naturally said 'all of them'.

All twelve concerts were a double bill with Billy J Kramer and The Dakotas and at one of the shows I was told to get some more programmes to sell during the interval. Not knowing the layout backstage, I entered the stage door and instead of going down the stairs leading to behind the stage I started going up and who was coming down but Billy J Kramer. Just imagine my embarrassment. A comedian whose name I've forgotten had the unenviable

Above: the Fab Four relaxing in a (rather cold) swimming pool at their Margate hotel, in between gigs. Below: Billy J Kramer, July 1963

slot immediately after the intermission of holding the audience at bay whilst waiting for our idols to take the stage. He was so funny and he held the audience completely in his hands by doing a skit about Christine Keeler.

The amazing music that followed couldn't be heard for the screams of the audience and at every performance the balconies seemed to be moving as the fans jumped up and down – it was quite frightening! I'll never forget that amazing week. I saw all 12 concerts and got paid for the privilege.

I WAS THERE: DIANE ALGER (AGED 20)

Diane Alger (left) set off the standing-on-seats trend at one of the Margate gigs

I first heard of The Beatles in Dreamland Ballroom. The DJ played 'Love Me Do' and we were all spellbound. The DJ had to play it seven or eight times after that as we were all blown away with the sound. I remember the show I saw as if it were yesterday. We were all shouting and screaming and, being short, I stood on my seat because I couldn't see them on the stage very well. The next thing that happened was that everyone else was standing on their seats.

I wondered why John Lennon was squinting with his eyes half shut. It wasn't until years later that I read about the fact that he needed glasses and could only see the front row beyond the stage. A few of us stayed after the show in the hope of getting The Beatles' autographs, but we were told that they had gone. I shall never forget that night at the Winter Gardens.

I WAS THERE: TONY CARPENTER

I went twice to see the show. On the Wednesday evening the ticket cost three shillings and sixpence [18p] and I bought a seat in the auditorium. On the Saturday evening there were still some seats available and I went with a schoolmate, Nobby Marcroft, whose parents had a small hotel opposite the venue in Fort Crescent.

This time the ticket price was seven shillings and sixpence [37p] and I bought a seat in the right-hand balcony looking at the stage. The place was really rocking. It was the first time I had seen dancing in the aisles.

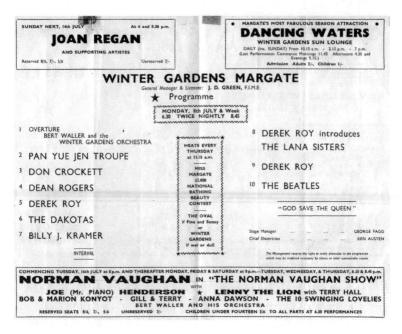

Over the week, momentum had gathered in the district and the school bus was very animated in the mornings – the girls were having heated discussion as to their favourite Beatle. I recall that Paul seemed to come out at the head of the list!

I WAS THERE: WENDY HOLLETT (AGED 17)

In July 1963, my 21-year-old brother Vincent asked me if I wanted to see The Beatles at the Winter Gardens in Margate, as he had two tickets. The tickets cost 8/6 [43p]. At the time I liked Cliff Richard and The Shadows. I said yes! Before the night that we were going to see them we went to see the theatre just to stand outside and listen. A couple were coming out of the theatre and they said, 'You can go inside as there's no one at the door,' so we went in and saw them for a few minutes for free.

On the night, we walked into the Winter Gardens noticing that they had built a wooden rostrum at the back. As soon as The Beatles came on the noise was deafening, with girls screaming. I was young too but I didn't like the screaming. I wouldn't have minded if it was after a song had finished, but not during the performance. They were also banging their feet on the rostrum. My brother and I were knocked out by The Beatles but we went there to listen to the music and I could never understand what all the screaming was about.

After the concert my brother and I went round to the back of the theatre, to catch The Beatles getting into a blue car. Ringo wound down the window and he signed my book. I then asked Ringo if I could have John's autograph and he passed my book to John. John signed it and passed it back to me and said, 'Here you are, luv', and he went off with my pen. I didn't mind! It was such a good evening. I went back again at the end of the week for 3/6 [38p].

I WAS THERE: JANET PILCHER (NÉE FURBY, AGED 21)

I don't remember much about the night I saw The Beatles at the Winter Gardens, Margate, except moving from my seat to get a better view and leaning against the radiator situated by the entrance to the toilets and joining in the screaming. I went with my friend. I can still see them on the stage but I can't remember afterwards. I was probably traumatised by what I'd seen. What a night. After that evening I became a Beatles fan!

I WAS THERE: TONY LAMPERT (AGED 17)

I went to one of those Beatle shows in 1963 at the Winter Gardens in Margate. It only came about because my father had died in a car accident a few months before. We were living in Sandwich, and after dad died we had to move so I went to stay with my grandmother in Ramsgate, which is where I had originally grown up. I renewed an old friendship and, with my friend's friends, started to go to pop concerts.

There were many in Margate at that time and during 1963 we literally had an invasion of chart stars coming to the town, either to the Dreamland ballroom or to the Winter Gardens. The first band I remember seeing were Brian Poole and The Tremeloes and I was then hooked on live bands. Not small local bands but the big names that kept appearing almost week after week.

To understand the impact of The Beatles then you have to look at the music that had been in the charts up to that time, and why it changed so dramatically. We'd had a diet of Cliff and The Shadows, Adam Faith,

Billy Fury, Helen Shapiro, etc. All good pop music of the early Sixties, but a bit bland. I remember listening to 'Love Me Do' on the radio and not liking it much, although DJs were starting to mention The Beatles because they sounded different. Then they appeared on TV singing 'Please Please Me' and it was like a bolt of lightning. I love pop music and this song performed by them was out of this world at the time – instantly catchy, very melodic, beautifully sung and so exciting to watch. Also they were witty, intelligent and able to handle themselves in interviews.

Tony Lampert, hoping for some Sixties sunshine in Ramsgate

❝ The boys went for the music but the girls for the sex appeal ❞

Then of course they came to Margate. The *Please Please Me* album had been released and tracks were being played everywhere – in the clubs, on the radio. People couldn't get enough of the new sound. The Winter Gardens show happened in July, as the *Please Please Me* album captured the nation, so we got The Beatles at full throttle. In the Winter Gardens there are the main seats at the front, some raised seats at the back and some balconies. I sat somewhere in the middle, maybe a dozen or so rows back, in those front seats. I can't remember who I was with but I had a good view of the stage. Apparently it was a variety show but I have no memory of anything else and The Beatles closed the show. I imagine it was just the excitement of seeing them that excludes everything else.

My most distinct memory is of John Lennon singing 'Twist and Shout', which closed the act. He was directly in front of me and, as he jumped up and came down again, his hair lifted up and down. It's a funny thing, but that's what I remember most vividly. Oh, and the girls screaming. I remember looking around and being amazed at how they just screamed and screamed and screamed.

I think we know now why girls did that, because they couldn't have been listening to the band. I think the boys went for the music but the girls for the sex appeal. Those girls were absolutely hysterical. Quite an experience though. I think Paul McCartney said he eventually broke up the band because he couldn't stand those girls screaming so much and because it meant he couldn't hear himself any more. Looking back, I should have bought a programme but didn't. I did eventually get a programme the following year when I went to the *New Musical Express* poll-winner's concert at the Empire Pool in Wembley, where they topped the bill along with Cliff Richard. I still have it.

> **Something special was about to happen. I remember a feeling of almost tension amongst the audience**

DAVID NORMAN (AGED 19)

It wasn't until about '63 that listening to our pop songs became a regular feature. Before that it was mainly coffee-bar jukeboxes. Or, if you were lucky, a rock 'n' roll social hall. One such 'hall' offered this for us teens twice a week. There was a sign to the effect of 'no alcohol or high-heel shoes allowed'. I had previously been to the Winter Gardens to see top-name artists. And, one Christmas Eve, the Marty Wilde Christmas package show, which was all rock 'n' roll, and I loved it. So when The Beatles started to achieve their fame, starting with 'Love Me Do', I wasn't totally committed to this 'new wave' of music. The same applied to my buddies at that time. We were still into Gene Vincent, Marty Wilde, Cliff and Elvis. That night, we went as a party.

For my own point of view, it wasn't just to go and see a band called The Beatles but for the promise of a good evening out. It was obvious, as soon as we walked into the Winter Gardens hall, that something special was about to happen. I remember a feeling of almost tension amongst the audience already there. It was fairly obvious that the majority of the audience were teenage girls and I felt almost as if it was their music that was about to be played. Which, in a way, it was. The music scene was changing fast with a mix of beat ballads and one or two rock 'n' roll songs in the charts. But also groups such as The Beatles and Billy J Kramer and The Dakotas and Brian Poole and The Tremeloes were beginning to be the start of the new pop trend.

> **The music scene changed that night ... I had witnessed the emergence of a band called The Beatles**

With this in mind, I remember when I walked in and settled down in the front row of the balcony that I had been there and experienced it all as far as knowing how to enjoy a good night out. Even if The Beatles, then, were not quite my first choice of pop artists. But that soon changed.

Billy J Kramer and The Dakotas finished their act to loud applause and screams. I remember the curtains pulling back and there they stood. The Beatles – four fresh-faced youths, perfectly groomed in matching suits and each with luxuriant mops of hair. They didn't at that moment quite match up to my expectations, or maybe I was still making comparisons with the rock 'n' roll stars which I still listened to. They launched into their first number – a Chuck Berry song. They sang nine songs. And what before had been deafening screams from the audience now rose to produce an almost constant bombardment of sound.

I remember leaving after the concert and thinking that I had just seen something special. It put a new perspective on the singers and groups which previously I had held in such high esteem. The music scene changed that night. Although it wasn't until some time later, when The Beatles started to achieve national prestige and international fame, that I realised just why and how that evening had been so special. Because on that evening in 1963, as soon as The Beatles had stepped onto that stage at the Winter Gardens, in the seaside town of Margate, I had been there and witnessed the emergence of a band called The Beatles.

I WAS THERE: MARION SIMPSON

I saw them with my friend Jenny. She went backstage to meet them and I didn't. We had front-row seats, possibly on the Thursday. I mostly remember all the girls screaming. I didn't scream, as I wanted to listen to them. I remember hanging around outside a lot, hoping to see them but only saw Billy J Kramer's band. Sadly my memorabilia got thrown away when I lived overseas and my parents cleared out their attic when they moved. I had so many magazines, plus the programme.

I WAS THERE: BARRY SOLLY (AGED 12)

I consider it an absolute privilege to have seen them in my home town at the Winter Gardens. Because it was never a concert venue. It was a ballroom. You've got concrete pillars all over the place. It's all flat. A couple of balconies. But it was a ballroom.

We hadn't got a television. We got all the magazines. We'd seen pictures of them in the *New Musical Express* and the *Record Mirror*. We'd heard them on the radio. We listened to *Pick of the Pops* with Alan Freeman on a Sunday teatime. And we became aware of all this different style of music, of music changing. I was very lucky. Mum took me to the Winter Gardens and all the stars of the day were there. In 1963 Gerry and The Pacemakers had the first national number one of the beat boom era. And then at the beginning of June we had Jet Harris and Tony Meehan at the Winter Gardens. And they had been at number one with 'Diamonds' and had a hit with 'Scarlett O'Hara'. We sat there in awe looking at them. I remember when we came out of the Winter Gardens we saw a poster and I said to my mum, 'Look that's that new group they've got coming, called The Beatles.' And straight away she went and booked up.

And it was the anticipation – even now it tingles me to think of it – the anticipation of seeing them live. And then we were aware that they were going to be there for the week. All the stars of the day stayed in a big hotel in nearby Birchington, and it became clear that they'd be in the area and we would see them on the night of the concert. We went to see them on the second night, the later show. In those days it was more of a variety show. So you got a comedian, a juggler, probably an acrobatic troupe, an impressionist, a lower-grade comedian and a compere. And then the top stars.

There was usually a good support act that would finish the first half. In this case it was Billy J Kramer and The Dakotas. And it was tremendous to see them because they'd suddenly become popular and we'd all heard of them and they were there on stage. I remember seeing them standing there in their suits and ties and shirts – so smart. And these songs that we'd heard on the radio. And then, all of a sudden, everyone realised that in the second half The Beatles would be there.

❜ I thought, 'How lucky we are. We're going to see The Beatles!' And the curtains went back and all hell was let loose ❜

There were a couple of acts after the interval. I think it was the comedian. And then Derek Roy, who was the compere. He came out and said his bit. And everyone just started shouting and screaming. And he said, 'Right that's it – no more. The Beatles!' And the curtains went back and all hell was let loose.

They stood there and they sang their songs. You could hardly hear the songs. But it was the sheer excitement and the anticipation that The Beatles were going to be there. It was tremendous. Bear in mind this was before 'She Loves You' was released, before 'I Want to Hold Your Hand' at the end of the year. They'd only had 'Please Please Me' and 'From Me to You'. And they were singing all these other songs. They sang what is still my favourite Beatles song, although it was geared more towards the female fan. 'Thank You Girl'. And they sang that as an encore. Twice.

There's nothing like the beat music of that era. Nothing like it at all. On the night we were well aware something big was happening in the music industry. Even then I thought, 'How lucky we are. We're going to see The Beatles.' And all of a sudden they appeared.

For sheer excitement nothing comes close to seeing The Beatles live. I think the important thing was we were lucky enough to see them right there at the beginning when everyone wanted to see them. No one really knew what they were all about. As the years went on, I loved The Beatles for what they were then, from '63 to about '64, '65. Once they got into psychedelia, *Rubber Soul* and *Magical Mystery Tour* – I really wasn't into that. I just prefer them for what they were. Three guitars and a drum set, singing beat music live.

So much happened in 1963. We were just coming out of a horrendous winter. People had just about got over the war. A bit of money in their pockets. Televisions, cars, things like that. Plus of course Margate in the Swinging Sixties. Tremendous summer times on the beaches. And then all of a sudden the music changed. And the youngsters had got something to cling on to. Obviously, a year later, 1964, it went a bit haywire with the mods and rockers. 1963 was the catalyst for the next few years, music-wise. Fate dealt me a great hand. I was there.

I WAS THERE: WENDY STILWELL (AGED 17)

I went with my friend Margaret but we never heard them because of the screaming! We both got their autographs. They were signed in their dressing room whilst we waited outside. I sold mine in the 1970s for about £30 through the Exchange & Mart. Margaret sold hers recently for £2,500. I should have waited!

BLACKPOOL, RHYL & WESTON-SUPER-MARE

After Margate, The Beatles played shows in Blackpool and Rhyl and then commenced another week-long residency in the seaside resort of Weston-super-Mare.

I WAS THERE: DES HENLY (AGED 16)

ODEON THEATRE

22–27 JULY 1963, WESTON-SUPER-MARE

I was in a band called The Iveys. That night we had been playing a gig a few miles out of town at Rossholme School for Girls at Brent Knoll. After our gig we made our way back to Weston. I was on my Triumph Tiger Cub motorbike with Bob on the back, Remo was on his Vespa scooter with his brother. Mario's dad had managed to get all of our gear on the back seat of his Rover 90. Riding into Weston, we were astonished to see thousands of highly excited people surrounding the Odeon cinema. Then it clicked that The Beatles were in town and had just performed their first night of a week-long series of concerts at the Odeon.

Although they were the biggest band around in 1963, they had not yet reached the extraordinary heights for which they were destined, hence their week of concerts in Weston-super-Mare. It was obvious from the crowds that The Beatles hadn't yet left the Odeon so we parked up to savour the moment. After five minutes, the hubbub from the crowd turned into a roar as a white 15cwt Thames van backed up to the exit opposite the Bristol and Exeter pub. The Beatles were about to exit the building.

Their long-time friend and driver, Neil Aspinall, was at the wheel and was gingerly reversing the vehicle through the crowd, trying to position it so that The Beatles could jump straight into the back from the stage door. Not an easy manoeuvre given the frantic crowd. The Fab Four burst through the exit and dived into the van, still finding time for a smile and a wave to their fans. The back door slammed shut and they were away. We jumped on our bikes and followed in hot pursuit. We soon realised they were hopelessly lost and were going around in circles and getting nowhere. On their second excursion into Wadham Street the van stopped. They must have seen us following them as one of the back doors opened. George Harrison's head appeared

One of several photos taken of the Fabs by the pier at Weston-super-Mare

> George Harrison's head appeared and he asked me in his unmistakable Liverpool accent 'Can you tell us the way to the Royal Pier Hotel please?'

and he asked me in his unmistakable Liverpool accent, 'Can you tell us the way to the Royal Pier Hotel please?' Trying not to show my excitement at this unexpected encounter, I said 'Sure, follow us.' We headed off with The Beatles in tow until we reached the hotel and, still grasping the moment, followed them inside.

However, we felt a little awkward standing in the reception with them. Not knowing what to do, we turned and said good night. John Lennon looked at us. 'Thanks very much lads – good night!' Still excited, I thought that was the end of our Beatles experience, but it was only the beginning!

We had booked our tickets for the second night's concert months before. I knew one of the Odeon's managers and that night he asked me, 'Was that you on the motorbike last night?' I said 'Yes' and he said 'We just can't get The Beatles away after the show. The crowds are far too big. So we've made a plan. We are going to use decoy vans at one of the other exits. If you can be backstage each night, we will decide which one we intend to use at the last minute. You can be there waiting with your bikes to guide them to their hotel.' We jumped at the offer, and for the rest of the week became The Beatles' official outriders!

'Girls? Where are the girls?'

John Lennon

One night The Beatles spilled out of the designated exit. We were waiting for them but the van didn't appear. There we were on the pavement with the Fab Four with thousands of screaming fans just around the corner looking for them. Any second we expected someone to shout 'There they are!' and for us to be engulfed. George said what I thought was 'Let's get the car.' It so happened that, that week, George had put his Mark 10 Jag in for a service at Victoria Garage, which had an entrance directly opposite the exit being used that evening.

Mike Millington, one of our team, was a mechanic there and held the keys to Victoria Garage. We all ran across the raised grass plantation to get to the garage's entrance on Alexandra Parade. On the way John Lennon fell over with a curse. I helped him up and we carried on running, genuinely frightened we would be spotted by the mob at any moment. We entered the garage, Mike took the band to George's car and they all looked bemused. There we were with the four Beatles, still in their Beatle jackets and Cuban-heeled shoes with their ties firmly in place, standing in a dimly lit garage in Weston-super-Mare. It was surreal!

George asked, 'What the hell are we doing here?' I replied, 'You said "Let's get the car". George: 'I said cab, not car!' But they all jumped in George's car and we escorted them home safe and sound. Being backstage with them for the next four nights, we had many conversations and ended up on first-name terms.

When some of my friends realised we were in such a privileged position, they naturally tried to take advantage of this and get closer themselves. We delivered many love letters, along with fluffy toys and other presents. On one occasion, as I handed Paul McCartney a love letter with hearts all over it, the sender had asked me to tell him exactly which seat she would be sat in that night. 'Paul, this is from a girl with blonde hair who will be blowing you kisses from the third row.' John, coming down the stairs from the dressing room, overheard me and said 'Girls? Where are the girls?' 'I thought you were married?' I said. Being just 16, I was taken aback by his response. 'So what?' Until he followed up his comment with a broad grin.

Every night we spent at least 15 or 20 minutes alone with The Beatles waiting for our exit instructions. There was many a conversation, and many memories: John Lennon composing on a piano backstage (composing what, I wonder?); being told off by all four of them because the brake light on my motorbike wasn't working and having to promise to get it fixed; a long and animated conversation with George about his love of cars, particularly his Mark 10 Jag; the time their van stopped at traffic lights, girls recognising them and screaming, only for Ringo to grin at me, pointing vigorously to his chest and assuring me that the girls were screaming for him not me.

And lastly, backstage at the Odeon I watched every performance from the wings and was never more chuffed than when Paul glanced at me and gave a wink of recognition.

I WAS THERE: PETE BROWNETT (AGED 15)

As a very young and naïve 15 year old, I was just starting my job as an apprentice photographer and was helping out on the assignment of taking a set of photographs of The Beatles when they visited the town. I was allowed to take one photograph in amongst the set that was taken. It was my birthday three days after the shoot and I managed to get the 32/6 [£1.75] needed to buy the latest album, which took some doing as Weston-super-Mare was closed on a Thursday.

But determination prevailed. Armed with the album, and a considerable amount of pride, I proceeded to get autographs from all members of the group. I was an awestruck teenager but clearly remember discovering that the four of them were down to earth human beings with a wonderful outlook on life and respect for their roots.

This made a lasting impression on me and gave me a philosophy by which I have lived and worked ever since.

I WAS THERE: ANN BAXTER (AGED 13)

Ann Baxter: such a determined autograph-hunter that she scrambled up to the balcony of The Beatles' hotel

My best friend Judy and I lived and breathed pop music. We danced for hours around my red Dansette record player to Cliff Richard and The Shadows, Elvis, The Tornados, Frank Ifield and Susan Maughan. But nothing prepared us for the sounds of John, Paul, George and Ringo. Imagine our excitement when we read in the local newspaper that The Beatles were billed to appear at the Odeon cinema! We rushed to buy our tickets for the performance on 23 July 1963. We could talk of nothing else.

Finally the day came and we caught the bus to the Odeon. Considering that The Beatles were already making quite a sir, the queue wasn't too long – but the buzz of excitement was unmistakable. We took our seats and sat through a supporting cast of Tommy Quickly, Gary and Lee, Dan Thompson and Tommy Wallis. The other group appearing was Gerry and The Pacemakers. The odd scream could be heard as Gerry Marsden sang 'How Do You Do It?' and then 'I Like It'. But the screams were deafening as the time came for The Beatles to be announced. They ran on stage and the audience erupted. It was wonderful. We just had to join in with the screaming and singing. I'd been a rather reserved young lady until that point but I couldn't contain myself.

The boys sang 'I Saw Her Standing There', 'Love Me Do', 'Please Please Me', 'From Me to You' and 'Twist and Shout' along with other tracks from my treasured copy of *With The Beatles*, and we enjoyed every moment. Afterwards, we waited at the stage door but they'd left by another exit. We couldn't leave things like that. We found out they were staying at the Royal Pier Hotel at Anchor Head and the next day, armed with our autograph books, cameras and my *Beatles Monthly* magazine, Judy and I caught the bus to the hotel.

❝ Hanging on for dear life, our autograph books and magazines were passed round ❞

Just as we got off the bus right outside the hotel, we caught sight of Gerry Marsden in the foyer.

I rushed across with my camera and snapped a magnificent photograph with my Brownie 127 and he also gave us an autograph. A few other fans were hanging about with us, but nothing was happening. Judy and I decided to wander to the back of the hotel. How lucky could we be? We could hear the voices of John, Paul, George and Ringo and a transistor radio playing on a balcony about ten feet above our heads. So near and yet so far, but nothing was going to deter me now.

Judy gave me a leg up and somehow my head just about reached the balcony and I was able to see the boys with their wives and girlfriends. They were so friendly at what must have been a great invasion of their privacy. With just a head showing through the railings, and hanging on for dear life, our autograph books and magazines were passed round and autographed. John even asked my name, and if I hadn't been perched so precariously I would have swooned.

I walked all the way home clutching the autographs on my *Beatles Monthly* magazine and my autograph book. I will always treasure the one that says 'To Anne, love John Lennon.' I was invited, along with some other Beatles fans, to tell our story on TV on the sad occasion of the fire at the Royal Pier Hotel in Weston-super-Mare some years later. The hotel was virtually burnt to the ground and we were invited to talk about our experiences as the hotel was smouldering.

I WAS THERE: SYLVIE BROOMHALL

I was working in a salon called Lloyd and Osborne, which had a wig room at the top of the building, a ladies salon in the middle and a gents salon on the ground floor. It was a really exciting time and I went to see The Beatles at the Odeon, but it was even better when they came into the gents salon one day to have their famous hair cut. We in the wig room went mad with

Sylvie Broomhall worked in the wig room of a salon that The Beatles visited: she could have made the most authentic Beatles wigs ever

excitement and wanted to go down to the salon but our boss wouldn't let us, understandably now.

But I wished I had swept the floor and saved the famous hair! My son and friends are so envious when I tell them all about that time, which I will always remember.

> ❝ They came into the gents salon one day to have their hair cut. I wished I had swept the floor and saved the famous hair! ❞

I WAS THERE: LESLEY WELLS (AGED 10)

I was one of many that went to the Odeon in Weston in '63. I remember everyone was screaming so much. As I was only 10 at the time I had to go with my mother. She had to put her hands over her ears for all the noise that was going on around her. I can remember where we sat in the stalls. Funny how you remember things so many years ago. The Beatles stayed at the Royal Pier Hotel in Weston. Sadly it is no longer there, as it was pulled down after a fire.

I WAS THERE: CHRISTINE PIERCE (AGED 15)

The Odeon auditorium was lovely and big, with a large stage. The Beatles were grouped in the centre, with Ringo behind Paul, George and John on a podium. I wish I could remember how they sounded because it's extraordinary, recalling now, how small the single amps – one for each guitar – were and how sparse the stage was, especially compared to how things are today.

When I bought my ticket they were the new 'buzz' and it had been easy to get a front-row seat. When I arrived for the concert, only a short time later, they were the new 'rave' and so the house was packed and the screaming had begun, so they weren't that easy to hear.

Christine Pierce had to avoid flying tins of toffees at The Beatles gig she went to at the Odeon

I particularly remember tins of sweets flying through the air. Someone had reported that one of them liked toffees, which were dangerous enough being thrown individually – both for them and for us in the front row. But some of the girls decided to throw tins, one of which caught Paul on the bone above his left eye. I can imagine what kind of language that would provoke now but, after recoiling and still playing, he clearly mouthed to no one in particular, 'I wanna go home.' The old Jack Vowles riding stables had the pleasure of their company during their visit. I remember being furious because my mum – of all people – saw them riding near our house!

I WAS THERE: DAVID VENN

I have vivid memories of The Beatles' appearance at the Odeon in Weston in 1963. I went with my future wife to see them on the Thursday during their week's stay here.

We were driving home in my little 1938 Morris 8 Tourer, and as we passed the Royal Pier Hotel we saw The Beatles pouring out of the back of a white van outside the front entrance. We pulled up and,

David Venn, in the very same 1938 Morris Tourer in which he encountered three of The Beatles, and (below) relaxing at home

grabbing the programme for the show, I ran across and managed to get Paul and George to sign it. I approached Ringo but a roadie grabbed him around the waist from behind and pulled him into the door and into the hotel. I have no recollection of John being there, only the other three. I would have loved to have got all four of them to sign.

I WAS THERE: MARK TILLEY (AGED 17)

BREAN SANDS

27 JULY 1963, WESTON-SUPER-MARE

I met them on the beach at Brean when they were clowning about taking a very famous picture of them playing leapfrog. I was down on the beach with my mother and family. I said, 'I wonder what they're doing down there?' because I could see there were two or three people with cameras and The Beatles were at Weston at the time.

They'd come out to Brean to take photographs. I didn't actually like them at the time, although I have since come to enjoy them. At the time I was very much a Buddy Holly fan. I was wearing one of these great big straw hats which was about two foot across. And they took the mickey

One of several photos taken of all four Beatles larking around in classic beach garb on Brean Sands, 27 July 1963

out of me a bit. But I wasn't worried about it. I can't remember if they actually had a photograph taken with my hat. But I got it back. They weren't rotten. They didn't take it away from me. But they were clowning about. I can't remember which one put it on.

I know I got three of their autographs. The hat's gone. It was one of my mother's hats for the beach. One of these straw-type hats with a very wide brim, almost like a Mexican-type hat. People say of those photographs, 'Oh, it's at Weston.' No it's not – it was at Brean. And I know – because I was there!

I WAS THERE: STEVE GOMERSALL (AGED 14)

QUEEN'S THEATRE

4 AUGUST 1963, BLACKPOOL

The Beatles were the first band I ever saw. There were four of us went from school. We were all from Blackpool. And we went to Tyldesley

*Queen's Theatre,
Blackpool, 1960s*

Secondary Modern School. Basically The Beatles took over our lives
when they hit. 'Love Me Do' got to 17 in November 1962 and that didn't
really register that highly with most of us, but when 'Please Please Me'
hit number one the whole school – the girls and the boys – we'd just
never been influenced to such an extent. The girls wanted to be with
The Beatles. And we wanted to be The Beatles. Plus the fact they were
northern lads who had an incredibly dry, sarcastic sense of humour. And
they thought nothing of authority so we loved 'em from day one.

I was always a music freak from being a child. My parents bought me
the Shadows first album in '61. My grandmother was a wardrobe mistress
at the Grand Theatre and the Opera House and I got Tommy Steele's
autograph. I've still got his 78s to this day. My friends and I were obsessed.
We were potty about music. And of course Blackpool – in those days we
got everybody. The Beatles were a phenomenon. They were the punks of
their era. Because you'd got Bobby Vee and all those kind of characters.
When The Beatles came along, plus the fact they wrote every single they
had a hit with, which was unprecedented, we thought 'These are real and
they're ours. They're knocking the Americans out of the hit parade.'

We were obsessed with the fashions as well. I remember buying a pair
of Beatles boots from Stead & Simpsons. 72/6 [£3.63]. I had bought a
Beatles suit. Not the rounded collars but the first ones they wore for the
publicity shots for 'Please Please Me'. They had velvet collars and velvet
cuffs. And I got one of those and I remember another kid in Blackpool
being very, very annoyed because I'd beaten him to it. But it was this
insane kind of dedication really. I suppose kids still have it now for boy
bands and stuff like that. But we'd never seen anything like that, because

before that it was distant heroes – Chuck Berry, Little Richard, Elvis Presley and the like. They were people we couldn't identify with because we'd never seen them and we'd only seen rare black and white footage of them.

> **The Beatles were a phenomenon. They were the punks of their era**

So with The Beatles it was 'What is this?' And even the Stones initially were never in the same bracket as The Beatles. They were gods. Marianne Faithfull said that when she was with Mick Jagger, Paul McCartney used to go round to see them and Mick Jagger was the pupil and McCartney was the teacher. And they could play. That was another thing. They could play. And they were innovators. George Harrison had a 12-string Rickenbacker before anybody else. They were using tone pedals before anyone else. Sitars, for God's sake. They were outstanding. Their energy was incredible.

And the fact that they didn't take themselves seriously either. They were fearless. The first opportunity I got to go and see them, I did. There were four of us went and unfortunately, like a lot of people, we didn't hear much of the band because of the screaming and the poor amplification. It was an incredible atmosphere, and when it finished there were girls that were like vultures swooping round the place trying to get a view of them, wondering whether they were going to come out and try to escape. I don't know how they got out of the building because the girls were circling the building.

So we put our collars up at the back and ran down this back alley. We couldn't resist running like lunatics. And the girls started following us because they didn't know who the hell we were. We went around a couple of corners and we eventually stopped and turned around and started laughing. And the vitriol that came out of their mouths when they found we weren't their treasured boys – oh dear, oh dear, they didn't like that at all! We were buzzing for ages afterwards.

I WAS THERE: JOHN MOORHOUSE (AGED 17)

I was 17 when we saw The Beatles at Blackpool. Me and my mate were working for the local Co-op grocery department while his sister was a secretary. The noise was certainly hard going. I remember the girl who was sat next to me being on the verge of losing herself and turning to me and saying, 'Aren't they great?' Their last song, which just about brought the house down, was 'Twist and Shout'. I'm fairly certain it was an all Liverpool show with the likes of Cilla Black and The Fourmost. Although late getting home, we made it to work on time. When we were waiting to go into the theatre, a girl was selling programmes. David put me off buying one. He said, 'I'm not buying one at that price. They are nearly as dear as the seats.'

THE CHANNEL ISLANDS

In early August 1963 The Beatles flew to
the Channel Islands.

I WAS THERE: CAROL CHARLTON (AGED 17)

SPRINGFIELD BALLROOM

6, 7, 9 AND 10 AUGUST 1963, JERSEY

*Carol Charlton, devoted Beatles fan,
cut her hair in a Fabs style. Her cabbie
dad transported The Beatles' luggage
to the hotel*

I had to plead with my parents to let me go. What a wonderful
evening it was. I stood right at the front of the stage, in line with
Paul McCartney, who was my favourite. The place was packed. The
Beatles were brilliant and the time went very quickly. It seemed
unreal that I was actually seeing them live! I was lucky to go
backstage at the end of the evening and sit on Paul McCartney's
knee while getting all their autographs! A really memorable night. I
became an avid fan – my mum made me a black collarless corduroy
jacket like theirs and I had my hair cut in a similar style and collected

every conceivable article and fan club magazine, the LPs, etc. In fact I still have most of it all! My dad was a taxi driver up at the airport who was asked to take The Beatles to Swansons Hotel when they arrived. He said he would take their luggage but not them as he didn't want his car damaged with screaming fans surrounding his car! I didn't know this until he came home and mentioned it.

I was horrified! Fancy missing out on the opportunity to say that The Beatles travelled in my dad's taxi. Can you imagine how envious my friends would have been?

I WAS THERE: JOHN HENWOOD (AGED 17)

John Henwood thought he was 'pretty cool' when he was 16, with his faux hanky and his white Triumph Herald convertible

I was 16 and just started work when 'Love Me Do' exploded into our world and 'Please Please Me' and 'From Me To You' had been released by the time they arrived in Jersey. 'She Loves You' was soon to be released and I have a feeling they may have previewed it at Springfield. They did a lot of other artists' material at that time and, as a fan of Chuck Berry, I'm not sure I altogether approved of all of it, but there's no denying they did it well, really well.

I was one of the lucky individuals who saw The Beatles at the Springfield Ballroom, although to refer to the venue as a 'ballroom' was conferring a status on it that it didn't deserve. Springfield was what we would today call an event venue and it hosted everything from trade fairs to livestock shows and, yes, it did from time to time act as a concert hall. In truth it was a bit of a dump and, although

George Harrison takes the mic, on stage at the Springfield Ballroom, Jersey, 6 August 1963

one or two tears of nostalgia might have been shed, few objected to its demolition some years later. Today it's a sports venue and grandstand overlooking Jersey's principal football pitch – our little (very little) Wembley. Those were the days when headliners still toured minor venues, playing to audiences counted in hundreds rather than thousands. Indeed, a thousand Beatles fans squeezed into Springfield would have broken all fire regulations and even the somewhat sketchy health and safety rules of the day. I'd guess the audience on the night I saw them was around 500.

To say I remember it really well would be to stretch the truth, but I was probably wearing my pale blue Prince of Wales check suit, with very tight trousers and what my mother called a 'bum freezer' jacket, because the style was to cut the jacket – no vents – just below the waist. I probably had a faux hanky in my top pocket – just four peaks of white cotton showing with, inside the pocket, a piece of card stapled to the fabric. My car – a white Triumph Herald convertible – was parked outside and I thought I was pretty cool. It was pretty crowded inside but there was just about room to dance. Not that many girls wanted to dance. They preferred to squeeze in front of the low stage and just swoon at their idols. I certainly don't recall the screaming and near hysteria that was to mark some of The Beatles' later gigs.

I worked for Channel Television as a trainee, drafted in to do everything from making the tea to pushing a TV camera round the studio floor. It was a really privileged opportunity and I worked in the industry for the next 38 years. Channel Television had a connection through common shareholdings with EMI and when we started doing a local pop programme, *Now Look Hear*, EMI made available artists

Three of the Fab Four, clad in their collarless jackets

signed to their labels. I was at that time training as a sound recordist and went as part of a crew to EMI's headquarters in Manchester Square, London, to film a series of interviews with their artistes. I can't recall whether it was there, or in Jersey, but I recall we did an interview with The Beatles.

Many years later, when Channel Television was about to celebrate 50 years of broadcasting, they hunted high and low for that film without success. They called me and asked if I knew what had happened to it. Well, I don't know for sure, but there was a time when the film library was running short of space and someone – I know who it was, but won't name him – took the view that a lot of old material was no longer of any value and it was dumped. I'm fairly sure The Beatles interview, along with countless others with pop stars of the day, plus irreplaceable scenes of Jersey and Guernsey in the 1960s, was destroyed. A little tragedy.

I WAS THERE: SUSAN BLYDE

They were lounging outside Springfield Hall. I was also waiting for a cab. There were three of us. The cab pulled up, and as we were getting in the band asked if they could squeeze in. We all set off to St. Helier. They were being very normal, and we all chatted about music.

I WAS THERE: BRENDA PIROZZOLO (NÉE EVANS, AGED 13)

I was one of the many young girls who attended that event and I remember the evening very well. I managed to be standing right in the front of the stage. I clearly recall that they were fabulous and that the girls behind me were really annoying as all they did was scream and did not listen to the music.

I went with my friend Janet Langlois, who is unfortunately no longer with us, and at the end of the evening we were told we could get autographs if we went to the side of the Springfield opposite Le Coie Hotel. We queued up outside the door and some guy took my *Beatles Magazine* up to the Fab Four and they signed it for me.

Brenda remembers The Beatles being fabulous, despite the annoying screaming

I WAS THERE: ALEX OLDHAM

GAUMONT THEATRE

19–24 AUGUST 1963, BOURNEMOUTH

The Beatles were booked for a week at the Gaumont in Bournemouth before Beatlemania struck. They performed every night with two matinees on Wednesday and Saturday. On the first day they were there, I was walking towards the stage door and the man on the gate opened it for me to walk through. I've often wondered why: whether it was because I had a Beatle haircut and wore the fashionable clothes or, which is quite likely, whether it was because I resembled Tommy Quickly who was also on the bill.

Was it Alex Oldham's resemblance to Tommy Quickly that got him in to every Beatles gig at the Gaumont?

Anyway, as a result of this I saw every performance that week from the wings because he continued to open the gate for me every time I approached it. He was an older chap and I think we all looked the same to him. As a result I met most of the musicians playing and also George and Paul. They knew I was only a fan but didn't care. Paul was messing about on the drums one afternoon when I stopped to watch him and he openly chatted to me as he would. George I met only briefly but he was friendly also. They were such happy days. A couple of years later, The Byrds played there and I saw them from the wings of the stage by using the same technique to gain entry!

The Beatles were staying just a few doors away from the Gaumont, in the Palace Court Hotel. They were there for the whole week and it was in the ballroom of the hotel that the iconic cover photo for *With The Beatles* was taken.

A few months later, in November, I saw The Beatles twice at Bournemouth's Winter Gardens – once on the bill with Helen Shapiro and once when they headlined. I queued all night for tickets for that show and we were in the second row. It was where I first heard John do his infamous 'rattle your jewellery' joke. Beatlemania was such an exciting time. I'd live it all over again if I could.

A WEEK IN SOUTHPORT

At the end of August 1963, The Beatles began another week-long residency, this time in the seaside resort of Southport.

I WAS THERE: THERESE HOWARD (AGED 13)

ODEON THEATRE

26–31 AUGUST 1963, SOUTHPORT

I was there. At that time The Beatles were still in their Liverpool homes and we got all the gossip, but after 'She Loves You' gave them fame and launched Beatlemania they moved to London, leaving their Liverpool fans behind. When they came back to Southport they were top of the bill and supported by great Merseybeat groups like The Big Three and, of course, Gerry and The Pacemakers. What a great concert!

I had not been to The Cavern at that time, being only 13 years old, but older family members and neighbours were talking excitedly about this group called The Beatles, and I already loved the music. So when my friend's older brother told us about this concert and offered to take us, we didn't hesitate. They lived across the road to me so we often shared games and bought records between us. My parents allowed me out at night if accompanied by older friends and family. I remember feeling really excited and totally absorbed in the music. Gerry sang 'How Do You Do It' and may already have reached number one in the hit parade. He then introduced The Beatles and the crowd went wild.

I don't remember too much screaming at that first concert – I also saw them at the Liverpool Empire in 1965 – so we could hear their wonderful unique sound clearly. Most of the songs they sang were their early hits – 'Please Please Me', 'Love Me Do', 'Thank You Girl', 'PS I Love You', slowing down to Paul's solo 'Til There Was You'. From then on Paul McCartney was my favourite, my teenage passion.

The tempo built up again with John Lennon taking the lead after the tantalising build-up to 'Twist and Shout'. The fans were going wild by the time their latest release, 'She Loves You' was introduced, I think by Paul, to end a really memorable performance. It was a real treat for Liverpool fans just before The Beatles were to become a musical legend, far removed from them.

From then on The Beatles, The Merseybeat and live music at The Cavern Club were at the centre of my teenage years and helped to make them memorable and magical. I bought the first LP *Please Please Me* at NEMS music store in Whitechapel, Liverpool soon after, followed by every other LP, EP and single. I joined the fan club and bought the magazines. It was a happy and exciting time.

I WAS THERE: MIKE RIMMER (AGED 13)

I saw them at the old Gaumont Theatre. It was then the Odeon cinema and is now Sainsbury's supermarket on Lord Street, Southport. The Beatles were the final act on a variety show which included a comedian and jugglers, plus sets from Sons of the Piltdown Men, The Fourmost and Gerry and The Pacemakers. I was born in June 1950, so too young to see The Beatles in their pre-famous early Cavern Club days. The Beatles only came to my attention through the media, after their recording career was underway.

Mike Rimmer and friends, inspired by The Beatles like so many of their peers

My earliest recollection was chatting with school friends about their first release 'Love Me Do'. This was late 1962, when I was only 12 years old, but I remember I wasn't all that impressed with the tune! The first 45rpm single I ever bought was 'From Me to You'. In fact I bought two copies and gave one to my girlfriend, Linda Sawyer. I can't remember how it was that Linda and I later came by two tickets to see The Beatles live in Southport. Many of the cinemas at that time had been converted from earlier theatre venues. Therefore the cinema could easily be 'morphed back' into a theatre facility for a stage presentation. One such venue was the Odeon cinema in St George's Square, Lord Street.

My only recollections of the Beatles gig at the Odeon are a number of mental snapshot images. In keeping with entertainment trends of the time, the gig was a variety-show format. Linda and I were sat in the front stalls, towards the right of the stage. I remember there was a compere/comedian and a juggling act, plus several bands.

The Fourmost were particularly entertaining, with lots of chat and jokes to the audience. The first half of the show was closed by a set from Gerry and The Pacemakers. My next memory is of The Beatles themselves on stage, with John Lennon directly in front of us. The Beatles were dressed in their iconic, collarless Beatle suits and wore heavy stage make-up. I remember being surprised that they actually looked like the photos and TV images I'd seen of them.

The noise from the audience was surprisingly loud, with screaming girls all around us and up in the balcony area. The performance was slick and well presented. The lads tried to talk to the audience between songs but we couldn't hear anything over the shouts and screams. The energy of performances and live music element of the show definitely left a lasting impression on me. Up until then the only live stage entertainment I'd experienced was Christmas pantomime shows as a child. Circa 1964 there were bands everywhere and a lot of live music being played in those pre-disco days.

Many of my friends were learning to play guitar. By 1965 I'd joined my first 'proper band' and I've been gigging for most of the following 50 years. Over the years I've played in about 18 different bands from rock 'n' roll to blues to country to folk. I still love playing live music. It can all be traced back to that first Beatles gig and the energy of live

The lucky Mike Winters got to see The Beatles when he was just 12 years old, thanks to his older sister

music venues in the 1960s. I did have the programme for the evening, but sold it to a collector about 25 years ago.

I WAS THERE: MIKE WINTERS (AGED 12)

I went with my sister who was then 20. I don't recall much about the other acts, even Gerry and The Pacemakers who I think had been top of the charts by then. I recollect all the screaming but you could still just about hear the band. I particularly remember John introducing their new single 'She Loves You', which had only been released a few days before.

My other memory is of leaving the Odeon and standing outside when a car raced from the car park at the rear and sped off down Lord Street carrying the band. It must have been driven by Neil Aspinall. About a week later I was walking past the Odeon and a guy was taking out the concert poster, which I asked for. I had it up until about 15 years ago when I sold it.

'SHE LOVES YOU'

'She Loves You' was released as a single
in the UK on 4 September 1963.

I WAS THERE: ROY TAYLOR (AGED 16)

GAUMONT CINEMA

4 SEPTEMBER 1963, WORCESTER

*Roy Taylor (right) will
never forget that gig at
the Gaumont*

The bill included Gerry and The Pacemakers, The Fourmost and
The Dennisons. The Beatles and Gerry alternated between shows as
to who would perform 'Twist and Shout'. The show I saw was the
first of two that day and Gerry sang it. The MC began to introduce
The Beatles and got as far as 'John, Paul...' when the dam burst and
the screaming was unleashed! They looked fabulous and sounded
wonderful – from what I could hear.

I recall 'Til There Was You', 'From Me to You', 'Please Please Me',
'Boys' (sung by Ringo) and 'Love Me Do'. They opened with 'Here's
Hoping', a song by Carter Lewis and The Southerners. I'm not sure
about the rest – I was too busy looking at the way they stood. George's

red Gretsch, Ringo's unique drumming style, Paul's handsomeness and John's whole attitude. What a night!

I WAS THERE: SANDRA LONGMIRE

By now they were very famous, but I suppose they still had commitments to keep. On this occasion we didn't go to the show but waited around the stage door, having run home from school and changed into our black polo-neck sweaters. I think I had embroidered 'PAUL' on the front of mine, as if he would notice!

Once again we handed our books in at the stage door as they didn't come out between shows. We listened at the doors to hear the end of the show and then ran to the front of the theatre – we were quite savvy by then. Our local knowledge paid off and we were able to catch them as they ran to their getaway car via the main entrance. I actually touched Paul McCartney – and he smiled at me!

I WAS THERE: CHRISTOPHER BEVAN

GAUMONT CINEMA

5 SEPTEMBER 1963, TAUNTON

In 1963 I was at school in the Lower Sixth and we had lessons on Saturday so I was not able to listen to *Saturday Club* on the radio. It was down to the *Teen and Twenty Disc Club* on Radio Luxembourg and possibly the *Six Five Special* for pop music. Many up and coming groups travelled to smaller venues around the country and lots came to Taunton. A school friend who was a regular reader of the *New Musical Express* usually sorted out tickets for us.

The Stones had only been going a short while and really the only thing we had heard about them was that Bill Wyman hadn't had his hair cut for a year – we had to have a short back and sides in those days.

186

The Beatles were in top form but most of their music was drowned out by screaming girls.

ODEON CINEMA

6 SEPTEMBER 1963, LUTON

Terry Allen, film critic of the Tuesday Pictorial, was granted an impromptu interview with The Beatles after the gig

I was a young reporter on the *Tuesday Pictorial*, sister paper at the time to the *Luton News*. The show was one of a series of concerts in a mini-tour granted by Brian Epstein after he cancelled a number of Mersey Beat nights earlier in 1963. The promoter of these shows was John Smith, the compere was Ted King and the supporting acts were Ian Crawford and The Boomerangs, Mike Berry and The Innocents, Freddie Starr and The Midnighters, Rocking Henry and The Hayseeds. The Beatles reputedly earned £250 for the show, equivalent to £4,775 today. A relative bargain, you might think, but those were different times.

At that time I was a general reporter but had a full page to fill every week as the *Tuesday Pictorial*'s film critic, which involved reviewing each week's movie offerings at Luton's four cinemas of the time – the Odeon, Ritz, Savoy and Gaumont. In truth, I rarely got to see the films in advance of their release and relied on industry PR and previously published showbiz reviews to give readers some insight to the films' relative merits. One reader told me at the time he found my reviews invaluable in planning his weekly cinema excursion – any film I panned (like the *Carry On* series) he knew he'd enjoy, and any film I praised he avoided like the plague! However, as a result of this work, I was on very good terms with the managers of the four Luton cinemas and the Odeon's Tom Phillips

❛ What do you think of Luton?
Terry Allen

We arrived in the dark and we'll be leaving in the dark, so you tell me, son!
***John Lennon* ❜**

was my personal favourite amongst this group of uniformly colourful characters, all of whom granted me access to see any film I wanted.

On the night that The Beatles performed at the Odeon, my girlfriend and I were ushered into the auditorium by Tom and watched the warm-up acts, followed by The Beatles. It was an unforgettable experience, not only seeing such a legendary band perform live but also witnessing the now infamous howling crescendo of screaming girls that virtually drowned out their music. The Beatles' fame came at a time when sound equipment wasn't what it is today, and the venues were also relatively small compared to today and were typically packed. The Odeon officially housed 1,958 screaming fans, though I suspect a few more sneaked in. The drowning of the music was, in truth, an absolute travesty.

But The Beatles were used to it and played on regardless. To my surprise, at the end of the concert, Tom sought me out in the auditorium and asked me if I'd like to interview The Beatles backstage. Without even thinking, I obviously agreed and he escorted me backstage and showed me into their dressing room, before introducing me to the Fab Four. I had no idea in advance that this was going to happen, which meant I was completely unprepared for it and I must admit the enormity of the situation overwhelmed me.

I recall spluttering a few random questions, which were almost exclusively dealt with, quite warmly in fact, by an ever-smiling Paul McCartney. The others took little interest. In fact, throughout the brief interview, as I remember it, George Harrison sat half-smiling – half bored, I suspect – and said nothing, while Ringo Starr was even more detached, just staring at the floor. John Lennon made the odd, slightly caustic interjection, and showed his character when I feebly asked what the group thought of Luton. John fixed me with a withering look and replied, in his Merseyside twang, 'We arrived in the dark and we'll be leaving in the dark, so you tell me, son.' The whole episode left me feeling slightly embarrassed and disconsolate at having blown such a unique opportunity, mainly through the lack of opportunity to prepare, mixed with my youth and inexperience.

Thoughts of *A Hard Day's Night* and *Help!* crossed my mind, but I consoled myself with the fact that I could not have anticipated getting this opportunity to interview The Beatles. I was thrust into it at a moment's notice, though my two sons subsequently regard this as a highlight of my career and my 15 minutes of fame. I think they've dined out on it with friends far more than I ever have.

Nonetheless, it was a rare experience simply to meet the Fab Four, who were literally a global phenomenon – an accolade the like of which is thrown around too casually with others nowadays – and I'm grateful to my old friend Tom Phillips for giving me the opportunity.

There was an interesting postscript to the story. The following week, when I made my customary call to see Tom Phillips and get information on the subsequent week's film screening, he told me that The Beatles had turned up prior to the concert at the front entrance to the cinema, which led to the back of the auditorium, of course. There were no police, no security, no barriers, and the Fab Four just got out of the car and sauntered up the front steps. Fortunately, the audience was oblivious inside the auditorium because had all those hysterical girls realised this, there would have been absolute pandemonium and I doubt whether The Beatles would have ever have made it on stage in Luton that night.

The quick-thinking Tom Phillips ushered them back outside and along the facade of the building to a small side door leading to the rear of the stage. Being a cinema, this door was totally inconspicuous with no signage announcing 'Stage Door', as you would get at a theatre. The design of the Odeon and the fact it had a stage perhaps indicated that it was originally built, in 1938, for vaudeville entertainment as much as for movie screenings, but in all my time there seeing films, I honestly never knew there was a stage door, and it was so innocuous I would actually have guessed it was part of Evelings – the adjacent toy store. Had I learned of this earlier, 'Beatles Almost Mobbed in Odeon Foyer' would have been a great lead story in the paper, but Tom told me about it the following Monday, which was the day the *Tuesday Pictorial* went to press. So we were too late by just a few hours and nobody was ever the wiser – except for Tom and me, my wife and two sons, plus anyone else they've told since.

PUBLIC HALL

13 SEPTEMBER 1963, PRESTON

I managed to see The Beatles a second time at Preston Public Hall in September 1963. Although it was great to see them again, Beatlemania was in full swing by then and the place was full of screaming girls. They kicked off with 'Roll Over Beethoven', sung by George, and I remember Paul dedicating 'I saw Her Standing There' to David John Smith (Miffy), who was lead singer with local band David John and The Mood, who was a mate of The Beatles. John called him 'Letters' because he was always writing to the music papers telling them how good The Beatles were.

A group called the Thunderbeats, whose drummer was Keef Hartley, supported The Beatles when they played the Floral Hall in Morecambe in January 1963. The Thunderbeats' van's lights stopped working and

David John and The Mood: lead singer Miffy (second from left) was nicknamed 'Letters' by John Lennon because he kept writing to the papers enthusing about The Beatles

*Backstage at the Public Hall,
Preston on 13 September, 1963*

Paul suggested that they follow close behind him and Ringo on the way back to Preston, which they had to go through to get back to Liverpool.

This done, Paul and Ringo stopped off at Miffy's house in Skeffington Road for a fry-up. My brother was one of a few lads from Preston who went along to support the Thunderbeats and ended up at Miffy's too. After the meal, Paul got on the old upright piano with Ringo banging rhythms out on an old armchair. They played about for hours, leaving about 7 a.m.

My brother remembers Paul playing loads of rock 'n' roll, and 'I Saw Her Standing There', which seemed to be a new song he was still working on. Maybe that's why he dedicated it to Miffy eight months later at the Public Hall.

I WAS THERE: MIKE DRYLAND

They were still at a stage where they could mingle with the fans. I went backstage and can remember John Lennon pulling his trousers on – the usual dressing room scene. We had a drink in the Public Hall and Paul McCartney was there. He was very genial, a very pleasant sort of guy. If they had faded into obscurity it wouldn't have meant very much. But you did realise they were unique.

I WAS THERE: MICK GARRY (AGED 13)

I'd never been to anything like that before. They'd just released 'She Loves You' and the place was packed. There was condensation running down the walls and we couldn't hear a thing they were singing. I was near the stage and I have this vivid memory of the boots that George and the others were wearing. They were scuffed and the heels worn down. George had mentioned in an interview that he liked jelly babies and we were throwing them at him on stage. The following day my brother was in hospital because he'd fallen off the slide on Haslam Park. When he came round, the first thing he did was to ask whether I'd brought any jelly babies back home.

I WAS THERE: ALAN FORRESTER (AGED 14)

CARLTON THEATRE

6 OCTOBER 1963, KIRKCALDY

As a schoolboy, Alan Forrester used to harmonise with his friend on Del Shannon and Everly Brothers songs. For him, The Beatles changed everything

Before The Beatles came along I had a couple of Elvis Presley singles – 'Teddy Bear' was one I liked. Johnny Duncan's 'Last Train to San Fernando', which I broke in the kitchen drawer, 78s being what they were. I had placed it in the kitchen drawer and I opened the drawer too fast and it broke in the middle. On the jukebox in the village I lived in I was punching in The Searchers – 'Sweets for My Sweet', 'Sugar and Spice', the 'Ain't Gonna Kiss Ya' EP. I loved the harmonies. My friend Chris and I would both sing. We would harmonise. Up until then we were harmonising on Del Shannon – 'Little Town Flirt' and stuff like that – whilst going to school, walking to the school bus. And Everly Brothers stuff.

But they were all lacking any meat and the meat, to me, came in the bass line. If you've heard McCartney singing 'Long Tall Sally' on the EP or heard Ringo's drumming. When he gets to the last verse or chorus, McCartney hits it straight away, better than Little Richard did. And this is what they were doing. They were consistently taking covers and making better versions, with a cleaner sound.

Many of the early rock songs are still fabulous songs but listen to the production. Chuck Berry – there's a double bass. The electric bass had been invented and by and large the productions are fairly clean but they're not exciting, other than his lead part. The Beatles were taking that and giving it a real kick. You wanted to hear it. You wanted to see it. You wanted to sing it. To understand the success of The Beatles you have to understand all that was deficient in terms of sound quality. There was Roy Orbison and his voice, but the production and so forth really just wasn't there. Neither lead guitar nor bass part. They were well played but they just didn't leap out of the speakers.

I got my tranny in late '63, early '64 for a fiver. My uncle bought it for me. It was tiny. You were holding it to your ear hoping to try and hear Radio Luxembourg. The musical changes were absolutely driven by The Beatles. Because they had taken American music that we hadn't heard yet. They were buying records that were coming into Liverpool on the ships. And they were hearing them in Hamburg, from the ships. This is how they got the Motown stuff early.

You could hear bass. For the first time you were hearing proper bass. There was a tightness in the production and in the sound quality. Now at the same time as this was happening, you were getting Phil Spector doing this huge Wall of Sound. But you didn't get four guys, a mini orchestra really, that was so tight, so rehearsed and melodic. It seemed like every time a record came out you could enjoy or love every song that was on the album. You used to get 12 tracks on an album and you would like almost all of them.

So what came through was their adaptation and their modification and transformation of American music, distilled so that British society could take it. It was John's driving rhythm and Paul's bass. I think his bass playing was ahead of most people, and that's down to the sheer hard work they put in in Hamburg. They just got ahead of everybody else. The Beatles were an experience. It was an emotional experience as well as a musical experience. It was huge excitement. You waited.

You waited. You heard them on the radio. You'd see them on TV. They were funny.

So the fact that they were coming to Kirkcaldy – I came into school waving these two tickets saying 'I've got them! I've got them! Seven and six!' – it was fulfilled excitement as well. And The Beatles came through and the sound was just terrific. Barbara Dickson, the singer, was in the year above me at Woodmill High in Dunfermline before I moved to Kirkcaldy and she was at the concert and she paid the same price as me, which was 7/6.

It's just a great memory of the sound. I was in the gods. The Beatles sound, although it was there, you could hardly hear it for the shrieking. We were in the balcony, right up in the gods. My recollection is that it was two or three rows from the front of the balcony, and maybe four or five from the back of the balcony. Houston Wells and The Marksmen were a country act who had had a hit with 'Only the Heartaches', which they played. And The Fortunes were fantastic.

And when the guys came on I swear I didn't hear any of the first song. I started to hear a little by the third or fourth song in. I found out in the playground the next day, because I was in high school, that they'd opened with 'Roll Over Beethoven', which at that point I'd never heard. When the *With The Beatles* album came out, of course, I clocked the song. It was just phenomenal. The queues. The atmosphere was electric. I was a 14-year-old boy and the people around me were girls of 10, 11, 12 right up to late teens. Everyone wanted The Beatles. They were getting calls for The Beatles while these other acts were on. Then it was just everyone standing up, hands in the air from song one to the end. With hindsight you think, 'We paid that money and we never heard it.' But we were there!

I WAS THERE: ANDI LOTHIAN

CAIRD HALL

7 OCTOBER 1963, DUNDEE

We got them back to Scotland for three concerts in October '63 and then we had them again in '64 for another three. In Dundee there were two houses. The Caird Hall very very rarely sold out. Even Frank Sinatra

Signed tour programme for the Scottish dates of autumn 1963

didn't sell it out. And we sold out both houses. We could have sold them out ten times over.

I WAS THERE: BRIAN MECHAN (AGED 19)

I spoke to Ringo Starr. He was staying at the Salutation Hotel in Perth, just before the bridge on the right-hand side if you're driving through. I was a hairdresser and I was working in a salon which was about 200 yards away. Ringo Starr was my favourite Beatle at that time and I'd read that at one time Ringo had wanted to be a hairdresser. This was the afternoon before the first Dundee concert. And I thought, 'I'm gonna try this', so I phoned the Salutation and asked to speak to Mr Richard Starkey, thinking if I'm going to get through, this may work.

And it did. I explained who I was, and where I was, that I was going to the concert that night and that if he had a chance to get out, to come across. He said he would if he was able to. Security-wise, I suppose, there wasn't a hope in hell. The receptionist probably just didn't think. He probably didn't sign in as Ringo Starr. I went to the concert with a friend. We were only about seven rows from the front. So we heard the first two songs over the screaming, but you just couldn't hear a thing.

I WAS THERE: FRASER ELDER

I drew a cartoon of The Beatles at the Caird Hall. I was the resident cartoonist for the *Dundee Courier*. I was also their very first pop editor/ reporter. I was sent along to meet The Beatles before they came into

Dundee and they were living in Perth at the time at the Salutation Hotel so that's where I did the drawing. On the afternoon of the show I took it down to them at the Caird Hall and they stood alongside me in line just like the drawing and I gave them all a drawing each.

And the Dundee Courier printed ten autographed copies of it and they made it into a competition. That cartoon went all around the world in some shape or form. About 30 years later one of the drawings was auctioned and it realised £8,000. I had the original drawing and it is now currently in Liverpool in The Cavern museum. The Beatles also autographed a special one for the kids in the Dundee orphanage. I actually met them several times. They came back to Dundee the following year.

First time around they shared top billing with an American soul singer called Mary Wells. And then the next time they came into the Caird Hall they did a one-band show and I went on tour with them in Glasgow, Perth and then Newcastle. I liked George Harrison the best of them all. John, I thought, was a bit of a smart guy – he was always coming away with one-liners. And Ringo was probably the least intelligent of the four of them. McCartney at that time was greatly under the influence of John Lennon. But in later years obviously all that changed. They were good guys. I liked George the best because out of the four of them he was the most accomplished musician, technically, by a mile. And he talked good music. He was a very pleasant guy and that's why I had a lot of time for him.

I WAS THERE: DANIEL FERGUSON

I worked for Dundee District Council for 35 years. Early in my career our office was situated behind the Caird Hall stage, with a door access to the stage. When The Beatles came to Dundee we were able in the office to hear them practising. When all went quiet we went on stage and picked up broken guitar strings and of course everybody came to believe them as having been used by The Beatles. I still have

Daniel Ferguson: proud owner of guitar strings broken by The Beatles (probably)

my guitar strings after all these years. Late in the afternoon came a knock on the common door and who should come into our office but Paul. He asked us if he could use our phone and sat for quite a while chatting away. We could hardly believe it!

I WAS THERE: ANDI LOTHIAN

I had to take the group through the back entrance of this fairly long concert hall, walking over huge coal bins to the least used service door to escape the manic throng awaiting the group outside. My claim is that the word Beatlemania is my word. It happened at one of the Beatles concerts in October '63 when the fans were rushing the stage and we were about to be overwhelmed. We were all trying to keep them all back, including the St John's Ambulance men, and we were losing the fight, as it were. And the BBC reporter stood beside me turned to me and he said 'For God's sake, Andi, what's happening?' I said 'It's ok, it's only Beatlemania.' Ten days or so later it appeared in the national papers, having been picked up by one of The Beatles' managers at another concert.

I WAS THERE: KATHLEEN MASON (AGED 15)

I went to see them in the Caird Hall. We did meet them backstage and I got their autographs on my arm. I didn't wash that arm for about two days. I loved The Beatles. I still have quite a few of their records. We got backstage because a cousin of mine's husband was a reporter at the time. A couple of years ago there was a picture in the paper of myself on Ringo's knee.

I WAS THERE: WILMA HART (AGED 17)

My friend and I were 17 years old. I don't remember much about the show other than the excitement, the noise and the thrill of seeing them in person. Mary Wells was also there, singing her hit song 'My Guy'. When we came out at the end, we'd both been temporarily deafened by all the noise. Once we'd had a juice in a local cafe, our hearing gradually returned. At that time I was working in the offices at DC Thomson, the publisher. The morning after the concert, I learned that one of my work mates had been invited by some of the reporters to a party at St Fillans in Perthshire, where The Beatles were staying. Most hurtful to me was the fact that she wasn't even a Beatles fan. Unlike myself, who was in their fan club and had all their records as well as scrap books full of photos of my heroes.

I WAS THERE: MORAG THOMPSON (AGED 15)

Having a pal who worked at the box office meant Morag ended up with front-row seats.

I was still at school and this was my first concert. My pal had left school and was working next to the box office so offered to get the tickets. Thanks to her we had tickets for the front row, centre right. We could see Ringo's grey streak. We were carried away with it all and joined in the screaming like everyone else. We came out after in a daze and our ears ringing.

Next morning there were photos of the audience in the *Courier* and the girl sitting next to me was there screaming her head off. My parents were horrified but I didn't let on that I was next to her and also in a similar state. I was quizzed but assured them that I was sitting quietly! Next day at school it was all we thought about or talked about.

I WAS THERE: NORMA MCGOVERN (NÉE WARD, AGED 12)

I was allowed to go with my brother Tommy, who was 14 at the time. I can remember wearing a green mohair coat and stopping in to a sweet shop in Reform Street and buying a packet of toffees. My family were not well off at the time so we were in the cheapest seats at the back of the balcony. The tickets were 5/-, or 25p in today's money. It didn't bother us being in the cheap seats. We were just so glad to be there. You couldn't really hear the boys for all of us young girls screaming.

My husband Jim is an even bigger fan of The Beatles than I am and he goes green with envy when I remind him that I actually saw them live. I am now a local councillor and if they were to come back to Dundee at this present time I might have been able to wangle a backstage pass. Well, a girl can dream!

She may have been in the cheap seats, but Norma still got to see The Beatles in '63

PALLADIUM THEATRE

13 OCTOBER 1963, LONDON

The Beatles appeared live on *Sunday Night at the London Palladium*. As it was a TV show, one could arrive and queue and hope to get in. I arrived early afternoon and was almost first in the queue. I think we were allowed in about 7.30 p.m.

The first ten rows were reserved and I got a seat in the eleventh row! They came on at the beginning for a short while and for the rest of the show Bruce Forsyth kept teasing us until they appeared at the end as the top of the bill. I loved every minute of it, even though we were all screaming for most of their act! A brilliant experience that I will never forget.

I WAS THERE: SYLVIA ELLIS

ALPHA TELEVISION STUDIOS

20 OCTOBER 1963, ASTON, BIRMINGHAM

I used to go to the studios in Aston where they made the TV programme *Thank Your Lucky Stars* and I was in the crowd when The Beatles were appearing. It was mayhem, and when someone as much as opened a window we all screamed! I remember chasing a black cab down the road with my mates as we were sure we saw Paul inside. I was in the studio audience when they announced The Beatles were on the following week. I was so miffed that I missed them by one week. Crazy times – but happy times too!

I WAS THERE: JOHN FIELDS

LEEDS BRADFORD AIRPORT

NOVEMBER 1963

I worked at Hepworth & Grandage, an engineering firm making Rolls-Royce engines, near Leeds/Bradford Airport. One day a rumour went around at work that The Beatles were due to land at the airport. We were busy working when hundreds of young folk began to pass by. They were mostly girls on foot and were seemingly getting off the bus. More and more came, all heading for the airport. Some carried homemade banners saying things like 'We love you John', 'Lindsay loves Paul' and 'The Beatles Forever'.

John Fields witnessed the tragic spectacle of hundreds of tearful, disappointed teenage girls expecting to see their idols at Leeds Bradford Airport

We had to get on with our work but were still very interested in the fact that The Beatles had chosen to come to our small airport. We waited and waited. Nothing happened.

No one came, least of all The Beatles, and eventually everyone came back the way they had gone, now trailing their carefully made banners behind them.

Dejected and forlorn, some girls were inconsolable, crying broken-heartedly as they passed by. We were quite naughty as we began taking the mickey over these pretty young girls crying over a group that would probably never give them a second look. But that soon changed to dejection when we realised that no one had ever cried like that over us!

I WAS THERE: TERRY BAILEY (AGED 11)

ADELPHI THEATRE

5 NOVEMBER 1963, SLOUGH

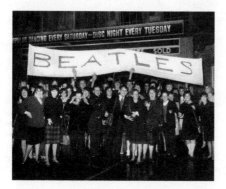

Fireworks of a different kind: fans gather outside the Adelphi, Slough, before The Beatles gig on 5 November

There was mass hysteria and they were using those little Vox amps you couldn't hear over the screaming. I do remember Lennon wearing glasses for some of the show which isn't always shown in the pictures of the time. I know subsequently people have written about the smell of urine as the girls lost control but I was only 11 and blissfully unaware!

I WAS THERE: ROD WATSON (AGED 17)

I went to that concert with a classmate called Andrew Clancy and his sister Charlotte, or Lottie as the family called her. I had just turned 17 in the October and was at Maidenhead College doing a commercial course prior to joining the Berkshire Constabulary as a police cadet and going on to be a police officer for 31 years. We were all from Windsor and caught the bus to Slough bus station and walked to the Adelphi. We were sat about 20 rows from the front of the stage. I think the Swinging Blue Jeans were the warm-up group.

❜ The screaming was unbelievable. You actually could not hear them playing or singing ❜

It was controlled mayhem but no one attempted to get on the stage. There were lots of hysterical girls though, even Andy's sister. The evening was full of excitement and screaming girls, especially when The Beatles came on singing 'Twist and Shout'. It got to a stage where your hearing started to suffer until they went off at the end. I did become a Beatles fan club member and wore a collarless Beatles jacket and Cuban-heel boots. I stopped short of combing my hair forward though!

I WAS THERE: HENRY WRIGHT (AGED 27)

I saw them at the Adelphi in Slough. I went with my wife Sheila. It was brilliant. The Troggs and Gene Pitney were there too. We had to queue a long way to get in but it was worth it. We didn't get very good seats. And cold an' all, it was.

I WAS THERE: NORMA ZACHARCZUK

I was there with my boyfriend, who I later married. We were about five rows from the front. The screaming was unbelievable. You actually could not hear them playing or singing, the noise was so bad. We also went to the Adelphi disco on Sundays to dance. We went to see everyone who came to the Adelphi.

My boyfriend also liked the Stones. They played a few weeks later at the Carlton in Slough High Street. I think that was on a Sunday afternoon. We went there regularly to the disco and sometimes to see live bands. We also went on Saturdays to Burtons in Uxbridge as they had live bands too. But not The Beatles. They got too big too quickly.

I WAS THERE: JACKIE GOODFELLOW (AGED 16)

ABC THEATRE

6 NOVEMBER 1963, NORTHAMPTON

I queued all night for tickets and the queue was so long I was way back around the corner. They sold the tickets on a Saturday so I did not have to worry about going to work. When the booking office was eventually open I got two tickets for my friend and myself and I could still only get on Row J, ten rows from the front.

In order to see The Beatles at the ABC in '63, Jackie had to queue all night

What an experience it was just to see them! You could not hear them through all the screaming but it was well worth it. I am now 69 years of age but the memories of seeing the fantastic four will be with me forever.

I WAS THERE: JACKIE SHORTTAND (AGED 11)

I was there! Although I got into rather a lot of trouble from my mother. I was 11 going on 20. An older girl who was a neighbour persuaded me and my best friend to say we were staying at hers for the night and instead the three of us spent all night queuing for tickets. It was very exciting and we were about fourth in the queue. When we got inside there was a plan of the seating and we were able to get front row right in the middle.

Unfortunately the *Chronicle & Echo* printed a photo on the front page the next day – and there we were for all the world to see! I wasn't aware of this until I got home from school the next day. All hell broke loose and my mother said I couldn't go. I begged and cried for hours. But by the morning my lovely dad had talked her into letting me go. My mum even bought me a new dress with a Peter Pan collar and a big red bow for my hair – I must have looked a sight!

On the night I was so excited. But because of all the screaming girls in the audience I didn't really hear the songs at all. I was however lucky enough to get the autographs of all four of them afterwards. My favourite Beatle was Ringo. Most of my friends couldn't understand why. I went on to see The Rolling Stones and several other bands at the ABC. Great times!

I WAS THERE: LINDA GROOM (AGED 14)

My mum was very kind, in that she went and queued for ages to get us some tickets, as we were at school. I went with my cousin Pat and my brother Ronnie.

I was about 14 and the others were about 12. At one of the shows, we had the fifth row from the front on the right-hand side, because John Lennon was my favourite and he always stood on the right. As soon as they came on and played the first chord, the room just erupted with deafening screams! In my naivety, I thought that if I didn't scream like

Ronnie Groom, who went with his sister to see The Beatles at the ABC in Northampton. Behind him can be seen a poster of the Fab Four on the beach at Brean Sands

all the others John would notice me and look at me! I gave up in the end and joined in.

At the end of the show everyone stayed outside to see if they could catch a glimpse of them, but as mum was picking us up to go back home, about 10 miles away, we weren't allowed to. I think we had to go to school the next day. I still have the two programmes, but not the tickets. I did find my diary of 1963, and as

❝ There was a photo of me being held back in the aisle, arms outstretched and screaming. My mother was not pleased and thought I would be expelled! ❞

it was a small area to write in, all I put was 'Caught bus to see The Beatles, they were Fab, couldn't hear much.' And the next day: 'Went to school, everyone was talking about The Beatles.' Little did I know how important that experience would turn out to be!

I WAS THERE: GEORGINA JEYES (NÉE TAYLOR, AGED 13)

I was there. As school girls aged 13 or 14 we hardly missed a concert. The Beatles, The Stones, Gene Pitney, The Kinks... A comedian also had a slot – I think he was Canadian Frank Berry. I can even remember one of his jokes!

We were all country girls and came into the Derngate bus station every day for school. Luckily my nan lived in The Drive so I was nominated to stay with her in order to be first in the queue for the tickets. We would go and hang about outside the Grand or the stage door hoping for a pre-concert glance or scream at our heroes. We would also rush to the stage door in time to see them being whisked away to a place of safety by a posh black car.

I cannot remember much of school learning but I can remember which of my friends fancied which Beatle and I still see these same friends over long chatty lunches. There used to be rugby players at the foot of the stage to stop us running down the aisle and trying to get onto the stage. After one Beatles concert there appeared a photo of me being held back in the aisle in the office window of the *Chronicle* at the top of the Market Square, arms outstretched and screaming. My mother was not pleased and thought I would be expelled! My nan, although thinking that the length of The Beatles' hair was disgusting, was brilliant and loved the tales when we returned.

I have always felt that those concerts were not acknowledged as important in the careers of so many legends, and if I ever talk about them I'm sure today's generation don't believe me as they buy tickets on line to groups who only perform in arenas. We also went to concerts to raise money for the Spastic Society (as it was then called) at Wembley. The Beatles and loads of groups all appeared, and by the end of the evening The Beatles had to climb over all the equipment to get to the front to perform. Famous stars of the day from shows like *Coronation Street* would walk about outside signing autographs. Somewhere I have Albert Tatlock's!

I WAS THERE: WENDY IRONS

My recall of the event was a long queue outside on the pavement with the police in attendance, but not as today as they were talking to us and did not understand the reason for all the excitement. We stood up once inside and were asked to sit but continued to stand. We were unable to hear most of the songs as the screams were so loud and girls were crying. It was over in such a short time, like most good events. My ears were ringing with all the noises from the concert as we made our way home.

I WAS THERE: JULIE CAUSEBROOK (AGED 14)

The second time The Beatles came to Northampton my best friend and I were ready. We had saved up our pocket money (half a crown a week) and the day before the tickets were sold we wagged school in the afternoon to go and queue outside the cinema where the tickets were being sold. I can remember we were about twentieth in the queue and we sat on the path outside the cinema, intending to stay all night until the ticket office opened the next morning.

I didn't tell my parents because I knew they wouldn't let me do this, but my friend had told her dad. We didn't think about food or a blanket to keep us warm, we just desperately wanted a ticket (my friend liked John Lennon but it was Paul for me all the way). At around 7 p.m. I

*Julie Causebrook, who planned
to queue all night for Beatles
tickets but omitted to share her
plans with her parents*

decided to go to my Nan's to get some provisions and as she lived in
Edith Street it was not too far away. Everyone queuing with us was so
nice and friendly and we struck up some new instant friendships with
like-minded girls. My best friend Glennis stayed and held our spot and
I walked to my Nan's. My Nan gave me some sandwiches and a blanket
and also a flask of tea – plus a short sharp telling-off for not informing
my parents where I was.

I went back up to my friend Glennis, who was getting on fine with
our new friends, and we shared the sandwiches around our close group.
Everything was OK until 10:15 p.m., when my dad turned up and
demanded I go home with him immediately. I begged and begged to stay
but he was not having any of it so I had to go home with him. My best
friend Glennis, however, stayed all night and in the morning, around
7.30 a.m., I went back taking her and our new friends some breakfast. I
was so grateful that they let me in the queue again because, really, they
need not have done.

Eventually the ticket office opened at about 10am. We got our precious
tickets and on the performance day we sat on the second row at the left-
hand side of the stage near to Paul McCartney. It was brilliant: the show
was terrific and everything I thought it would be. After about three songs
there was a surge to the edge of the stage and Glennis and I went too. I
was quite tall and my friend much shorter than me so I was the barrage

that made us a space. Paul came over to our side of the stage and for a brief moment he touched my hand – being so tall had benefits! I was thrilled, then it was all over, but Glennis and I were really happy.

We didn't see The Beatles live again and we didn't see any of the friends we had made in the queue either. Glennis's mum never forgave me for leaving her daughter to queue all night for my ticket and said I had led her daughter astray! But her dad was fine with me.

My mum was not too pleased with me either, but my dad understood and I was soon forgiven. My nan had got a bus up to my parent's house that night to tell them where I was (no mobiles or phones in every household then). That is the first and only brave thing I did – dangerous really, when you think of today's world. Still it is a memory that I will always treasure.

My love of The Beatles waned when they started to go all hippy and always in the background was my first love Elvis Presley, whom I have been a fan of since 1959. I still am an Elvis Fan, loyal and true but I will never forget the short couple of years and Beatlemania. By the way I named my son Paul, born in 1978, in tribute to Paul McCartney – and also as my husband wouldn't let me call him Elvis.

I WAS THERE: KEITH SHURVILLE

When the second visit to the ABC as headliners was publicised, it was obviously a major event in the town and I had to get my mother to drive me to Northampton early one Saturday morning to join a queue for tickets. Luckily I managed it.

I went with a friend but I can't remember which one. This time Beatlemania frenzy was in full force and even the lads were dressing up in Beatle tops and had Beatle hair-dos, including myself. Dressing in similar fashion to The Beatles, I resembled Billy J Kramer and was close to being mobbed when he visited the ABC.

At Keith's second Beatles gig in the ABC Northampton, Beatlemania was at full pelt

The queue to get into the ABC, 6 November, 1963

I WAS THERE: JAN DEAN

My friend Lynne and myself were 14 years old when The Beatles came to Northampton. We played the wag, as they called it, from school and we went to what was called Lynn's Cafe and went to the Ladies and got through a window and into the car park of the ABC. We then got into the back door of the theatre and made our way up the stairs and ended up hiding in a dressing room.

But after a while we thought, 'We can't stay in here as it would be ages before The Beatles would be in the theatre.' So we then went up more stairs and ended up on the roof of the theatre. After running across the roof trying to find somewhere to hide, unbeknown to us some workmen working on an adjoining building had spotted us and called the police.

The manager of the theatre then came up to the roof and they took us to the upper circle of the theatre and told us we were very lucky not to have fallen through the roof when we were running across it. They took it no further. It made the local paper – two girls being up on the roof of the ABC hoping to get up close up to The Beatles. My friend Lynne did not get to go to see them as her mum would not let her go. But I did. It was all great fun.

I WAS THERE: VALERIE CURTIS (AGED 20)

The curtain was about to rise amid the buzz of excitement. Instead, I was filled with dread at the prospect of them not appearing. The Beatles surely, having performed at the London Palladium, and with a recent number one record, would not now show up at this unknown venue in a small Midlands town.

My boyfriend had purchased the tickets earlier on in the year, having seen The Beatles support Tommy Roe at the same venue. Although we lived in the town, we would travel on our Lambretta scooter to see most of the concerts of the pop stars of the time. This concert felt different, as the popularity of The Beatles was unlike anything we had seen before. As a child I would get asked in the playground, 'Are you Labour or Conservative?' Now it was, 'Who is your favourite Beatle?' by the girls in the office.

We thought The Beatles had been a great support act and looked forward to seeing them in their own show. By then, however, they had suddenly it seemed become very successful. Previous pop concerts sometimes made announcements that certain artists would not be appearing for various reasons. None of my friends had been lucky enough to get tickets so I looked forward to reporting back to them. I was filled with excitement and also dreading a non-appearance. I found myself saying 'Please turn up!' over and over.

Suddenly there was the twang of their familiar chords and we were enveloped in a wall of sound. No words, just pounding beats deadened by screaming shouts to Paul, George and John. Ringo just smiled and nodded his head in time. He was my favourite! I was so happy and caught up in the excitement too. Soon I realised that the hysterical

Ringo was Valerie Curtis' favourite Beatle – 'he just smiled and nodded his head in time'

screaming was not going to stop, even in the gentler songs which I wanted to hear. The younger girls screamed until they were hoarse.

I remember feeling concerned and embarrassed that The Beatles would dislike Northampton after this! Seeing the way that they smiled and carried on with their numbers anyway made me realise that they were used to this reaction. My boyfriend was very amused by the whole scene but I longed for someone to intervene and quieten down the screaming. However we both knew that this was the best concert that we had ever seen and that we were witness to something unforgettable. Next day my father expressed his opinion strongly. 'Bing Crosby did not need all that amplification and no girls screamed the place down for him,' he said proudly. I understood then The Beatles' place in popular music and how lucky I had been to witness it.

I WAS THERE: MARGARET COLE

I lived in a village roughly 12 miles away, with my parents. They thought I was mad to go. I actually took my brother-in-law along. He drove to Northampton as he was familiar with town driving. It was so loud – everyone screaming and shouting. Getting outside afterwards, goodness – my head was ringing! We both had work next day: my brother-in-law at Wolverton railway works and me at a printing company. Great fun and never to be forgotten.

Margaret Cole's parents thought she was mad to go and see The Beatles

I WAS THERE: ROGER FRISBY

My girlfriend had got tickets near the front of the cinema and by this time Beatlemania had gripped the country; Northampton was no exception. The support included the Brook Brothers. This was my chance to use the loo, and going around the back seats a girl grabbed my shoulder and asked if I was Brian Epstein. I said that I was and she asked if I could get their autograph for her youth club in Moulton. I said that of course I would, and to 'Stay where you are.'

I now had a problem because I would have to go past her on my way back to my seat, so I had to go around the other way, all around the cinema, and had difficulty finding my seat again – and also explaining to the girlfriend what I had been up to. The show was noisy, but at least I had seen the Fab Four twice in eight months.

I WAS THERE: COLIN LITTLE

I went to see The Beatles at the Gayway dance club in Northampton when they were The Quarrymen and Pete Best was the drummer. I later went to see them at the ABC. My mother was an usherette there and she met The Beatles after the show and they signed their names on a programme for her. The show was incredible. Young girls screaming and dancing in the aisles. I was one of the first to have a Beatles suit made without a collar on the jacket. I don't know what happened to the programme and I no longer have the suit!

Colin Little

I WAS THERE: DI NEWBERRY (NÉE BENSON, AGED 13)

The second Northampton show, when they were at the height of their fame, I remember was brilliant. I don't remember too much of what they sang as I, along with most of the audience, screamed the whole way through it! I was in a picture on the front of the *Chronicle & Echo* looking wild!

I WAS THERE: KEITH WHEELER

I managed to get a ticket through Rodex Coats to see The Beatles at Northampton. Which turned out to be a complete waste of time. You couldn't hear a thing for girls screaming.

I WAS THERE: PETE SPENCER (AGED 13)

Their second performance in Northampton, when they were top of the bill – and after appearing there in March 1963 – was completely drowned out by screaming girls, including my sister. It was continuous and ear-splitting. I'm sure I never heard a note, certainly not from their instruments with the rudimentary amplification of the time.

 As soon as school finished we rushed out to get the bus ... I do remember feeling embarrassed about wearing my school uniform at the concert

Although I took up guitar soon after, and did the rounds of the folk clubs, my appreciation of The Beatles grew and *Abbey Road* is certainly one of my top ten albums – if not top five. Two years later I went to see Dylan at De Montfort, about two months before he went electric. Now *that* was a concert...

I WAS THERE: ANN TAYLOR (NÉE TODD, AGED 13)

I was just a month short of turning 14 years old when I and my twin sister Wendy saw them in concert. We were big fans and had all their records. We lived a few miles out of the village and had no chance to get home from school to change to go out. Instead, as soon as school finished we rushed out to get the bus from Moulton into Northampton. I do remember feeling embarrassed about wearing my school uniform whilst at the concert.

The Beatles sounded just like their records but there was so much screaming that my sister says she couldn't hear them play at all. When the concert ended we went straight to the old bus station in Derngate in order to get our bus home. At the time it was a great treat for us as usually we never had any opportunity to go out anywhere.

I WAS THERE: DAVE YOUDALE

I went to see both Beatle shows in Northampton in 1963. It was the boys in our group who got into The Beatles first. It was the boys who bought the first two singles, who got tickets to the Tommy Roe and Chris Montez tour, where The Beatles started off at the bottom of the bill but had a number one single by the time they had reached Northampton. It was three of us boys who forked out for their first LP on the day it was released – five weeks' paper round money! The girls stayed true to their idols – Cliff, Mark Wynter and co. For a time, anyway...

> ❛ We took it in turns to climb on the sink and be screamed at – Beatlemania first hand ❜

By November 1963, I was at work and we were in full-fledged Beatlemania. Now the girls were on board. Some would say overboard. I met my mates in a coffee bar called Guys and Dolls. It was in Albert Place just off Abington Street. As show time approached, we headed towards the ABC only to meet the first house coming away. A lot has been said about mass hysteria and, true, some were putting it on. But many were not. We passed girls we knew, who were in a daze and had no recollection of seeing us the next day. A lot has also been said about mass urination but I don't remember any evidence of that. Mind you, we were in the circle so perhaps only people in the stalls wee themselves.

It was a normal package tour with about five other acts, The Beatles only doing the last 20 minutes or so, but the girls screamed from start to finish no matter who was on. I had to ask some girls I knew who were sitting at the front what songs The Beatles had sung as I couldn't hear. During the half-time interval we went to the toilets, where we could hear the girls from the first show still outside, chanting 'We want The Beatles.' One of my mates climbed onto the sink and opened a small window. When he stuck his head out there was a load of screaming from below.

It was a dark November evening, the girls were gathered in an alley behind the ABC and the only lights were the toilet windows set high in the wall. We took it in turns to climb on the sink and be screamed at – Beatlemania first hand. I sometimes wonder if there are girls who have spent the last 50 odd years thinking their vigil in that dark alley paid off with a sighting of their heroes. It was a great time to be young. Today's kids can keep their Twitter and their Facebook. I wouldn't have missed that time for anything.

I WAS THERE: CLIVE GEDDES

I had the good fortune to attend the Beatles show in November 1963 at the Savoy cinema, Northampton, with my then girlfriend. Unfortunately, I didn't have any tickets so I asked my father, a police sergeant in the old Northampton Borough Police Force, if he could have a word with the manager of the Savoy. I knew he was in charge of the security operation getting the band in and out of the cinema.

He duly did so and I was told to ask for the manager at the front kiosk on the night of the concert. Arriving at the kiosk and saying who I was, the manager came, led the two of us into the cinema and down to the middle of the central aisle. Sitting there were two tables and chairs from the manager's office. No health and safety in those days! We had a uninterrupted view and room to dance.

The atmosphere was electric, but when The Beatles came on stage, the noise level was overwhelming. Constant screaming from the ecstatic fans made it rather difficult to hear the band singing. This continued from start to finish, but I realised we were privileged to be present at such a momentous occasion.

Leaving the concert, it took some time for my ears to get back to normal. Next day at work, where I was working as an unqualified teacher before going to university, the 11-year-olds were spellbound as I told them all about the evening. My street credibility was well and truly enhanced.

My father wasn't especially enamoured by them. After the concert, a dummy limousine went to the front of the Savoy. My father and others led the group through a back door and across the car park to a 15-feet brick wall. A ladder was placed against the wall. They went up the ladder and through Tricker's shoe factory, which much later featured in the film *Kinky Boots*. Waiting in

' My father, a sixteen-stone former heavyweight boxer, was not impressed by how lightweight they were when he helped them onto the ladder. 'Could have picked Ringo Starr up with one hand' '

The cinema/theatre in Northampton where The Beatles played was originally named the Savoy, before it was bought by the ABC Cinema group

St Michael's Road was the getaway vehicle, which departed with no problems. My father, a 16-stone former heavyweight boxer, was not impressed by how lightweight they were when he helped them on to the ladder. 'Could have picked Ringo Starr up with one hand' he informed me when I got home. Their music did not interest him.

It was amazing to see an early performance of such a worldwide phenomenon. Throughout my teaching career, all my classes heard my story when I regularly took assembly. I used their story as a way to inspire children to be interested in music and to learn to play an instrument. My children grew up listening to 1950s/1960s music while my grandchildren suffer the same fate! Indeed my granddaughters dance to music from this era in their dance shows.

I WAS THERE: ANNA CIVIL

My mother, Ann Edwards, saw The Beatles perform in Northampton in 1963. She remembers it well and says that her and her sister Maureen Tilney and their friend Rita Keedle were right near the front screaming their heads off! They also saw The Rolling Stones perform there too and

Alan Civil, the concert French horn player who played the solo on 'For No One', was Anna Civil's uncle

remember the audience laughing at their unusual long hair and scruffy appearance. Mum recalls a photograph that was taken at the time of them in the crowd, which was later in the paper – although we cannot find a copy of it.

My late uncle, Alan Civil, was from Northampton and played the famous horn solo on the track 'For No One,' from the *Revolver* album. I don't think many people are aware of this Northampton connection. Alan also played in the orchestra on 'A Day in the Life' on the album *Sgt. Pepper's Lonely Hearts Club Band*.

I WAS THERE: MICHAEL BAILEY

GRANADA CINEMA

9 NOVEMBER 1963, EAST HAM, LONDON

John at the Granada café, which was then opposite the venue, supplied food for The Beatles when they played. He later tried to auction off the unwashed plates.

I WAS THERE: SUE FLANAGAN

HIPPODROME

10 NOVEMBER 1963, BIRMINGHAM

The Hippodrome was manic. Screams and yells all through the performance. We didn't need drugs. We all just let it all out. There was nothing to compare it to. You had to be there. Do I remember the Sixties? Yes I do. Because I kept a diary!

I WAS THERE: DAVID LAWRENCE (AGED 12)

I saw The Beatles at the Hippodrome and again at the Odeon on 9 December, 1965, the day after my fifteenth birthday. I went with my school friend Paul. He had queued all night for the tickets.

In those days the sets only lasted about 25 minutes and my lasting memory is of the noise and the screaming. I'm sure we couldn't hear a great deal of what was being played.

I WAS THERE: MALCOLM REYNOLDS (AGED 16)

I'd gone to the show on my own because I wasn't dating a girl at the time. I had a good seat in the circle and remember The Beatles looking very smart. The amplifiers behind them and the PA speakers were small compared with present-day gear. Consequently, when they started playing it was difficult to hear them because of the screaming of the girls in the audience.

In the back of my old exercise book of reel-to-reel tape recordings from the Sixties, I pencilled a list of the numbers that they performed and the order that they played them. I was interested in this because I was learning to play guitar at the time and was a fan. They played: 'I Saw Her Standing

Above: David Lawrence and his friend Paul Luton, who queued all night to buy Beatles tickets. Below: Malcolm Reynolds, who noted down which songs The Beatles played that night

There'; 'From Me to You'; 'All My Loving'; 'You Really Got a Hold on Me'; 'Roll Over Beethoven'; 'Boys'; 'Till There Was You'; 'She Loves You'; 'Money'; and 'Twist and Shout'.

I was really pleased to hear them do 'All My Loving' as it was only released the previous month on the *With The Beatles* LP and I really loved

Ringo, John and George sign autographs for the local Birmingham police, who had helped them escape the concert venue

it – and still do! I remember the concert programme being very nice and having a bright orange textured cover. Unfortunately it was thrown away with my ticket stub and a lot of other concert programmes in the Seventies.

When the show had finished I made a quick exit to catch the last Midland Red bus back to Sutton Coldfield, which wasn't part of Birmingham back then. The Birmingham Corporation buses only travelled to the city boundary, so if I'd missed that bus I would have to have walked the last four miles or so.

The following week the local paper, *The Evening Mail*, showed pictures of the boys after the concert wearing policemen's helmets. Apparently they had borrowed them to try to disguise themselves to make an easier getaway. I still play guitar in a group and we do 'I Saw Her Standing There', 'Roll Over Beethoven' and 'Money', amongst others.

I WAS THERE: GERALDINE LAWRIE

ABC CINEMA

13 NOVEMBER 1963, PLYMOUTH

I lived in Bude in Cornwall and went to see The Beatles in Plymouth. My father was a Conservative and, much to his disgust, I joined the

Young Liberals as they were doing a coach trip outing to see The Beatles. It was wonderful!

I WAS THERE: CHRIS GALE

ABC CINEMA

14 NOVEMBER 1963, EXETER

When they came to Exeter for a second time they were big. My wife actually met them and turned their autographs down. She knew one of the policemen that had escorted them in, because her father was in the police force. He asked, 'Do you want to come in and meet the group?' and she met them and said 'Hello'. And they asked her, 'Do you want our autographs?' and she replied, 'No, not really.'

I WAS THERE: LYN HOPE (AGED 16)

I went to the concerts in Exeter on 14 November 1963 and 28 October 1964. I still have the programmes, and stuck the ticket stubs inside the cover. The first concert was 10/6 [53p] and the second 15/- [75p]. I was lucky enough to be in the third and fourth rows as I remember from about six rows back everyone stood up and it must have been very difficult to see or hear a thing, not that we were really bothered. Just to be there was enough! I remember there was great consternation before one of the concerts as Paul had the flu and there was a possibility that it might be cancelled. A

Lyn Hope thought Paul having flu might mean a Beatles performance in Exeter would be cancelled

friend of mine was lucky enough to get all the Beatles autographs – I think it must have been at the first concert when they were not top of the bill. She was in the dressing room of one of the other performers getting their autograph when in walked Paul, carrying a bottle of milk, and he got all the autographs for her. I was a pupil at the Maynard School in the 1960s and we went up to the ABC after school one day in full school uniform and asked a policeman standing outside if The Beatles had arrived yet. He looked us up and down and said, 'I should have thought girls like you would know better!' I can't remember what we said in reply, but it is astonishing to think how The Beatles were viewed then as they look so neat and well dressed. Even the newsagent where I ordered the *Beatles Book* every month told my mother he was surprised she bought it for me!

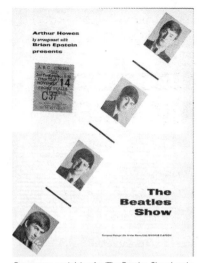

Programme and ticket for 'The Beatles Show' at the ABC in Exeter

I WAS THERE: TIMOTHY TREE

All the top groups appeared in Exeter at some time in the Sixties. In 1963 The Beatles were certainly well known but there were other groups that were more prominent than them at the time. I lived in a place called Sourton. I used to play in a group called The Thunderbirds. We couldn't drive ourselves. My dad used to drive us. We used to go around in an old Austin Sheerline ambulance and we took quite a number of the people from our village to see those shows.

My mum used to run a youth club called the Twist Club where we used to play. So when we saw The Beatles were coming in mum bought block tickets for both years so we all got in to see them. There was a then unknown compere compering the show called Jimmy Tarbuck. He was brand new and he was very good. I wasn't terribly impressed with the Beatles performance, what you could hear of them, which was not a lot because of the screaming and shouting. Their live performance wasn't up to the standard of their records.

They were on with Peter Jay and The Jaywalkers, who used to mimic other groups. As the lights went down and the curtains drew across, Peter Jay and The Jaywalkers struck up the tune to 'Twist and Shout', which was exactly like the record. The girls went screaming mad because they thought The Beatles

Left: Peter Jay and The Jaywalkers: their vesrion of 'Twist and Shout' fooled the audience into thinking they were The Beatles. Below: Timothy Tree, guitarist for The Thunderbirds

were on. And then the lights came up and the curtain went back and they saw it was Peter Jay and The Jaywalkers and it all went quiet! There was screaming at the Rolling Stones shows exactly the same as the Beatles shows. But not quite as loud – you could actually hear what they were playing. But with The Beatles it was very difficult to pick out what they were playing. Being a musician I could hear them. Whether because there was so much noise they weren't putting in the effort I don't know, but it wasn't what I would call terribly good the first time. Certainly they looked the part. Afterwards all the girls were expecting The Beatles to come out of the main side entrance and they sneaked them out of the back entrance of the ABC so they were all disappointed. The car went past and they were all in it.

I WAS THERE: JILL PHILLIPS (AGED 16)

COLSTON HALL

15 NOVEMBER 1963, BRISTOL

I had been crazy about The Beatles ever since I saw them on *Juke Box Jury*. When I found out they were coming to Bristol as part of their 1963 tour I was beside myself. I worked opposite the Colston Hall where they would be performing so I spent the entire day hanging out of the window waiting for them to arrive, much to my boss's annoyance. I did not care. My patience was rewarded when suddenly a large black car with blacked-out windows appeared and the side gates magically opened and they were in. Gradually the crowds built up until it was impossible for any traffic to move. Bristol was brought to a standstill, which was a very strange sight and one I had never seen before or since.

Jill Phillips: thanks to her opening a toilet window, there were a few more people than there should have been at that Beatles gig!

I told my parents I was going to see a play as they strongly disapproved of The Beatles because they had taken over my mind! I was very glad my friends and I had already bought our tickets. Because of this we were able to push past what seemed like thousands of people and take our seats. I was later to become ashamed of my behaviour twice that evening, although I did not think so at the time.

The first time was when unfortunately we had to sit through several acts before we got to The Beatles, as they were top of the bill. I only remember two of the acts, who were Millicent Martin and Roger Whittaker. Through all of the supporting acts the audience were shouting 'Off off off!' and I joined in until we had drowned out their singing. That seems so cruel now, but we were only there for one reason. The second time was during one of the support acts. I decided to visit the loo, only to find loads of people outside the frosted windows begging to be let in. So I opened the window and people immediately piled in. Someone opened all the other windows, causing a stampede. When I got back to my friends I told them I'd done something terrible.

What seemed like a lifetime later the MC announced 'Now is the moment you have all been waiting for!', and I heard nothing after that. My ears were popping because of the high-pitched screaming, most of which was coming from me! I cannot tell you what they sang – I didn't hear one word or one note. John Lennon said later that they could have been singing nursery rhymes and no one would have known.

People were dropping like flies and the St John's Ambulance people were very busy ferrying people out on stretchers. I also remember one girl getting on the stage and making a beeline for John, only to faint at his feet. John picked her up and carried her to the wings. He went back a couple of times to check she was all right, which only provoked louder screaming. I was cursing that I hadn't managed to get tickets for the front row. I thought my ears would never return to normal, but on leaving the venue I remembered there was a small side street behind the Colston Hall and we might be able to get sight of them. A few other people had had the same idea. Just in front of the railings was a window with a light on and curtains drawn.

I started shouting for John and, to our amazement, the curtains parted and the window opened and there was a smiling Ringo. He stretched out his arm, which I grasped, telling him that I wanted to hold his hand.

I WAS THERE: CHRISTINE McDERMOTT (AGED 12)

ARDWICK APOLLO

20 NOVEMBER 1963, MANCHESTER

I only went once to see The Beatles, but I still have my ticket. It was the first performance at 6.30 p.m.. It was called the ABC cinema at the Cinema Ardwick at the time. My mother wouldn't let me go unless she accompanied me to the door of the cinema. And she waited outside for me to come out because she wouldn't have me wandering around at night on my own. I went in the theatre on my own. I went on my own because no one else would come with me.

I'd seen The Beatles for the first time on an early evening Granada news programme. They used to have a music slot. And the first time I saw them they'd just released 'Love Me Do' and I was absolutely floored by the record. I'd never heard anything like it and I was really, really keen on them right from that point. I went out and bought the single and then, when I realised they were touring, I just had to go and see them. And I finally persuaded my mother to let me go on the condition that she accompanied me. She gave in and said, 'You can go.' I got front stalls seats. I was in XD35 and it cost me 10/6 [53p]. My friends would have liked to have gone but none of their parents would let them go.

We lived in Ardwick. My mum and dad had an outdoor off-licence shop, a 24-hour open-all-hours type shop. By then I was going to school on my own, crossing over Manchester on two buses. But it was the night time that mum didn't like the idea of. And so she said she would come over with me and wait outside for me, which was amazing really. It was just an amazing experience. I'd never been in anything like that before. And the noise when they came on was just incredible. I was on the side of the stage near Paul, which was a bit of a disappointment because I was a real John Lennon fan and he was on the other side of the stage. But it was just amazing. You couldn't hear a thing that they were playing, you really couldn't. Because the screaming and the noise was just so intense and I think you were just so amazed by it all you just stood and stared. You couldn't take your eyes off them.

Why did everyone scream? I think it was the reaction of the time. In that period, we were all expected to be little replicas of our parents. And the music was beginning to get quite exciting because you'd had Cliff Richard and Adam Faith and Lonnie Donegan and Tommy Steele and

For Christine McDermott (above), The Beatles were a revelation that changed everything. Below: the ticket for that night in November, preserved in her scrapbook

all that. But that was all very parentally approved, in a way. And they came on and they were just so totally different. For a start, there was four of them and they all appealed to different people, especially girls, and I think it just gained momentum.

They had quite a following in the north-west anyway, so you were very aware of them if you were old enough to be going to concerts and gigs. There was definitely a sort of following around them and a buzz about them. It was something to do with the fact that there was a type of music, especially an English type of music, that was yours and that was definitely for you and not for your parents. Because your parents didn't necessarily approve of it. And it was all bound up with the fashion, with Mary Quant, and everybody was suddenly conscious that you could dress differently from your parents and you could be somebody different from your parents.

I remember my mother still buying me clothes that really were almost like clothes you found in fashion magazines that were meant for older women. You had to wear the miniature version of it. And then all of a sudden the whole thing blew up. And it became a thing about fashion and music and everything. That's certainly how I felt – that all of a sudden I could see a freedom to be somebody different and it all became very exciting.

And I think that excitement engendered the whole frenzy around the groups, both The Beatles and the Rolling Stones. And, of course, in Manchester we had The Hollies and Wayne Fontana and The Mindbenders. Eric Stewart used to live in the next street to me. He was in the Mindbenders and he used to let his sister Debbie know when we could go over and get into *Top of the Pops* in Dickenson Road when they were filming it. And it was all that sort of excitement, and the collectivism of a cinema full of girls roughly between the ages of 12 up to 16, 17. The hysteria thing, the excitement, bred the initial scream and then it just got hysterical. But it was an amazing experience. It was a truly wonderful time to be a teenager. It was brilliant being in Manchester and it was probably the same in Liverpool because you had a really vibrant music scene.

The thing was, they were all people you vaguely knew anyway. My cousin went to school with both Eric Stewart and Wayne Fontana. So you had a knowledge of all these people. Two of The Hollies worked for my uncle in his furniture shop in Salford. And when they got the recording contract, they just came in and said, 'Harry, we're leaving.' 'What do you mean, you're leaving?' 'Well, we've got a recording contract.' And he thought they were mad.

I WAS THERE: GEORGE MORLAND (AGED 15)

GLOBE THEATRE

22 NOVEMBER 1963, STOCKTON-ON-TEES

We went to see them on the day that Kennedy was assassinated. I was still at school. I knew The Beatles were coming to Stockton. But I didn't have a ticket so I thought I'd go and queue for one when they were on sale. I lived in Middlesbrough at the time. Tickets were on sale at the Globe in Stockton, which was about a four-mile bike ride for me. There was no chance of me queuing overnight because my mother and father probably wouldn't let me go anyway. So I got up about six o'clock in the morning and set off and cycled over to Stockton and waited in the queue to try and get a ticket, but unfortunately by the time I got round the corner from the entrance they had sold out. So that was it as far as I was concerned.

But luckily for me a lad who lived over the road from me said his brother was a driver for a local coach firm and they were down to take people to the show and he got given two complimentary tickets. So he gave them to his brother and his brother said to me, 'Do you fancy going then?' And I said 'Of course I do!' The only trouble was with complimentary tickets it was right at the back in the stalls, in the downstairs. The audience was mainly girls. The show wasn't too bad but as soon as The Beatles came on you couldn't hear a thing. The screaming and what have you. You could barely make out what songs they were singing. I do remember one because it was going to be their next number one hit – 'I Want to Hold Your Hand'. They played that that night and you could just about make it out, what it was.

We were chuffed we'd even got in. To actually see them on stage, you know? When we came out, because we went to the first performance which was six o'clock, I think it was just after eight. We were going across the road and this policeman stopped us and he says 'Did you enjoy the show?' We said 'We couldn't hear a bloody thing, mate.' And then we walked down to where we would catch a bus home. We got on the bus and that's when we found out that Kennedy had been shot. And my mate kept asking, 'What's gonna happen now? What's gonna happen now?' On Monday I went back to school and people asked if I'd been to see The Beatles but people weren't really interested. All they were really interested in was talking about Kennedy.

I WAS THERE: BARRY PARKIN

When The Beatles appeared in Stockton I did not get to see them on
stage, but myself and three pals were driving through the High Street near
the Globe Theatre when we were stopped by a policeman. We thought
we were in some sort of trouble, but to our surprise a large black limo
came out of the alleyway next to the Globe and passed in front of us.
The policeman waved us on and as we followed the limo we noticed that
John Lennon and Paul McCartney were looking out of the rear window
laughing and waving to us.

As we tried to catch the limo up, the driver suddenly accelerated
and Lennon and McCartney stuck two fingers up and then waved us
goodbye. That's as near as we got to seeing The Beatles!

I WAS THERE: CHRISTINE PINDER

ABC CINEMA

24 NOVEMBER 1963, HULL

The Beatles played at the ABC
cinema in Hull in November 1963
and October 1964, and I was there
on both occasions, my friend's mum
having queued all night to get us the
tickets. The now demolished ABC cinema
was at the corner of the only access road
to Hull's central bus station. Despite the
police's efforts to control the huge crowds
of fans, they spilled out right across this
road, bringing the bus services more or
less to a halt for the rest of the evening.
In 1963, the support acts included Peter
Jay and The Jaywalkers, The Brook
Brothers and The Vernons Girls. In
1964, the support acts included Sounds
Incorporated, Tommy Quickly and
Mary Wells. I can't remember any of
these at all – only The Beatles. Once

*Barry Parkin was almost there – he and
his friends pursued The Beatles' limo and
got the finger from Lennon and McCartney*

they came on stage, as you'd expect, we couldn't hear anything at all except screaming, including our own!

After the second concert of the evening in 1964, The Beatles were taken in a police van to the local Gordon Street police station, until the fuss died down. Whilst they were there, they changed out of their stage clothes in one of the offices, and then went to the nearby chippy in Redbourne Street. My friend lived down Redbourne Street, and was furious and very upset that The Beatles had been within yards of her house whilst she was still on the bus coming home from their concert!

Christine Pinder, saw The Beatles both times that they played in Hull

I WAS THERE: SUSAN YORK (AGED 15)

RIALTO THEATRE

27 NOVEMBER 1963, YORK

When the tickets went on sale I was at that time attending York College of Commerce doing a course in commerce, shorthand, typing and book-keeping. As my mum did not want me to miss lessons to get the tickets she queued all day for them for me and three of my friends to go to the concert. She sat on a little chair with her flask of tea. My cousin was called Joan. I actually don't remember any of the other acts that were appearing at the same time as them, but I do remember screaming throughout most of The Beatles' performance! I don't think we listened to the music.

I WAS THERE: DUNCAN CURRY

When I saw them again in November you just couldn't hear them. We were out on the balcony and all you could see out from the Rialto was just people as far as you could see. People who couldn't get in, hadn't got tickets.

And anybody who went to that window of that balcony – well, the screaming just went mad outside because they thought you were The Beatles looking out. Any face that went to the balcony to look out. You could hardly hear them at all. It was just screaming non-stop when they came on. They had gold Beatle suits on.

Nº 23 U

MECCA Ltd. – RIALTO, YORK

ARTHUR HOWES presents

THE BEATLES

Wed., 27th Nov., 1963

at 8-45 p.m.

SECOND HOUSE

STALLS 8/6

Tickets cannot be exchanged or money refunded.
No responsibility will be taken for the loss of this ticket.
THIS PORTION TO BE RETAINED

I WAS THERE: EUNICE HAINSWORTH (NÉE WADLEY)

I was a 5th-form pupil at Queen Anne Grammar School and in November 1963 I was lucky enough to see The Beatles. I say lucky as getting the tickets was difficult. They went on sale during the morning on a school day, so of course we couldn't all miss school to buy them. I think there were three girls who volunteered to go to buy them, and who pretended to have dental appointments.

Of course, girls from most of the classes also skipped school to buy tickets. Unfortunately teachers weren't fools and soon realised that rather a lot of girls were missing. Some of the younger teachers had heard about the sale of tickets for The Beatles. When the girls returned they were stopped and asked if they had bought tickets. Some admitted they had and the tickets were confiscated. However, the girls from our class put on sad faces and said that all the tickets had been sold and had none. I don't know if the other tickets were returned. The concert was amazing but I don't think I heard a single word of the songs for all the screaming. But I can say – I was there!

I WAS THERE: GILLIAN THOMPSON (AGED 14)

The Beatles appeared in what was usually a cinema but in those days was used monthly for pop concerts, as they were called then. My parents owned the Edinburgh Arms, which was almost directly opposite. It was the nearest hotel to the Rialto. So anyone who was bottom of the bill used to stay with us, and as a result we often got free tickets.

I have got their autographs in my autograph album, which I got at the time. I went to both the March 1963 and the November 1963 concerts. In March they weren't top of the bill but were somewhere near the top, and I know that we got free tickets. In November we didn't because they were then exceedingly popular and I truanted from school to get

❜ When the girls returned they were stopped and asked if they had bought tickets. Some admitted they had and the tickets were confiscated. However, the girls from our class put on sad faces and said that all the tickets had been sold and had none ❛

the tickets. I got into major trouble for doing it. I got two tickets – one for myself and one for my brother. He was younger than me. And he said that if I went I was not allowed to scream because it would be an embarrassment.

I loved them from the time that they did 'Love Me Do'. That was a wonderful record and it was at that point that people started screaming at concerts. Before then people didn't usually scream at concerts. People were screaming and tears were rolling down their faces. And it hadn't happened to such a large extent before The Beatles started. My dad was quite a well-known publican at the time. He was in the York Licensed Victuallers Association. He and my mother always went over to the concerts after the pub was closed. And in those days pubs closed at half past ten on Tuesday, Wednesday and Friday and closed at 11 on Monday and Thursday. Because in those days we had a cattle market and on cattle market days they were open later. Mum and dad met them because they went over to the Rialto as they knew the manager. And so they went over and spent time with them at the end of the concert.

ABC CINEMA

29 NOVEMBER 1963, HUDDERSFIELD

In 1963 I had been working for around six months. My best friend from school and I worked together as jewellers and we had money of our own to go dancing and buying records. We lived in Halifax and the Sixties were a magical time for us. We were mad on The Beatles and when we heard they were to appear at Huddersfield we immediately decided we must get tickets to see them.

However, all was not as easy as it sounded. We had seen on the television that all the concerts were booked out and people were queuing all night to get tickets and many were coming away disappointed. We were only young and lived a bit of a sheltered life, and although it was supposed to be the Swinging Sixties, the 'swinging' bit had not yet reached us – if it ever did! There was just no chance my dad or my friend's mother would allow an all-nighter on the streets of Huddersfield. We came up with a plan and we each told our respective parents we were staying at each other's houses and, after smuggling out a blanket and a flask, we headed over to Huddersfield the evening before to join an already enormous queue of mainly young girls from all over the north that had been forming for some time.

We joined the end of the queue and it was thankfully policed by the local bobbies, who chatted to us most of the night, and we were also moved as more and more people joined the queue and the police started to worry. The first few hours passed fairly quickly but sitting on the cold flags was really uncomfortable and, as time passed, the singing of Beatles songs trailed off as some managed to get to sleep while others sat there, numb, wondering if it had been a good idea to come at all. Similar thoughts were going through mine and my friend's minds too. Even the man selling 'Beatle Soup' (it was Oxo) had packed up and gone. We were moved again, but as luck would have it they moved a chunk of us and placed us nearer the front on the steps of the cinema, which up to then had been kept clear. This cheered us up no end, but trying to sleep on steps was never going to happen.

We overheard a couple of the police talking. They estimated that the amount of people in the queue would mean some would not get tickets and they were contacting the manager to get the staff down early to open up for selling. I'm not sure what time they did open up but I think it was something like 6am rather than the 9 or 10am it was supposed to be, as the police were concerned for some of the girls in the queue who had not wrapped up warm and were freezing. Also more and more people arriving meant the police were finding it difficult to manage us all. They opened the doors when my friend was asleep and she was trampled on by someone wearing heels and, as they surged forward, she got shoved into the corner as I got pummelled by some around me fighting to get through. It was horrendous and I felt faint.

A part of me was so exhausted I just wanted to give up, but events overtook me as I nearly passed out and was swept up by the Red Cross or similar who had been called out to take care of us. They were only letting a few in at a time to the box office, and with everyone shoving it all got a bit hairy and the ambulance lads were helping

Linda Kitson's signed fan-club photos (top); Linda in the Sixties (centre and bottom, Linda in the middle of the trio)

you through past the ticket box so I took the opportunity to just join the queue. The young lads were saying, 'You should have a lie down' and, although the camp beds in the make shift room looked inviting, I replied 'Oh no, please. I've waited all night and there's no way I'm going home without tickets.' I managed to get tickets – you were allowed to buy four each. I then went out to find my friend still in the corner so we headed back home. I fell asleep on the bus going home and arrived home looking like something the cat dragged in. I went straight to bed and slept all day, so pleased I'd got the tickets. My dad never told me off either. He was just glad I'd arrived home.

The anticipation leading up to the concert, which was due to take place a few weeks after, was just so exciting we could hardly wait. The night of the concert arrived and the four of us set off for Huddersfield, my friend and I and my sister and her friend all excited to be seeing The Beatles.

My favourite was Paul and my friend liked John. We all got settled into our seats and as soon as The Beatles came on the screaming was horrendous and you couldn't hear them at all. We were screaming too! And then everything was over in a flash. I couldn't even tell you what they sang as we couldn't hear them, but it didn't matter. We were there and we saw them.

When it finished, we called out for more and they played us on for a bit that they were coming back out, but I think it was to give the group time to get out of the building. By the time we ran around the back they had gone. We all lost our voices with the screaming. I couldn't speak for days after. My friend had a job interview the next day for a telephonist at the GPO and she had no voice. We still don't know how she got the job, but she did.

When I married from home six years later, I took some things with me from my room and my mum was nagging me to take the rest of my stuff. I ignored her and eventually she threw out some of my memorabilia – Beatle jumper, photos and stuff. All I have left is a few things from being a member of their fan club.

I WAS THERE: JENNY MASKELL

The second time we went to see them in Leeds, it was just Beatlemania and people everywhere, and that continued when they

Paul and John, on stage at Huddersfield ABC

came to Huddersfield. It just blew up really quickly. When they were on in Huddersfield I queued all night. I slept on the pavement with my mum. We queued all night to get tickets for that particular one. My mum was a big fan. She was only about 33 or something. My dad, who was about the same age, thought we were both mad. It was like when I went to see the Rolling Stones. I didn't actually hear The Beatles at all in Huddersfield. We heard them when they went to The Cavern, obviously, but when it got to Huddersfield and beyond we didn't hear anything.

I WAS THERE: LAURIE STEAD

Gorden Kaye and I were in hospital radio. We teamed up to go around doing interviews. He wasn't an actor at the time but he went on to become the star of TV's *'Allo 'Allo*. Gorden's from Huddersfield. And we did an interview with The Beatles. On all the occasions I've gone to previous shows we'd been able to take our photographer with us, but on this one only two of us were allowed to go backstage. So we didn't get photographic evidence of it.

With previous interviews it had been by arrangement with the management of the venue. But on this occasion, with The Beatles being the biggest band around at the time, I decided to write to Brian Epstein to see if we could get permission and I got a letter back from Brian Epstein giving us permission. And if I hadn't have had that, I don't think we'd have got backstage. Because that sort of opened the door as it was, because security was really, really tight. We got to interview all four of them. At that time it was the height of Beatlemania. They got so fed up with people asking them questions they did tend to send the thing up, the usual sort of zany Beatles banter really. But we managed to get some comment from all of them.

' We got to interview all four of them. At that time it was the height of Beatlemania. They got so fed up with people asking them questions they did tend to send the thing up '

And when we ended up editing the programme we had about a 20-minute programme out if it, because we went the previous month when they started selling tickets and we interviewed some of the crowd. So we edited it all together to make a complete 20-minute programme that was broadcast on hospital radio in Huddersfield.

I never thought we'd actually get permission to do it. It was rather a daunting experience, when you're going to interview the biggest band around at the time. Very nerve-wracking. The two of us went backstage and I did speak to all of them. I got some of them to introduce record requests, which they did in a silly way. We did the interview backstage and we stood at the side to watch them in the theatre. It was really all noise. Everybody was screaming so you didn't hear a great deal of it. You could make out what the songs were, but it was this constant barrage of noise and screams. I sold the interview and the Brian Epstein letter and a signed photograph of The Beatles some years ago at Christies'.

I WAS THERE: JENIFER TAYLOR (AGED 15)

The Beatles put their feet up, at the Huddersfield ABC

I saw them at The Ritz. It used to be the ABC. Whichever way round it was. I can't remember now. So top of town. Market Street. It was much like you'd expect those concerts to be. It was heaving. We had to get the tickets by having a rota from school. We were at high school at the time, Huddersfield High School for Girls. I was in the fifth year. I was 15 going on 16.

The tickets were going on sale the following day but we knew that people would start queuing. And they were starting queuing the full day before, so whatever day of the week it was we decided we'd set up a rota. Because some of us had free periods during the day, where you were supposed to go in the library and work or do your homework or whatever. We said, 'Well, if you've got a free period go and stand in the queue and then whoever else gets a free period the next one will come down on the bus to the Ritz and take over from you in the queue and you can go back to your lessons.' And it worked! It seemed to work really well. And you'd stay there all night. Well, we were supposed to stay there all night. But I bottled out. I think it was the threats from my parents – it was 'ridiculous' and 'You're not supposed to do it!' In the end I didn't. Now my friend Jean did stay, and in the morning when they opened the doors it was just a free-for-all. You might just as well not have bothered queuing.

It was a nice long queue that went all round the back of that building and all round here, there and everywhere and it was a proper queue. But in

> If you've got a free period go and stand in the queue and then whoever next gets a free period will come down on the bus and take over from you

the morning Jean just said it was ridiculous. Everybody piled in: it was like the old football matches, when everybody was pushing and shoving to the front. But we did get tickets. We did get our tickets.

The only thing I can remember is it was just absolutely packed to the ginnels. And there were stewards standing down the aisles. So of course

> ▌ It was bedlam really. You pretend to faint but you're not really doing it. It was just fun ▐

we screamed because that's what you did. We weren't very far back We were in the first ten rows, if not nearer, and I was more than happy because we were to the right of the auditorium so I was in front of John because he always stood on the right. It used to be Paul, George in the middle and John on the right. So I was chuffed to bits because he was the one for me, John.

It was bedlam really. You know, you pretend to faint but you're not really doing it. It was just fun. It was all fun. But they were very, very good. Even in those days. It was just the excitement of it all. It was great. I remember the scenes on television when they went to America and things like that, and when they came back on the planes and everything.

It was great really to be part of that. They were national events really. It was good news in those days. Being a kid I wouldn't take notice of anything political or anything like that. But there seemed to be a lot of happy, good news. And that's what we concentrated on of course. We got loads of people at the ABC when it was taking off in the Sixties. Then everybody started going to Batley Variety Club. Big acts were going there. I went to one or two there but it never seemed the same as just popping down to town on the bus, because our bus used to stop on Market Street right outside the Ritz.

We used to hang around outside the side door. If you stood on Market Street, looking towards where the Ritz was, you were able to go up the side. There was a little snicket that went up the side and there was a back door to the Ritz and a car park for the cinema. If we went to the cinema my boyfriend always used to park there. If you didn't get into the show to see whoever it was that was on, we just used to go down and hang about there, in the car park. Because the back door was there and sometimes they'd come and everybody screamed and ran over to the back door. And if you didn't get to see your heroes, sometimes the doorman would come and you'd pass your autograph books in and get your own back if you were lucky. And it'd be signed by loads that you didn't know, like backing bands and parts of the groups that you really had no idea who they were. But I got a few decent autographs – they were good days.

John was my favourite. He was sharp. And I don't know whether that appealed to my sense of humour. It probably would, even now.

I never liked Paul McCartney much. He looked all right, but to me there just wasn't enough substance to him. I thought George was lovely. He was quiet and serious-looking. And he had a lovely smile when he smiled, a bit of a shyish smile.

And Ringo used to sit there and shake his head while he played the drums and it was like: 'It's Ringo: he's just a bit of a lad really – a bit funny, a bit of a joker.' But for me it was always definitely John. And I liked him all the way through his career as well. Apart from when he married Yoko Ono, which I thought was a travesty.

When any of the songs from those groups come on the radio) now I know the lyrics from back to front. I used to buy the weekly magazine *New Musical Express*. And we used to go into Woolworths on a Saturday afternoon and buy this thing that gave you all the lyrics in this little magazine. When new songs came out that week you'd get the lyrics so we just used to buy that every week and we just used to sing along and learn all the songs. And bopping of course – everybody bopped.

At school lunch hours we were lucky because, being in the fifth year, we weren't kicked out to play after lunch. We were allowed to play music, play records in the hall. So we used to just dance all together, bop away to all these songs. They were good days. I think we had a lucky childhood, a happy childhood.

I WAS THERE: JENNIFER BENTLEY

I never saw The Beatles. I used to sit in front of the TV whenever they were on, screaming my head off. I had jigsaws, necklaces, photos, etc., of them but I wasn't allowed to go to see them as my mum said I was too young at 13. I think I'll always regret it. Then the Stones came along, and I'm afraid I switched allegiance to them and then also to The Kinks, who I did see back then.

ODEON THEATRE

7 DECEMBER 1963, LIVERPOOL

I was a member of the TA in Fraser Street, Liverpool. The Beatles were playing at the Odeon cinema in London Road. The queue for tickets was reputed to be a mile long but later in the day there was no queue and tickets were still on sale. I telephoned a mate and he said that he would like to go so I bought two tickets and we both went to see The Beatles. Unfortunately we couldn't hear the music because of the screaming girls.

FUTURIST THEATRE

11 DECEMBER 1963, SCARBOROUGH

When I was in the sixth form at Scarborough Girls' High School, I saw The Beatles in concert at the Futurist in Scarborough. They all wore pale grey mohair suits with Chanel-style high necks without collars, white shirts and narrow black bootlace ties, in contrast to the Rolling Stones, who wore casual clothing. Charlie Watts alone wore a suit.

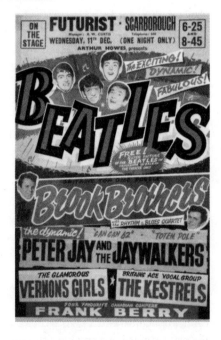

I could not hear anything of The Beatles singing as girls in front of me just stood up and screamed.

I WAS THERE: CHRIS EVERETT

ASTORIA THEATRE

24 DECEMBER 1963–11 JANUARY 1964, FINSBURY PARK, LONDON

I went to see *The Beatles Christmas Show* with a girl I really fancied. A few days later I went to see The Rolling Stones at Tooting Granada when they appeared with The Ronettes. Although I liked the Stones I was more interested in The Ronettes because they were very sexy and 'Be My Baby' was a big hit at the time. It was obvious to people of my age that the times they were a-changing! Pop music was changing and so were attitudes and you could just feel it. They were heady days. There was a lot of optimism around. Bands like the Stones and The Beatles were quick to give credit to their heroes, who were all black – Marvin Gaye, Chuck Jackson, Howlin' Wolf, Muddy Waters, Chuck Berry, Bo Diddley, BB King. And those people were able to launch and relaunch their careers by coming to Britain and Europe thanks to The Beatles and the Stones.

I WAS THERE: MALCOLM PAUL

I last saw the group live with a group of friends including my younger sister, who was a George Harrison fan. Supported by Cilla Black, Tommy Quickly, Billy J. Kramer and The Fourmost amongst others, they used their second LP, *With The Beatles*, as a source for most of their songs, although as ever 'Twist and Shout' closed their performance.

I WAS THERE: FRANCIS CROUCHER

There were about ten or twelve of us that had the chance to go to the Astoria Finsbury Park, London. I remember it was very cold. I could not believe the amount of girls queuing to get in. I remember seeing The Fourmost and Cilla Black as support groups. There were others, but I cannot remember them. At the end of the night The Beatles came on and the place erupted. Everyone made a dash for the front of the stage. A lot of us were standing on the seats to see.

You could hardly hear them for the girls screaming and fainting. The highlight of the night was that a few of the lads I was with had had a bet with one of them that they could walk on stage and shake hands with

John Lennon. Our mate Sid did it! John Lennon was playing the piano. Sid calmly walked over, held his hand out and John Lennon shook it with no problem. The theatre erupted again. Sid calmly turned round and walked off stage. Believe it or not no one stopped him or even questioned him. Mind you, he was a big bloke.

The other thing I remember was that when we came out you could not hear a thing. You couldn't hear the traffic, just a pinging noise in your ears because of the screaming. Oh what memories. Brilliant times.

I WAS THERE: CAROL ALLEN

SCALA THEATRE

23 MARCH – 31 MARCH 1964, LONDON

As a teenager I worked in Charlotte Street next to the Scala theatre where The Beatles filmed their stage scenes for *A Hard Day's Night*. I worked with a friend and, as you can imagine, knowing that our heroes were next door was almost too much to bear. Our supervisor took pity on us one day and let us finish early so we could wait at the stage door. We stood for quite some time, but in the end we were rewarded. Out the Fab Four came. We were within touching distance.

They all got into a black limo and the icing on the cake was when John Lennon wound the window down and offered me a Polo, which I obviously took! That's my claim to fame. No one believes that story but it is true. My friend and I also saw them at the Finsbury Park Astoria.

I WAS THERE: MOIRA MORRIS (AGED 13)

ABC CINEMA

29 APRIL 1964, EDINBURGH

I was 13-and-a-half when I heard that The Beatles were coming to Edinburgh so naturally I wanted to see them. The only way to be sure of getting a ticket was to camp out, but my mother was a bit over-protective: as I was an only child and she was not keen to let me go. One girl had camped out for three days and had missed school and there was no way that I would have got to do that. On the Friday I pleaded again and was told 'no' again. Well, I went to my room and sobbed solidly for about three hours. My father couldn't stand seeing me so sad and pleaded with my mother to let me go, as by that time my friend was getting to go if I was allowed. I can remember him saying to my mum that I didn't ask for much and that they would never hear the end of it if I didn't get to go. By this time my mum had said she had had enough and didn't care any more so the next thing I heard was my dad knocking on my bedroom door, telling me that I was getting to go.

My friend and I headed up to the ABC cinema where they were due to play and we sat on the pavement along with hundreds of other girls. My friend's mum came up later on with fish suppers and they were the best I had ever tasted as it was March and it was cold. My mum said she wasn't giving me any money and that she would come up the next day with money for my ticket. However, because we were near a dance hall and there were drunks about the place the police decided to get the cinema to sell the tickets 12 hours earlier than they had intended to. That was OK, apart from the fact that I had no money for a ticket, so guess what? I burst into tears again. This policeman saw me and asked what was wrong and I told him. He said not to worry and that I would get a ticket. They would keep it for me for a day as there would be a lot of people in that position. He then pushed me near the front of the queue although there had been loads of people in front of me. After a wait of ages, I was at the desk and managed to get a seat eight rows from the front – I remember the seat number, H33 – and they told me they would put it in an envelope for me to collect the next day.

I was excited, to say the least. My friend and I walked down Lothian Road and along Princes Street to get home. There were no night buses at that time and we had no money anyway and we got home about 6am. I had to ring my doorbell as kids didn't get keys then, and of course my parents were not expecting me back at that time. When my dad answered the door I screamed 'I've got a ticket!' and my dad said 'OK, I know you're excited. Just calm down and get to your bed.' So the next day I went to school and was ecstatic. It was a big deal as only three people in my class had a ticket and I had the best seat.

I went after school to get the ticket and my mum told me to give it to her for safe keeping. It cost 12/6 [63p]. The first two rows were

15/- [75p]. I'll never forget the concert. I couldn't see, but there was a boy at either side of me and they lifted me on their shoulders so that I could get a view. I screamed myself hoarse but it was great. I didn't try to get on the stage as the bouncers were throwing girls off, not bothering too much, and some of them got hurt. I was quite light so didn't fancy getting flung about.

It's something that'll stay in my memory forever. When we were going out of the theatre quite a lot of the seats were wet, but I managed not to pee on my seat. I also went to see them in October that year but there was no camping out allowed. You had to send a postal order and it was first come, first served. I still got a seat in the stalls but it wasn't so near and it cost me 7/6 [38p]. The concert was just as good. It's hard to believe it was over 50 years ago.

BEATLES IN OZ

May 1964 was spent on holiday. Then The
Beatles commenced their first major
overseas tour. On 11 June 1964 they
arrived in Australia.

I WAS THERE: RAY BARWELL

CENTENNIAL HALL

12–13 JUNE 1964, ADELAIDE

I could not believe the number of people outside the town hall. It was
gridlock. There were thousands and thousands. You could not fall over
if you tried. Everything came to a standstill. You could not think for the
screams, the cars, the trams, everything.

When they came onto the veranda at the town hall, girls were
fainting and medics were trying to revive them. I know it was a long
time ago, but I'll never forget seeing The Beatles on stage. They
were fantastic.

I WAS THERE: BRENTON MONTGOMERY

I went to one of the concerts, but can't recall which one. There were four
in all – two on the twelfth and two on the thirteenth. I was a member of
the UK-based Beatles Fan Club and through a promo on Channel 7 won
a free ticket in the front row!

I WAS THERE: KARINA KAY BILLETT (NÉE MORESEY)

My father, Desmond Thomas Moresey, was a police officer. He
was awarded the Australian Police Medal in 1987, just before he
passed away, for his outstanding service to the community. I had a
look through his duty logs and I found two brief entries that state
he was there. He got the job of crowd control at the town hall and

Far left: George Harrison on stage at the Centennial Hall, Adelaide. Left: Paul McCartney, enjoying himself at a reception for the organisers of the Australian Beatles fan club

pulling hysterical and fainting girls from the front of the stage at the Centennial Hall, because he was so tall.

I can remember him telling me that he was on crowd control and on stage with The Beatles at their Adelaide concerts. I also remember him not being so complimentary about the band, although this may be an age and an era thing. He said, 'They were long-haired Poms' and he couldn't hear a word of what they sang because of the girls screaming. 'Why go to a concert and scream?'

I WAS THERE: SANDRA ADAMSON (NÉE WYATT, AGED 22)

I was 22 years old when I was excitedly taken to the Wayville showgrounds, Centennial Hall, to see and hear them by a boyfriend whose name I have forgotten. My seating was in the centre of the hall about halfway back from the stage.

Everyone in the audience was standing up and jumping around and not being very tall – about 5' 4" – all I could see was the topmost part of their heads. The entire concert was a yelling and screaming crescendo of noise so that I heard none of their music or singing. It was a huge disappointment for me and the only concert that I have ever attended since because of this. I might as well have been at a football match.

I WAS THERE: LIZZIE ARMSTRONG

I went to The Beatles concert in 1964 with my brother and some girlfriends. We camped out on North Terrace overnight to get tickets. We were six rows from the front!

I WAS THERE: SANDI HOGBEN (AGED 17)

My father got the ticket from a friend who I did not know. I went with his daughter and her friend. The seats were two rows from the stage – dead centre. Lucky me! Being a young lady at the time, I went with the attitude of not getting caught up with the hysterical girls screaming. However that changed immediately when those gorgeous, handsome, well dressed, swanky young Englishmen with their accents opened their mouths. Oh yes – I screamed as loud as anyone!

I fell in love with George. Paul, John and Ringo did not get a look-in. I can still see them before me in their black stovepipe pants, jackets, tie, white shirts and iconic Beatle clean-cut hairstyle. My boyfriend, now my husband, wore the same style at the time. Paul was the frontman, with general banter from John and George being more reserved. The stage setting was simple, with speakers, equipment and microphones all in black. I have the official souvenir Australian tour programme, which shows Johnny Devlin as supporting artist, a popular Australian rocker at the time.

I have a signed photo of Johnny which my older brother got for me. I don't remember the support artists apart from one of the bands, who had a saxophone player who blasted the songs out. Needless to say I went home exhausted, my throat sore and my voice hoarse, re-living every moment. To this day I am excited to think I was there and so very fortunate to have the perfect seat. Thank you, dad!

I WAS THERE: SUE CURNOW

My husband and I were at Centennial Hall for that performance all those years ago. My husband slept in the street to get the tickets, much to his mother's disgust. We were five rows from the front. I still have the original programme and some black and white photos I took myself with my Kodak Instamatic camera.

I WAS THERE: SAMELA HARRIS

Who could forget? The hall was packed. The audience was predominantly young and female, like me. I had a good seat four or five rows from the front. It was all very happy, excited and generally nice – until The Beatles came on stage. Perfectly normal girls suddenly went completely mad. They started to scream – and they did not stop. They bounced and jumped and screamed ear-piercing, deafening screams. The Beatles played, looking amused and bemused, but one could hear only snatches. Amplification was not as huge as it is these days. I was not a screamer and I was really annoyed at the whole phenomenon. I was thrilled to have seen my pin-ups in the flesh but I just could not understand then or now why all these fans would rather scream than listen.

I WAS THERE: NICKY CONNOR

Nicky Connor (on the right) stayed out all night to get her ticket – for just 30 minutes of Beatles

I slept overnight outside Allan's Record Shop in Rundle Street to get an even row – Row B, second row from the front. The supporting acts were Johnny Chester and Sounds Unlimited, plus a few more top bands that I don't remember. The Beatles came on for 30 minutes.

They sang ten songs of three minutes each – 'Please Please Me', 'Love Me Do', 'I Want To Hold Your Hand', 'She Loves You', 'From Me to You', 'Can't Buy Me Love', 'Rock'n'Roll Music', 'A Hard Day's Night' and two other songs I don't recall. I never remembered too much about it because I was screaming the whole time and never heard anything!

I WAS THERE: HELEN JORASLAFSKY

I wagged school, slept in Grenfell Street to get tickets, and our tickets were in the very last row! As we were in the back row of

Centennial Hall we had no reservations about standing on the seats so that we could see above the waving arms of those in front of us. I can't remember whether it worked! What do I remember? All that screaming! I don't think I actually heard a note or a word during their performance. And Roy Orbison was their support act – who would have thought?

I WAS THERE: JULIE TOLLEY (NÉE BENNETT, AGED 14)

I was one of the very lucky ones at the Beatles concert at Centennial Hall in 1964 and I remember it very clearly. I went with my very first serious boyfriend Gary Saunders, who lived next door to my mother's friends Uncle Jack and Aunty Lila Dawe on Bundarra Avenue, in the northern suburb of Blair Athol. Although unrelated, in those days the terms 'aunty' and 'uncle' were a sign of respect. Gary's mother would drive him to my place at Dover Gardens, in the south and near the coast, and we would sit in the lounge room and listen to 45rpm records whilst my mum and Gary's mum would sit in the kitchen chatting and drinking tea. Gary gave me a ticket for the concert for my fourteenth birthday. I do not have any recollection of getting to Centennial Hall, but either his or my mum drove us there and picked us up after the concert finished.

Our seats were about five or six from the front. Despite what the newspaper and TV reports said, the only screaming was between songs. While The Beatles were singing, everyone was listening. I suspect this was for several reasons. Firstly we were polite and it was polite to listen. And the tickets were probably expensive, although I never knew the cost. Plus we were just spellbound by the appearance of a fabulous group from overseas, not just local acts such as The Twilights (who later become the Little River Band), The Easybeats or Johnny Farnham. The hall has since been demolished.

I WAS THERE: JENNY LESLIE (AGED 16)

It was my first concert. My parents bought me the ticket from a neighbour who couldn't go, for 30 shillings as a birthday gift. It was the best gift ever. I was seated seven rows from the front and everybody screamed, which did make them a bit hard to hear at times. The acoustics in Centennial

The Beatles was Jenny Leslie's first ever concert

Hall weren't the best, but who cared? Along with them were the group Sounds Incorporated and Johnny Chester, who wore red shoes. I always remembered that. I took my dad's binoculars but didn't need them. I became the twenty-first member of the SA Beatles fan club. Always loved them. George was my favourite. Didn't get to see Ringo – Jimmy Nicol filled in. I've never forgotten that night.

I WAS THERE: JO ROGERS (AGED 20)

They weren't actually gonna come here. But radio DJ Bob Francis got a petition up because they were going to miss out Adelaide altogether. My younger sister and her friend went and queued up. They queued up as soon as they finished work Friday night. They were queuing up outside the market, the big stores that were selling the tickets, and they queued all along North Terrace, which is quite a long street, and they went right round the corner and right down one road and round the other road. There were crowds of them for four days. They did a procession up King William Street, which is a main street, to the town hall.

And I was on the median strip and I put my foot out just to see and a copper was coming round on his motorbike. I put my foot out and of course I ended up with it under his footpeg and around his knee. And I ended up with my elbow on his shoulder because he stopped. He had to stop. So the cars stopped. I think it was an open-top Rolls convertible. And we were taking photos of them but none of them came out. It was such a mess, it was just so shaky. It looked like someone's operation actually. Terrible. This poor policeman – I let him go in the end. But it stopped the parade. I stopped the whole parade with my foot!

We got front-row tickets both nights. mum came with us the first night but we were sitting just at the side in the front. We were right in the front the next night, right in front of the microphones. But they needn't have sung really, even when we were sitting right in front, because there was so much screaming you could only just about hear them. But not much. The three of us walked home and that was a fair old way because it was a half-hour drive. We got offers of rides but we were walking on cloud nine singing all the Beatles songs going along the road. That was absolutely great.

The only thing was, Ringo wasn't there. I think he had tonsillitis. Jimmy Nicol was there instead. When they left, my dad and mum took my sister and I to the airport. But we didn't go to the airport. Going down to the beach, along the side, there's all this grass and hedges. There it was all fenced off and dad parked there because you could just about see the planes from there. And he stopped.

So Sis and I both got out and we jumped the fence and we ran across this paddock and jumped down the ditch before anyone saw us. And then we got up and ran again to get to another ditch. And these guards saw us and made us go back. So that's as far as we got. So we didn't see them take off. But there were crowds. There were so many people. And they reckon that even though they weren't going to come to Adelaide they got the best reception here of anywhere in Australia. They were so natural and down-to-earth. They weren't putting on any airs and graces. With Australians that doesn't go down too well anyway. I think it was just that everyone found they were just so easy to get on with. And there wasn't all this prima donna stuff that you get with a lot of people. That's why Adelaide liked them.

I WAS THERE: GILL RIBIS (AGED 19)
FESTIVAL HALL

15–17 JUNE 1964, MELBOURNE

In June 1964 I won a competition to watch The Beatles live on stage – an Elnett hairspray competition. We were living in Melbourne at the time and I worked in a pharmacy and got to know about the Elnett competition. You had to answer the question 'Why do you use Elnett?' and I can't remember what I wrote, but whatever it was I won it!

I took my eldest brother. We couldn't hear. We could hardly see. But I did see it on television afterwards and it was fantastic. The atmosphere was great. They were just coming up at that time. Paul was my favourite Beatle.

I WAS THERE: JOYCE ALLAN (AGED 13)
THE STADIUM

18–20 JUNE 1964, SYDNEY

My friend and I took the day off school when they arrived in Sydney. We spent the day under umbrellas and an awning of the Chevron Hotel, opposite the Sheraton Hotel, waiting for them to appear, which they finally did in the afternoon. The young policemen who were keeping us in check were very friendly and there were no hassles. We were just so excited. Two girls from our school went to the airport and were on the front of the *Sydney Morning Herald* the next day.

Despite the fact that their mothers had given them notes saying they were sick, the school was very accommodating with teachers asking if they had fun! My mother had queued up previously to buy us the tickets for the show. This was an unusual thing for her to do, as she was usually more interested in us getting on with our studies. Four of us went – my sister and her friend – who was four years older than us but mad about John Lennon – and my school friend and I. We were in the middle section of the stadium, mesh fences between us and ringside, but with a reasonable view. We had such a great time. We were thrilled that Ringo had been able to come in time for the Sydney show after his illness. I had binoculars and remember him wearing lime green socks!

When they came on the screams were deafening, but we all swear we could still hear them singing. Mum and dad came to pick us up and said they saw The Beatles leaving in their car. I think they had a quick getaway quite a while before we were all let out of our seats. mum always says she wishes she had gone too. It had reminded her of her own teenage years when she was mad about Frank Sinatra. It was such a special time and I'm only sorry now that I didn't keep my scrapbook and ticket for posterity. Years later, when I was coming home from work and heard about John Lennon's death, I immediately thought that my sister would be upset, so had to write to her in London to say how sorry I was. It all felt like they were people who were special friends.

I WAS THERE: GEOFFREY OGDEN BROWNE (AGED 13)

I went to the Sydney Stadium by some sort of serendipity. My elder sister Mo was married at the time to a colleague at Radio 2SM, who was given two ringside seats to The Beatles concert but could not make it, so I went with her instead. The tickets we had as a comp cost 37/6 each, which was quite a lot of money in those days – you could get a pie for sixpence. Even outside the hysteria had started. I had just turned 13 and could not in my wildest dreams have seen so many nubile teenage girls, especially that night as it was Paul McCartney's birthday. The smells when we got to our seats were amazing. It was a mixture of lust, musk and pheromones. The stadium was like a huge barn. The seats were ancient. The air of anticipation was electric, absolutely electric – you could actually feel it. We were seven rows from the front but the noise from what were called 'the bleachers', i.e. the cheap seats at the back, was getting louder every

A prized ticket for The Beatles at Sydney Stadium

minute, a bit like a thunderstorm approaching. Sounds Incorporated, the support act, came on and did a decent set and by and large the audience gave them due respect for their efforts. But no one had come to see Sounds Incorporated! Then you could practically hear the pounding heartbeats of all the girls as the lads came on. It's so very hard all these years later to describe it... let's just say the room went from 240 volts to about 10,000. It really was a case of 'you had to be there'.

The boys looked so natty and clean by today's standards, but in those days the haircuts alone raised eyebrows as well as derision from anyone over the age of 30. I remember George having a go at counting-in the first number. I heard 'She was just 17 and you know....' and then the screaming really started! It was deafening, truly on the threshold of pain.

From then on they may as well have been miming. In true stoic Liverpudlian spirit the boys soldiered on. They were battle-hardened by this stage, having just been to America. But they make 'em tough in Liverpool. In just over half an hour it was all over. Or was it? I had witnessed something I have seen to this day only on film and that was mass hysteria. In the stadium that night on those wooden seats everyone was standing. I was in disbelief as if I were observing from another world. The teenage girls were right next to me crying, sighing, screaming, and some most probably wetting their pants as well! A medical person would call it rapture. In those days there were no drugs as we know them today, nor even much pre-fuelled alcohol. It was just pure unadulterated fun. Carefree.

Part of my life changed that night. For days I ran it through my head trying to figure out what had happened. I remember one thing above all about that night at the Sydney Stadium: I knew even at the age of 13 I was witnessing history. I shudder to think, though, about what I did when given the album *A Hard Day's Night* one Christmas. I took it back to the shop and exchanged it for *Beethoven's Fifth Symphony*, played by The London Symphony Orchestra.

I WAS THERE: TONY CHAPLIN (AGED 15)

I was in the third year of high school when I went to the Saturday show at the Sydney Stadium. I think there were two other acts that night – Johnny Chester and Johnny Devlin and a great English rock band called Sounds Incorporated. I remember The Beatles running on to the rotating stage and them singing about ten songs. You could just make out the words above all the noise. Then they ran off the stage. There were no encores. The place was packed and I loved the show.

I WAS THERE: SANDRA DEE (AGED 16)

My friends and I were there at the Sydney Stadium to see The Beatles and we were four rows from the front. Ringo wasn't playing as he had tonsillitis. We didn't take photos – there were no mobiles or videos then. We were 16 years old and my friend's sister was 11. I felt so very fortunate to be there. The tickets were £12 each and, no, we didn't run to the Sheraton Hotel afterwards!

I WAS THERE: GAIL FAHEY (AGED 15)

I was 15 years old and came over to Sydney where I stayed with my aunt and grandmother and while I was living with them, they took me to nearly every show that came to the stadium. I can remember the gate man saying to my grandmother that she was the oldest person to go through the gate that night. She would have been 62 years old.

We entered through a very small door into the stadium that day. I think it was because I was with the older people and a man took us with him to avoid us being shoved around. I had a wonderful time. We were about 15 rows from the front and could see very well. Everyone was screaming and having a wonderful time. The Beatles looked immaculate in their suits on the stage of the old building. My biggest regret was I didn't keep the tickets. I don't know if I even saw the

The Fabs on stage, amidst the hysteria of the Sydney Stadium shows

tickets, as my aunt would have had them and in those days I would never have thought of keeping the tickets.

I WAS THERE: JUNE GRANLAND (NÉE CONNELL, AGED 14)

I went with a girlfriend to the Saturday matinee show. To this day I can't believe my mother let me go. I don't remember how we got the tickets. I think my friend had a relative in the entertainment industry. We caught a train in from Parramatta. I can't remember what station we went to but I remember walking a fair way in new high-heel T-bar shoes which were all the rage.

On arriving at the stadium there were thousands of people – mainly girls like us. We had to stand behind wooden barriers waiting to go in. Then all of a sudden The Beatles' car pulled up and out they got. I could reach out and touch George. He was my favourite! Everyone was screaming but I was just in total amazement that I was so close to them. We were ushered to our seats. Ours were in the bleachers so they were only tiny specks on the stage and the noise of the girls screaming was unbelievable. But I remember them singing 'I Saw Her Standing There'. It was incredible.

I WAS THERE: MARGARET HYDE

My father worked for 2SM at the time. He came home and announced that he had tickets for the concert. My two brothers, my sister and I just about went ballistic and off we went – by public transport, I might add – from Lane Cove. We were in the third row from the front.

I WAS THERE: ROGER UNETT (AGED 20)

I had arrived from England on 22 December 1963 and was staying at the migrant hostel at Heathcote. As soon as we found out about the tour, me and some other lads at the hostel, including a guy called Jeff, arranged for a girl who was also a Beatles fan to go into Sydney very early and queue for tickets.

On the day, I drove three mates in my VW Beetle into Sydney and we parked as close to the stadium as we could get at Rushcutters Bay. We presented our tickets with much excitement and went into the Stadium. What I remember most is the revolving stage and the screaming. The

Roger Unett: he bopped so hard he broke his watch

noise generated was incredible. I was clapping throughout the concert so enthusiastically that when we got out I realised I had broken my watch.

I WAS THERE: NOELENE JOHNSTON

I was sat in the front row. Honestly, you couldn't hear a thing they sang because of the screaming from the audience. I wasn't one of them because I was with my boyfriend, who had said if he came I wasn't allowed to scream. I still have the original programme. I'm not sure why I have saved it all these years as none of my family are interested. They might be when I die, but it will probably just be thrown in a skip.

I WAS THERE: GERRY KEEFE (AGED 24)

I went with my friend Bob Muirhead. There were about 15,000 in the crowd and the females outnumbered the males by fourteen to one. Because of the continuous female screaming throughout the whole show I did not hear one word of the songs. Still – what a night!

I WAS THERE: SANDRA MILLHOUSE (AGED 16)

I remember it very well. I was standing up in the bleachers with my girlfriend. I kept lighting matches and calling out Paul's name. There were two guys that kept blowing out my match and my friend said, 'I wouldn't do that if I were you', because I was crazy and she didn't know what I would do.

Well, I put the match out on one of their hands. They didn't do it again!

I WAS THERE: LOUISE MORRIS (AGED 14)

I was a very excited 14-year-old in 1964 when my older brother bought me two tickets to see the Fab Four. It was a hard choice as to which girlfriend I would take! We left Drummoyne, where we lived, at 3 p.m. to head to the stadium – much to the concern of our parents, as we had to go up William Street and through Kings Cross. This in itself was an exciting adventure for two very naive teenagers!

It was a long wait until The Beatles came on at 9 p.m. to the deafening screaming of the crowd. There were no ear plugs in those days. I remember the advice from DJ Bob Roberts to stick your fingers in your ears and press forward to

Above: Paul, belting it out against the massed screams of Sydney. Below: Louise Morris, who bunked an afternoon's school to see The Beatles

eliminate some of the screaming noise, which was as loud and ear-piercing as a tree full of cicadas. It sort of worked. We were in the second-last row of the bleachers so the stage was very far away but we were able to see Paul – our favourite – shake his Beatlemop while singing 'I Want to Hold Your Hand'.

Such great memories. At school the next day we were the envy of our friends but in trouble with the headmistress as we had wagged school after lunch!

I WAS THERE: SANDRA ORSZACZKY (AGED 17)

I still recall the excitement of it all and the incredible wall of noise that endured for the length of the concert! I lived in Sydney in 1964 when the beloved Beatles arrived for concerts. I was 17 years old and, along with countless other young girls, completely in love with Paul. I was a working girl and so was able to invest in tickets to the most exciting night out I had ever had. I attended the show with a work girlfriend who shared my love of the band.

We arrived at the Sydney Stadium to find the place packed to the rafters. The anticipation was palpable! The old building shook when the music started and I can honestly say we

Sandra Orszaczky: a little more conservatively dressed than when she saw The Beatles in tight pants and fur-trimmed white boots

all heard no singing at all, just the screaming of a stadium full of lovestruck girls accompanied by a sprinkling of brave young men. The concert has remained one of my favourite memories of that time in my life and whilst those memories are no longer so sharp, I am so grateful to have experienced the joy of seeing The Beatles.

One firm memory I have is of my friend Lesley and I taking the train home and walking down the road singing at the top of our voices all the favourite songs we had seen but not really heard! I can even remember what we wore – tight black pants, sloppy purple jumpers and white boots with a fur trim. So cool!

I WAS THERE: DON BROWN (AGED 17)

I'll never forget that period. Parties in those days would play Beatles records only, even though there were only two or three LPs released at that time. It's amazing that we call it such a memorable event – but it was! I was there and so were The Beatles and that was all that mattered. It was June 1964 at the old Sydney Stadium at Rushcutters Bay. I drove there in my MGA.

I was working with an advertising agency and the social club organised the tickets, which might have cost 30/- [AUS$3]. I attended many stadium concerts in the late Fifties and the Sixties and The Beatles concert was without doubt the pinnacle of all of them. But it shouldn't have been, because I couldn't hear a thing other than the non-stop screaming of the girls for the duration of their stage appearance. It was unbelievable – the worst I had ever heard, and all of this in the giant chook house called Sydney Stadium.

The noise was the one thing that made it different to any other concert I had been to, and yet the atmosphere was electric. I think I went to a Saturday show, as we didn't take time off work, and possibly one that started in daylight hours. I remember that The Beatles didn't relate to the audience too much other than singing their five or six songs. And then they were gone.

I WAS THERE: MARGARET VINCENT

I was a lowly student nurse at the time, earning about four pounds a fortnight. I queued for hours to buy the tickets for myself and my sister, by which times the ringside seats were all sold so we had to be satisfied with terrace seats, which were just like long benches with numbers painted on them, which cost 17/6 [88p] each. They were elevated in long rows with bare ground underneath, so that if you dropped anything it was lost forever. We waited with great anticipation for weeks and guarded those tickets with our lives.

Several days before The Beatles arrived in Australia, a local radio station had one of their staff travelling with the group, and I listened to the radio every chance I got and hung on every detail. I was heartbroken when we were told that Ringo would not be coming for the first of the shows but would play Sydney. The same radio station then announced a competition for people to attend Paul's 22nd birthday celebrations. So I entered the competition – only finding out years later that my mother did not post the entry!

My father drove us to the stadium with strict instructions that we were to behave like young ladies and not talk to any strangers. He would return to pick us up after the show. It was pouring rain and freezing cold, with a very leaking roof and terrible acoustics. The stadium was constructed mainly of corrugated iron and the noise of the pouring rain on the roof often drowned out the singing. And if that didn't do it the screaming fans did. Sounds Incorporated were playing first and I think they were greeted with choruses of very loud boos.

From what I remember, the songs sung by The Beatles were not terribly good, the acoustics were terrible and they often seemed quite flat and/or out of tune. In hindsight, they seemed to be quite detached from the audience and reacted very little to them. They did their songs and just left the stage, which seemed quite anti-climactic. They almost looked to be reading a script some of the time. The stage was circular and the centre of it revolved, so maybe they were just dizzy.

Between the noise of the screams and the very loud rain and howling wind, it was very hard to hear anything much,

Margaret Vincent and her mates didn't quite live up to the conduct standards her dad would have preferred...

⟨ After the show, we piled out of the stadium for dad to collect us, assuring him that we did behave like young ladies ⟩

but – it was The Beatles! Who cared how bad or good they were? After the show, we piled out of the stadium past ambulance officers and fainting girls, into the weather for dad to collect us, assuring him that we did behave like young ladies. Not!

A group of us went down to Kings Cross on the Saturday morning and stood in the street outside the Sheraton Hotel (where they were staying) for hours, in the freezing cold, just waiting for them to make an appearance on the balcony. We were chanting and singing Beatles songs for hours on end until, at about five o'clock, some heads eventually appeared over the balcony railing. We were sure it was them! After a few waves from them and deafening screams from us, it was all over and they were gone. Of course, from a distance of about ten floors up, it could have been anyone up there, and we would never have known.

We lived very close to Sydney Airport, so I went down to the airport to see them leave, but the weather was still awful. I think they were driven out onto the tarmac and up the steps undercover. We won tickets to an early screening of *A Hard Day's Night* and the umbrella that Paul used at the airport was used as a lucky door prize. It was filled with confetti, which went all over the stage when the winner was announced. I didn't win the prize but I did get a piece of the confetti, which I carried around in my purse for several years.

My sister and I went to nearly all of the British Invasion shows at the stadium, artists such as Cilla Black, Gerry and The Pacemakers, The Searchers and just about anyone else of that era. I also saw the Rolling Stones' very first Australian show. I still love all the music of that era, and most of it since, and could not imagine life without it.

I WAS THERE: TED ORAM

My mate Max and I had bought our tickets some time before. The big night finally arrived and we trained into Sydney not knowing what to really expect as neither of us had been to anything like this before. Our seats were not bad considering the size of the venue, although quite small by today's standards. The first act was Jonhny Devlin, an Aussie singer. I managed to shout to Max 'what do we do when everyone starts screaming?' 'Dunno.' he said. It did not take long to find out. The next act up was Sounds Incorporated, the volume of the crowd increased and we shouted louder to match it. Sounds Incorporated finished their set and The Beatles were next. The feeling of seeing one's idols suddenly took hold of the crowd. The sense of expectation grew like something alive in that stadium. Words cannot really describe it. The sound and volume of the crowd went up to something I have never heard since. Then four mop tops could be seen trying to get through the crowd to the stage. We had heard of the term mass hysteria. Well, now Max and I were suddenly part of it. Standing on our seats, we screamed along with everyone else until The Beatles were finished. We did not hear much and did not see much – but what an experience, one that is still clear many years later. Hoarse from screaming, we came out not quite believing what we had just been part of. So much so that we took the chance and went back in to Palings Music store in Sydney the next morning, a Saturday, and managed to buy two more tickets. These seats were a bit further back than the night before but we still managed to go through the whole fantastic experience again.

I WASN'T THERE: CAMPBELL FORD

As a young man in the Fifties and Sixties I went to many a concert at the Sydney Stadium – Frank Sinatra, The Beach Boys and Spike Jones – but I didn't go to the Beatles show. Whilst I liked their music, I was unable to buy tickets as their performances were sold out in minutes! However, I did book for the premiere of a sensational new performance of *Henry V* on the same day, with a young John Bell and his wife Anna Volska as Katherine in an innovative in-the-round presentation in a pavilion tent erected in Rushcutters Bay Park, just across the road from the Stadium. All started well until The Beatles' concert began a few minutes later. The music didn't bother us – but the deafening screaming and stamping of the audience from across the road drowned out any other sound at all, including the dialogue of the actors on stage in the tent. John Bell and his troupe valiantly continued their performance but it was all in vain – nobody could hear a word! Fortunately the audience saw the funny side of it all.

I was in my mid-twenties and had been working as a film animator for TV for some time. I was booked to leave Australia to try my luck

Campbell Ford (far left) worked as an illustrator on The Beatles' animated movie Yellow Submarine. One of the main reasons he came to London was Diana, the Aussie girl he later married (above)

in England just a couple of weeks after this 'Beatles vs the Bard' event. I was also interested in a pretty Australian girl who was already in London. With several friends and a VW Kombi we sailed to India and,

Campbell and Diana, ex-pat Aussie illustrators for The Beatles

in true Sixties tradition, unloaded it in Bombay and drove overland to London where, by a strange coincidence, I was later hired to work as an animator on The Beatles' *Yellow Submarine* feature cartoon.

It was the most memorable year of my life. I met The Beatles briefly during production and found them easy to talk to and totally fascinated by the cartoon versions of themselves. The pretty girl also came to work on *Yellow Submarine* and we became engaged during production. We married back in Australia in 1969.

I WASN'T THERE: BRUCE HAMLIN (AGED 14)

In 1964 I was still at school way down in Narrandera and couldn't make it to Sydney, even though I had my accommodation booked with a family friend and had a mate willing to share the adventure with me. Being only 14 at the time, it was a little difficult to convince my parents to let me come to Sydney, although all of my life I had spent the January school holidays at Manly literally every year since I was born. I now live in the next suburb up from Manly, so I have always been a frustrated Beatles fan.

I WAS THERE: BARRY IDOUR (AGED 23)

TOWN HALL, DUNEDIN

26 JUNE 1964, DUNEDIN, NEW ZEALAND

I attended the Beatles press conference and reviewed the concert for the

Evening Star, the now-defunct Dunedin evening newspaper of the day. I was one of four *Star* reporters to attend the press conference and recall being staggered by the massive crowds blocking Princes Street outside the City Hotel, where The Beatles were staying. When they arrived they were literally thrown into the hotel lift by police as they battled against the crowd. I suspect John Lennon may have been mildly injured in this incident as he didn't make it to the press conference, although it was claimed a bit of flu was the reason. Apparently George Harrison said to a police officer that the police had badly underestimated the crowd control problem, to which the policeman replied along the lines of, 'Don't worry son, we know what we're doing. We looked after Gracie Fields when she was here.'

The conference itself got off to a grand start once The Beatles got seated when the *Star*'s chief reporter David Exel attempted to get things underway by saying, 'Right, now before we start can you tell us which of you is which?' The 100 or so people in the room erupted with cries of amazement and George summed it up by replying, 'If you don't know by now, what the hell are you doing here?' I felt sorry for Dave because in many interview situations like this it was probably a reasonable suggestion, but it was totally farcical in the context of The Beatles. Quick as a flash, Ringo announced that he was John, Paul said he was Ringo and George said he was Paul. This certainly eased the tension in the room. The rest of the session went pretty much without incident, although John's absence diminished things a bit.

On to the first concert of two in the 2,500-seat town hall. I and another reporter, the late Frank Campbell, were lucky enough to be the chosen reviewers, although in hindsight there was little to review except the crowd reaction. This was because the volume of the sound system coupled with the screaming crowd made it almost impossible to hear what The Beatles were singing.

Frank and I discovered early that if we put our fingers in our ears some of the music did filter through, but not much. Not that it really mattered as The Beatles were only on stage for 20 to 25 minutes. I don't know what all the audience around us in the dress circle thought about these two dorks sitting there with fingers stuck in our ears. It was an experience that has remained vividly in my memory, being an impressionable 23-year-old at the time, and it being one of the most exciting visits to the city.

BACK IN THE UK, 1964

Shortly after returning from their world tour,
The Beatles were given a civic reception at
Liverpool Town Hall.

SPEKE AIRPORT

10 JULY 1964, LIVERPOOL

Some of the planes that flew the London route were DC3s which required
only one cabin crew. The ground crew pushed the very heavy door
from the outside and the hostess was responsible for securing it on the
inside. On one occasion, the plane was taxiing down the runway when
to my horror the door opened, a bag was thrown in, followed by Paul
McCartney. He was very apologetic. I wasn't best pleased because in the
split-second that all this happened I had been wondering how I was to deal
with what seemed an emergency.

At the time, Liverpool was a homely little airport; I doubt the ground
staff or airline pilot of what is now John Lennon Liverpool Airport
would have been so accommodating.

Huge crowds
gathered in
Liverpool on 10
July 1964 to
celebrate The
Beatles' movie A
Hard Day's Night

I remember queuing up. The fire station on the corner by the old Speke Airport with Bryant & May, the matchstick factory, on the other corner: I was in that road there and I was looking through the mesh and saw them coming off the aeroplane. And then, when they came past in the Rolls-Royce, heading to the town hall, I saw them there as well. There were thousands of us, all lining the road.

TOWN HALL, LIVERPOOL

10 JULY 1964, LIVERPOOL

I went to see The Beatles at their civic reception at Liverpool's town hall. The crowds were phenomenal and the crush unbelievable. I was next to a police horse which continually bit me. The only way to escape it was to tell a first-aider, who took me to an ambulance. I was taken to the Royal Northern Hospital for treatment but I only sustained bruising and was able to return to the crowds.

Paul (above) and Ringo (below) being escorted to the town hall

My cousin, Ritchie Hughes (aka Ritchie Galvin), was a drummer with another band and was actually asked to become The Beatles' drummer when Pete Best was dismissed from the band. My cousin declined as he did not get on well with John Lennon.

I WAS THERE: CHRIS HORLOCK

HIPPODROME

12 JULY 1964, BRIGHTON

Singer Ray Charles appeared at the Dome in July, but this month in Brighton 1964 is remembered for Beatlemania taking the town by storm. 'The Beatles Show', as it was quaintly called, came to the Hippodrome and a ticket in the stalls cost 15/- [75p]. Most of those present say they couldn't hear what was being sung at all due to the screaming girl fans, and when the sound system packed up for a short period, no one noticed because of the din.

In fact no one interviewed about the concert can recall a specific song at all, such was the row. Getting The Beatles into the Hippodrome without being mobbed caused some managerial head-scratching until someone decided to utilise a garage building that stood immediately opposite the theatre. Middle Street was closed off and the van containing the Fab Four drove down West Street, which no one was expecting, then into the garage, which had a West Street entrance.

The group dashed through to the Middle Street entrance and ran across the street and through the Hippodrome's front doors, with the crowds getting all but a fleeting glimpse of them as they passed.

I WAS THERE: JEREMY KNIGHT (AGED 13)

I had a front-row seat, along with my 15-year-old sister Belinda. My parents would not normally have let me out at night, but even they recognised it was a major event and, as I was being chaperoned by my sister, they let me go. Some of her school friends had slept out in front of the Hippodrome for at least one night to be at the head of the queue for tickets. A couple of her

Jeremy (left) witnessed the strangest act of Beatle fandom: being hit by a Beatles car!

friends spotted The Beatles arriving by car and had chased it up the road. One of them was thrilled to have been knocked down by it. She wasn't hurt but she felt that she had actually sort of touched them.

I WAS THERE: FRED AVERY (AGED 23)

I was working in the London borough of Fulham as a quantity surveyor. In 1962 a colleague asked me if I had seen The Beatles yet on TV and what long hair they all had. They were a really weird-looking group. The Beatles show I saw in July 1964 was the second performance, commencing at 8.30 p.m. I travelled from Burgess Hill to Brighton by train with my 19-year-old brother Philip and our father, whose name was Horace but who was known by everyone as Syd.

We arrived at the Hippodrome half an hour before the show started and there were a lot of teenagers in and around Middle Street and outside the Hippodrome. Many of them were waiting to get a glimpse of The Beatles and some of them no doubt saw the first performance and couldn't go home! Our tickets were for the centre circle and cost 15/- [75p] each. My mother spent a very long time outside of the ticket agents in Burgess Hill a few days before, queuing and not knowing if there would be enough to go round.

The evening was compered by comedian Tony Marsh and opened with The Jynx, who were not mentioned at all in the programme. Marsh then introduced boy band Jimmy Nicol and The Shubdubs and then The Fourmost. After the interval we had The Jynx again and then The McKinleys, who were singing sisters Sheila and Jeanette. Then Tony Marsh came back on and introduced The Beatles. T

The Beatles were on the stage for about 40 minutes but it seemed like three hours! Most of the audience were teenagers – 80% girls and 10% boys, and another 10% were parents or other adults. The audience had little interest in the first eight acts, but when compere Marsh came on for the last time the screaming started – even before he could begin to announce The Beatles. By the time The Beatles appeared, the noise level increased to such a pitch that none of the music they were playing could be heard. It was at this point that several of the adults and parents got up and walked out of the auditorium with hands over their ears! Young girls tried to climb on stage and others passed out, and had to be lifted above the agitated – mainly female – young crowd so that they could be treated by the medical attendants outside of the theatre. Front-line girls were throwing jelly babies, which Paul McCartney reputedly loved.

The noise level never decreased even though The Beatles tried to announce the songs and, after they had finished, the ringing in my ears went on for half an hour after leaving the theatre. My father stayed throughout the performance but was heard to say, 'That's the first and last time that I will ever see The Beatles!' Of course, that was the same for all of us.

I WAS THERE: ROSALIND DAVIDSON (NÉE MERRIMAN, AGED 14)

The first time I became aware of The Beatles was when two classmates started singing 'Please Please Me' while we were lining up to go into a lesson at school. They were dancing together while singing and I thought it sounded pretty good. It must have been 1963. When The Beatles were due to appear at the Hippodrome the next year, someone in the class organised a rota to take turns overnight in the queue for tickets.

Hove resident Rosalind cycled from home to Brighton in the dark in order to queue up for Beatles tickets

I heard about this and was very keen to take part, and even though I was only 14 I was allowed by my parents to cycle from my home in Hove to the Hippodrome in Brighton in the middle of the night so that I could take my place sitting on the pavement. I recall being stopped on the way by a policeman who asked where I was going – the roads were dark and deserted – and when I told him he just smiled and waved me on. I ended up getting tickets for both performances, first in the right hand box and then in the left.

Of course, with all the screaming you couldn't hear much. I didn't scream. I just took it all in, spellbound. They were wearing those dark suits with the mandarin collars. l took some photos but there wasn't enough light and they didn't come out. How thrilling their music sounded to me then. I still get a kind of shiver if I hear it today, 50 years later. I saw the Rolling Stones at the Hippodrome later that year. I was in the stalls and remember getting up to dance in the aisle. They seemed so wild and unkempt compared to The Beatles. Funny how they don't seem that way at all now when you look at photos of that time.

I remember my dad sending off to the *Radio Times* for a large black-and-white print of The Beatles for me, saying knowingly that they'd be finished in six months. How wrong could you be?

I WAS THERE: PATRICIA HAWES (AGED 15)

I attended the Beatles concert. Alas, all I can remember is sitting in the stalls, near the front, in the northern part of the theatre and being extremely cross that the girls were all screaming so loudly I couldn't hear any of the performance!

I don't remember how I acquired tickets but I certainly didn't cycle in the dead of night like my friend Rosalind. How times have changed. I also saw The Rolling Stones at the Hippodrome. I think I attended with Rosalind again, who says we were dancing in the aisles.

I WAS THERE: GRAHAM FRANKS (AGED 16)

My recollection of seeing The Beatles at the Brighton Hippodrome is now rather patchy, although at the time it was a momentous occasion. I went to see them with a friend, an apprentice carpenter at the time called Chris Harmes. He was 17 and I was 16. I worked for the tailors John Collier's, so was able to have suits made with velvet collars on inspired by The Beatles. They influenced a lot of our fashion – shirts, suits, etc. – subject to what we could afford.

We both lived in Burgess Hill, about 11 miles from Brighton, so

The Beatles, with Jimmy Nicol (right) standing in for Ringo, in 1964

travelled down on the train that evening. I remember sitting in the stalls at the Hippodrome, a small venue for such a huge group by today's standards, and watching the support act, The Fourmost. Also on the bill that night was a drummer called Jimmy Nicol. He had replaced Ringo for a short while when Ringo apparently had tonsillitis.

The atmosphere in the theatre was electric, with people shouting and screaming. I remember looking at the closed curtains on the stage, again very old-fashioned compared with the O2. The curtains didn't quite touch the stage floor so we could see boots walking about behind the curtains. Was that The Beatles? The curtains opened to an eruption of hysteria and there they were on stage. It was almost surreal, and hard to believe it was actually them. They had amplifiers and speakers of course, but nothing by the standards of today's huge sound systems in auditoriums.

The screaming and shouting by the audience, including me, was intense, but you could hear them and I remember thinking, as they played, that they sounded just like their LPs and singles. It was very tight, professional music and you couldn't help but admire them. 'A Hard Day's Night' was high in the charts at the time and I remember it being played. After the show, walking away from the Hippodrome, I noticed all the discarded ticket stubs from the show littering the street. I wish I had known then what I know now and stopped to pick some up!

I WAS THERE: MIKE GRAVES

In the weeks before The Beatles performed at the Hippodrome, I and some young school friends thought up a small money-making scheme to profit us, all which revolved around six young Roedean School girls who wanted to go to the concert. My suggestion was would they like to queue for me for several hours to buy two tickets, which was the limit, for a few bob and my offering them one free ticket for their time. All went well and I finished up with six spare tickets, which I raffled at the local coffee bars – the Cottage, the Penny Farthing, etc. – making around £10 profit. When the

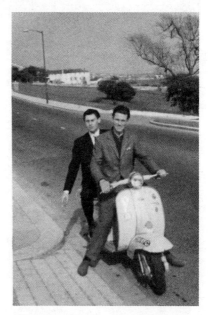

Mike Graves and friend. A scooter in Brighton in the Sixties? Well, I never...

day arrived, all of us were outside the Hippodrome to see and experience Beatlemania. The girls who got in said they could hear very little of the band's voices because of the screaming teenagers. Although I was not a fan, as I was into the Stones, it was an amazing experience just to soak up the atmosphere as they stepped out of their limousine!

I WAS THERE: LYNDA PEARCE

I was lucky enough to see The Beatles in Brighton at much the same time as I saw The Rolling Stones, but whilst it was a brilliant concert they really couldn't match the Stones! I went with friends and the main impression was that it was very difficult to hear because of the screaming! I do remember that lots of dolly mixtures were thrown on the stage. I assume at some time one of The Beatles had said that they liked them. I enjoyed being there but I was never a great fan and much preferred the Stones much lower-key – but much better – concert in Tunbridge Wells. When the Stones played everyone just stood and listened and it was a completely different atmosphere.

OPERA HOUSE

26 JULY 1964, BLACKPOOL

I was on holiday with my parents, brother and my cousin Jean at the Claremont Hotel in Blackpool. The show had been sold out weeks ago. However, the waiters in the hotel had tickets to sell and did not charge any extra for them. Our seats were on the balcony on the front row. The show was in the Winter Gardens complex. Paul, John, George and Ringo wore identical black suits to match their black hair, leading the way in fashion. There were no boys in my circle who dressed like them.

The audience was mostly young girls with their mothers. There were a few teenage boys. I don't feel I was into Beatlemania. I was keen on Elvis, Del Shannon, The Everly Brothers and Motown. But I was keen to see them so I could show off to my friends. From what I remember of the concert there wasn't a tremendous amount of hysteria. The boys sang about ten songs, mostly about boy and girl relationships like 'Love Me Do', 'PS I Love You' and 'From Me to You' to name a few. The show had other 'boy bands' taking part, and Gerry and The Pacemakers may have been one of them. A few of my classmates at Market Drayton Grammar School had elected to attend colleges and university in Liverpool because they were especially attracted to the Merseybeat sound.

The Beatles were good-looking and they were not copying or sounding like anyone else. Over the years I have appreciated them more and my favourite songs are 'Lucy in the Sky with Diamonds' and 'Paperback Writer'.

In my teen years I worked in a textile mill in Huddersfield and went with my mates to Blackpool every year for our holidays in late July or early August and nearly always finished up at the Tower every night. Brilliant times. One year, after arriving on the Saturday, on the Sunday morning one of the lads' dads came over from Huddersfield and told us he had won a lot of money on horses and bought seven tickets for us to see The Beatles. We couldn't believe it because we hadn't seen any advertising or heard they were coming anywhere. So, really excited, we went along to the Opera House.

Sandra Longmire's ticket, autographs and fruit gum – allegedly previously belonging to Ringo Starr

The accompanying groups which were on before them were The High Numbers – later to become The Who – who were fairly new and who did three numbers, smashing their equipment on the last one, and The Kinks. They were brilliant and then we got a countdown from ten to one for The Beatles. We could hardly hear the countdown for the incessant screaming from all the girls – and some of the lads! They kept this up until the very end of about ten numbers, finishing with 'Twist and Shout'. What a fantastic night – to see three top groups like them in one go. It was brilliant, even though we were up in the gods. There were even opera glasses attached to the seat for you to use at a cost of 6d [3p], if I remember right.

The other thing I remember was a bank of four Vox speakers on either side of the stage, which I thought was a lot. But if they had had 40 speakers it still wouldn't have drowned out the girls screaming. My parents didn't know I had been until I got home from the holiday, but they weren't surprised. I used to buy all The Beatles, Rolling Stones and Bob Dylan records at that time.

I WAS THERE: SANDRA LONGMIRE

I have The Beatles autographs from this show. Oh, and Ringo's fruit gum. I'm really not sure if it was Ringo's fruit gum, but it was given to me by Mal Evans [The Beatles' road manager] when they were packing the van. I was easily impressed at 14 years of age!

I WAS THERE: DAVID FELSENSTEIN (AGED 12)

GAUMONT THEATRE

2 AUGUST 1964, BOURNEMOUTH

I was on holiday with my parents in Bournemouth. At our hotel, I'd become friends with a boy of my age from Liverpool who was also there with his family. Interestingly, his family lived on Queens Drive in Liverpool, where Brian Epstein's family also lived.

The Beatles were appearing at the Gaumont Theatre that night and we had tickets! I can't remember who else was on the bill that night but I know that The Beatles closed both the first and second half of the show. We sat on the front row of the royal circle and although the other well-known pop acts on the bill were well received, I remember there was an excited air of expectancy as we waited to see the main act. At the end of the first half, when The Beatles were announced and they ran on stage, there was an explosion of screams and cheering so loud that even from our good seats, the volume from their Vox amplifiers wasn't enough for us to hear clearly what they were singing!

Nevertheless, they were amazing, and as they played all their hits, we were on our feet shouting and clapping along with everyone else! By the time The Beatles closed the second half, my pal and I were buzzing with excitement at how fab they were – and that we were actually there! The following morning, we rushed to the local Bournemouth record shop to buy Beatles records, including the *Twist and Shout* EP, which I've still got today. Since that night I've been a lifelong Beatles fan with a treasured collection of all their music, loads of books plus their movies. I've followed them all through their solo years and still get a buzz from anything Beatle-related.

The Beatles in their dressing room last night looking at the Echo pictures (see page 8) taken on their arrival at the Bournemouth Gaumont Theatre stage door, where they found themselves locked out and were besieged by fans for about two minutes until the doors were opened.

BACK IN THE USA, 1964

Having appeared on *The Ed Sullivan Show* in February 1964, The Beatles returned in August 1964 for their first North American tour.

HOLLYWOOD BOWL

23 AUGUST 1964, LOS ANGELES

It was a Sunday evening and it began what would be for me a long relationship with the Hollywood Bowl. At age 13, it was my first concert venture into the big city. The Beatles were playing the Hollywood Bowl. dad was always able, somehow, to procure great concert tickets for me and my friends. I never asked him, but in retrospect perhaps it was no coincidence that I made the front page of the *Los Angeles Herald Examiner* the next day, screaming my head off at The Beatles concert.

I don't really remember actually hearing them play as the screaming was so loud. But I noted visual details like their dark suits and quirky movements because we were so close to the stage. The Bowl is a smallish venue of 17,000.

THE GARDENS

27 AUGUST 1964, CINCINNATTI

Like most people I watched The Beatles on Ed Sullivan in February 1964. Being seven-and-a-half, I mainly wanted to watch because my siblings wanted to and I didn't care to watch the programme dad was watching on the other set. So we sat on the bed and I had my first taste

Cheri Bill

277

of The Beatles. I was hooked for life. I loved the music and the way they smiled while performing, each having their own unique style. And Paul McCartney solidified the fact that I am a heterosexual. He was the most handsome man I had ever seen.

So when The Beatles came to Cincinnati Gardens in August of 1964, I wanted to go too. Two of my sisters, my brother, my mom – yes, my mom – and I attended. We were seated upper deck, middle. The stage looked a long way off. Before the concert began, my brother leaned over and said, 'When The Beatles come out, don't scream.' 'Why?' I asked. 'Only idiots scream,' he replied. Not wanting to appear like an idiot, I agreed not to scream. And when the curtains opened and the light shone on The Beatles everyone began to scream, including myself. I just couldn't help it. It's what you did to release pent-up adrenaline. The girls in the row in front of us had binoculars and were kind enough to share them with us. My sister, having used them first, leaned over my brother and said to me, 'Cheri! I can see Paul's freckles!' She then handed the binoculars to me and, yes, I saw Paul's freckles too.

I WAS THERE: PAULA BROCK (AGED 11)

It was sold out. We had to sit in the seats that were assigned to us. At the Stones concert in the same venue just a little over a year later, it must have been more than half empty. I have a photo of The Beatles getting off the plane at Lunken Airport in Cincinnati, Ohio, and a photo of them performing on stage.

The radio station WSAI brought them to Cincinnati, Ohio and put out a magazine after the concert. There's a close-up photo of girls screaming outside of the glass doors leading into the Cincinnati Gardens before they opened the venue. I know this because I am in the photo – I am the shortest one on the left with dark bangs and mouth open, and my sister is the blonde in striped shirt to the right with her eyes shut.

It had to be 100 degrees outside and 120 degrees inside the arena. I don't think they had air conditioning. Electric fans blowing would have been it. I was pretty far back even though I had bought the more expensive ticket of $5.50. The cheap seats were $4.50 I think. It was very noisy. The Righteous Brothers and Jackie DeShannon were the opening acts. The Beatles were on stage for about 25 to 30 minutes. I couldn't hear a thing but I was screaming so much it didn't matter. Before the show started we were milling around and every time someone screamed, we would all start screaming, having no clue as to what we were screaming about! My future husband, who I didn't know back then but who was there too, told me that he told his youngest sister not to scream like an idiot. She promised she wouldn't but did anyway. He also said there was a guy walking around who looked a little like George Harrison, dressed in full Beatle attire, and he had all the girls screaming at him. He was lucky he didn't get hurt. Someone was selling small squares of bed sheets for a dollar and we were told they were the sheets The Beatles slept on at the hotel. I don't know if they even stayed in Cincinnati that long.

Above: The Beatles, arriving at Lunken airport in Cininatti, to be welcomed by thousands of fans. Below: American Beatlemania in action at the Cincinnati concert

I WAS THERE: THOMAS STALNAKER

In late August 1964 a classmate of mine came over to our swimming area at the subdivision where my family and I lived. He was all excited because he had four tickets to the Beatles concert. The good news was that he had an extra

– would I like to go with him and his friends?

Like an idiot, I made an excuse and turned it down. When my friend came back he told me that after the concert, and as he was leaving the venue, a car passed in front of him and through the window Ringo smiled and waved at him. Yeah – like that happened! After giving him a bad time about that story, he smiled and pulled out a photo of Ringo in a car pulling away.

I WAS THERE: ALBERT ANDRUS (AGED 17)

OLYMPIA STADIUM

6 SEPTEMBER 1964, DETROIT

I was a 17-year-old 11th-grader. I was living in Hamtramck, Michigan about 5 or 6 miles from the Olympia Stadium. I went with a friend who lived two doors away. It was the 2 o'clock show. We didn't call them concerts back then. We started out with balcony standing-room tickets, but the place got so crazy with screaming I ended up right at the stage front and took some really nice black and white photos. At the time, I was into film developing and made lots of copies that I gave to friends. But I have

Ringo, in mid-headshake, during the Olympia Stadium gig in Detroit, 1964

The Olympia Stadium, Detroit, 1960s

nothing now, not even a negative, and neither does anyone I remember giving a set to. We saw them again in Detroit in 1966.

I WAS THERE: WAYNE PARSONS (AGED 16)

MAPLE LEAF GARDENS

7 SEPTEMBER 1964, TORONTO

In 1964, like most 16-year-olds, I was consumed by the music and aura of The Beatles. There had been an NBC news report the previous November about the Beatles phenomenon in the UK and later a clip of the group performing 'She Loves You' on *The Jack Paar Show*, an American talk show. Then in February 1964 The Beatles performed on *The Ed Sullivan Show* to a record 70 million viewers. So by the summer of 1964, and after the release of the movie and album *A Hard Day's Night*, I was filled with anticipation of the impending visit by The Beatles to Toronto's Maple Leaf Gardens. I desperately wanted tickets to the show, and since my dad had worked at the Gardens since 1949, I thought for sure I would have the inside track to scoring a pair. Alas, he informed me that the tickets had sold out in a matter of minutes and not a single one was available, not even to him. I was crestfallen.

I had a friend called Linda White who – to my great surprise – had a crush on me. She came to my rescue. When she asked me to go to the concert with her, I couldn't have cared less how she got that pair

The Beatles show Canada a good time: live onstage at the Maple Leaf Gardens in Toronto

of tickets and, of course, I said yes. I had little interest in Linda as a girlfriend but even less shame in attending the show with her. Linda's tickets were in the second row of Greens, not the best seats in the house but certainly not the worst. I was on top of the world as 7 September approached. One week before the concert my dad had a surprise for me. He had somehow managed to get a single ticket. The seat was AA-1, the first seat in the first row, about ten feet from where Paul McCartney would soon be stomping his Spanish-heeled boots. What a dilemma. Take the best seat in the Gardens and take Linda's heart and break it (which I would later do anyway)? Or give the ticket to my best friend Dave and let Linda have her night with The Beatles and me that she had been hoping for? I did the right thing. And I have regretted it ever since.

Dave knew exactly where we were sitting, and every two minutes during the show he would look up in our direction with his best shit-eating grin while the Fab Four shouted, sang and pranced a few steps from his seat. Linda soon had a different crush in her bomb sights. Her broken heart mended in about an hour. The show and the experience were unforgettable just the same. While I sat in the Greens with Linda White, somewhere else in that crowd of 17,000 was a girl who would turn 14 a week later named Janice Cowan. Janice's parents were not happy about their young daughter going to her first concert with her friend Bev Ballantyne and no adult supervision. But ultimately they relented and gave their permission on condition that under no circumstances was she to go downtown to join the raucous crowd that was amassing at the King Edward Hotel, where it was rumoured that The Beatles would be staying. As her parents waited for Janice to come home for dinner before the big show, they settled down to watch the five o'clock news on TV only to see – in living black and white – their darling, sensible and well-behaved daughter at the King Edward Hotel. 'You are not going to the show' was the announcement that greeted Janice's arrival home. Her brother Rick was almost apoplectic with joy. Janice pleaded, wept, moaned and spoke in tongues and finally her parents showed some mercy and allowed her, at the very last minute, to go. Janice ended up having the best night of her life in the same building where I was and where we both would be, 14 years later, when we had our wedding reception at Maple Leaf Gardens. The reception was to be the second best night of her life – and the best of mine.

I WAS THERE: TED BRENNAN (AGED 15)

THE FORUM

8 SEPTEMBER 1964,
MONTREAL

I was 15 in 1964 when they played their only Montreal concerts. I remember a feeling of electricity up and down my spine while watching them. I kept thinking – I was in the same place and breathing the same air as them! Their set consisted of eleven songs, which meant they were only stage for about 30 minutes. Not much by current standards. My other memory is of the constant sound of screaming fans during the show, which resembled jet engines. It only subsided long enough between songs for me

Above: the calm before the storm of the concert at Montreal's Forum. Below: the Forum's audience

Onstage at the Forum, 8 September 1964

to hear Paul's voice introduce the next song, whereupon the sound of screaming would instantly rise again. It was almost impossible to hear them singing. In hindsight, a Beatles show was not so much a musical concert as a social and cultural experience.

I was also lucky to see them twice more, in Toronto in 1965 and 1966. The experience of these two shows was very similar to the 1964 Montreal show. My belief is that they decided to stop touring in 1966 mainly because most of the fans, especially in North America, only wanted them to remain as moptops frozen in time. They realised it didn't really matter what songs were played, there was no seeming end in sight to the screaming and hysteria. *Revolver* had just been released before the 1966 North American tour yet they chose not to perform any of its new songs on this tour. This decision to exclude their latest product went against every rule of marketing and promotion.

I WAS THERE: RICK DOESCHLER (AGED 14)

GATOR BOWL STADIUM

11 SEPTEMBER 1964, JACKSONVILLE, FLORIDA

I grew up listening to the British Invasion bands. I was very lucky to talk my parents into taking me and my brother to see The Beatles in Jacksonville. That changed everything for me. I was hooked on music and the guitar.

I WAS THERE: GAIL NASON (AGED 16)

BOSTON GARDEN

12 SEPTEMBER 1964, BOSTON

On 27 August I wrote in my diary 'I got in the mail today – I am almost too excited to write; when I opened the envelope I did a cartwheel and my mom thought I had gone mad – I got in the mail a letter. And in that letter there were words and the words read: Congratulations, etc.! I won a contest and the prize was two tickets to see The Beatles in person at Boston Garden. I was going to see The Beatles in person – The Beatles, the most popular singing group in the world! Thousands of fans gather wherever they go. It is something you dream about. I can't believe it!'

Above: Gail Nason. Below: the diary entry in which she excitedly described winning Beatles tickets

On the day, my friend Marie Ceramicoli and I stood outside the hotel for five hours hoping to get a look at them. As the kids got over-excited outside the hotel, some boys actually started rocking a parked car which brought the mounted police, who proceeded to rush at everyone with their horses. I actually had to climb over a car to avoid being hit by the horse. It must have been scary for the police too, as such screaming crowds were new to all of us.

We got in with ten thousand screaming girls. When we were finally inside the long halls of the Garden a few girls actually fainted and could not fall to the ground because we were packed in like sardines. That was scary. I didn't scream and neither did Marie. We wanted

285

to hear them. We could only hear a few notes because of the girls screaming, but they were beautiful. I will never forget the screaming kids who must have been jumping up and down, because the floor was shaking. The Garden actually vibrated from the sound of the screaming, jumping girls. Seeing The Beatles live was such an exciting thing. Of course, we were all mad about them.

You could see The Beatles but could not hear them. I could not understand them screaming like that so that you missed them singing. That summer was wonderful. My friends and I saw The Beatles, The Rolling Stones, Dave Clark Five, The Animals, and The Kingsmen. What an exciting time for music. So lively and upbeat – just what we all needed. Except, of course, our parents – who hated the look and the sound!

I will never forget those years. I have often thought about the 'madness' of it all, the screaming crowds. I think after the Kennedy assassination we were like balloons ready to explode. The Beatles' joyfulness allowed us to explode.

I WAS THERE: MAUREEN ELIZABETH SMITH (AGED 15)

I saw them once at Boston Garden and then again at a race track which is now gone, called Suffolk Downs in East Boston. I went with my best

friend. My mother and hers stood in line to purchase tickets while we were attending school.

My clearest memory is them running by me with their hair flying in the breeze as they scrambled to the stage, not to mention the screaming that I and hundreds of teenage girls took part in. I was only 15 years old then but a memory like that is hard to forget. But then again – who would want to?

Maureen Smith's beloved Beatles patch

I WAS THERE: SHAMO JANIE BISHOP (AGED 16)

I did not have a ticket and some friends did. I tried all summer and bought a ticket at the last minute from a kid who could not go. Of course, I dressed Mod like the British girls, with tweed skirt and vest and bangs. I didn't ever go to my seat.

I WAS THERE: JODY TUBERT (AGED 13)

I was almost 14 when I got to see The Beatles in concert. That was a magical age, a magical time. Little did I know that I would leave the Boston Garden that night with my very own autographed Beatles programme. The Beatles meant everything to me. Not only did I have their autographs, but I also had their drinking glasses, ash trays and cigarette butts. Wow! Back in early 1964 I was attending junior high school and starting to get boy crazy. Months earlier, the world had been grief-stricken and in total shock when President Kennedy was assassinated. I was pretty naïve and had not seen much in the way of tragedy. President Kennedy's death was devastating to me. The world would never be the same. Innocence was lost. The holidays were sad. Winter was upon us.

Then something magical happened. The radio stations everywhere started to play some new happy-sounding songs by a new group from Liverpool, England. 'She Loves You' and 'I Saw Her Standing There', about a young teenage girl just like me. The tide started to turn. The British had invaded. There were more songs and albums. Then the best thing happened. This new group The Beatles were going to be on *The Ed Sullivan Show* in February. They had taken the world by storm. The veil of grief started to lift. History was being made. A whole new era was about to begin. Music and life would never be the same. Yeah yeah yeah! Beatlemania had taken over. You could buy everything from Beatles bubblegum cards to lunch boxes and pins. Everything was The Beatles. The radio stations held contests such as how many words you could make out of the word 'Beatles'. One of my friends nicknamed herself Beatlette and would call into the radio station for requests. One of my younger brothers had his hair styled into the first Beatle haircut in the city.

It was a crazy time! It was electrifying and exciting. Late in the summer of 1964, while The Beatles were on their first US tour, my father – a reporter for the *Worcester Telegram & Gazette* newspaper in

Boston's Beatles fans queuing up for tickets in 1964

Massachusetts – received a dreaded assignment: 'Jack, go to Boston and interview these four moptop boys at the Boston Garden and find out what is causing all this hysteria!' Lucky for me, he was able to take four of his seven kids with him. Of course, we each had to buy our own $5.50 ticket, which at that time was an outrageous amount! The four of us did everything we could do to earn our $5.50, from mowing lawns, to babysitting – 11 hours at 50 cents an hour – to caddying at the local golf course. We were all huge fans and had been buying and listening to all The Beatles' albums and records since earlier that year.

Of course, our record player had to be shared with mom and dad and the likes of Frank Sinatra, Tony Bennett and Anthony Newley. The older folks just couldn't understand what the fascination was with these 'long-haired hippies' who sang such silly songs! Weren't they surprised when their crooners started singing some of the Fab Four songs themselves! Finally, the day arrived. We didn't own a car so my father had to borrow one. We drove into Boston and stood outside the Garden for what seemed like eternity. I remember a hotel close by and rumours that The Beatles were staying there. So we joined the crowd and just stood there looking up. Everyone screaming, pointing, believing we just saw 'them' peeking out the window. It was like the feeling you had as a seven-year-old when you know you just saw Santa Claus on Christmas Eve and heard the sleigh bells.

At some point in the afternoon, my father had to go to 'work' to interview The Beatles. Oh how I wished I could go with him! After the interview, he came to our balcony seats and surprised each of us with our very own autographed programme. There I was, sitting inside the Boston Garden holding my newly autographed Beatles programme, waving at the cameraman along with my siblings. We were in ecstasy and waiting anxiously for The Beatles to come on stage. What a night! Finally the wait was over. There they were, singing and shaking their heads and laughing and jumping around and waving. The pandemonium was indescribable. This is what they sang that night: 'She Loves You', 'A Hard Day's Night', 'If I Fell', 'Long Tall Sally', 'All My Loving', 'Roll Over Beethoven', 'Boys', 'Can't Buy Me Love', 'Things We Said Today', 'You Can't Do That' and 'Twist and Shout'.

My father's article appeared in the 'Feature Parade Section' of the *Worcester Sunday Telegram* on 15 November, 1964 – the day after I officially turned 14. I was the luckiest girl in the world. It was the opportunity of a lifetime and one that I will cherish forever. Priceless.

I WAS THERE: DONNA CERNOHORSKY-CASENOVE (AGED 13)

CIVIC CENTER

13 SEPTEMBER 1964, BALTIMORE

Imagine being 13 years old, never having been to a concert and being absolutely crazy about The Beatles. My mother took me, my sister and brother and a few friends to see them. The Civic Center was packed. We were so excited. When John, Paul, George and Ringo walked out onto the stage there was a deafening roar of screaming girls and thousands of flashing cameras. All I could think of was, 'They are in the same building as me, breathing the same air!'

Everyone was standing on their seats. The ushers couldn't get anyone to get down. I was so overwhelmed I thought I was going to explode. All I could do was cry. The Beatles were fantastic.

The Beatles-mad Donna, before her teenage bedroom wall

The concert ended. We all went home with the memory that will remain in our hearts forever. Even today, when I see pictures of The Beatles or play their music, that wonderful youthful feeling comes flooding back to me. I will love John, Paul, George and Ringo forever!

Donna and her sister Janis Pratt, with their treasure trove of Beatles stash

MEMORIAL AUDITORIUM

18 SEPTEMBER 1964, DALLAS

Rodger Brownlee and his sister Shela, who he took to see The Beatles after he was stood up

By the time The Beatles made their first concert appearance in Dallas, I was a full-blown raving Beatlemaniac. It began on a cold December day in 1963 while riding in a friend's car, when suddenly 'One, two, three, bah!' exploded from the radio speakers and the interior was flooded with the thumping beat and rhythm of 'Well she was just 17, you know what I mean.' That was how it started. I was hooked. I wanted to be a Beatle. Then came 6 February 1964 and *The Ed Sullivan Show*. America got to see and hear what The Beatles looked and sounded like and was given a live glimpse of the reaction of ecstatic Beatles fans.

My enthusiasm knew no bounds. I was extremely excited about this new sound and new look and wanted to be part of it in every way. So later that year when I learned that The Beatles were coming to Dallas, I knew I had to be there and be a part of the scene. In the intervening months I engaged in a flurry of activity, working on a construction crew by day and hanging out at the local hops on weekends. I learned where to shop for the right duds and soon had myself decked out in a Beatle outfit so I could at least play the part.

When the concert tickets finally came on sale, I was first in line and bought two – one for myself and one for the lucky girl I would ask to go with me to the show. Then the day finally arrived. I donned my Beatle outfit; slim fitting, black stovepipe slacks, white shirt with broad collar, skinny black tie and the crowning touches – my Beatle boots and collarless jacket. Completing the look, I combed my hair down all around just so. Striking a pose in the mirror, I fancied myself 'fab'. I was ready.

The lucky girl I had asked to the concert got cold feet and backed out so, as a last minute substitute, I gave in and told my 14-year-old sister Shela to come along. When I could get her to stop yelling and bouncing off the walls, I fired up my 1957 Volkswagen Beetle convertible and off we headed for Dallas and Beatlemania. I couldn't help but notice that girls outnumbered the boys by at least three to one. Not a big surprise there, but I was a little surprised that I didn't see any of the guys decked out as I was in full Beatle regalia, and I was a little more than disappointed that no one seemed to notice that I was!

We located our seats out on the floor, about 20 rows back from the raised stage, slightly right of center. I had a perfect view of the bandstand for filming with my Brownie 8mm movie camera. A row of wooden barricades encircled the front of the stage and the blue uniforms of the Dallas Police Department were everywhere, including the cordon they formed in front of the bandstand. The steady hum of conversation and clatter of chairs bounced from the walls and increased in volume as the excited fans filed the auditorium to capacity and the much-anticipated hour of show-time fast approached. My heart was thumping wildly with anticipation as the MC made his introductions and the show began, but subsided as the audience settled down and rewarded the show openers with ripples of polite applause, punctuated with shouts of 'We want The Beatles, we want The Beatles!' I don't remember much about the show that preceded The Beatles, except that there were two well-known artists, Jackie DeShannon, and Clarence 'Frogman' Henry, and an unknown girl trio known as The Exciters, who were three black women in the mould of The Supremes and who wore orange shifts loaded with concentric rows of fringe that really shimmied when they shook. They lived up to their name, doing uptempo numbers that really rocked the house, adding to the overall excitement that filled the air.

Rodger and his band The Elite

❝ I was surprised that I didn't see any of the guys decked out in full Beatle regalia, and I was more disappointed no one seemed to notice that I was! ❞

The opening acts were done and the lights went down as the last round of applause faded into a low-level hum of excited conversation that rattled around the auditorium. Then, stepping out into the spotlight, KLIF disc jockey Irving Harrigan introduced The Beatles and Ringo, followed by Paul, George and John, took the stage. From that point on, pandemonium reigned with a rising level of screams and shrieks coming from the throats of the 10,000-strong audience of mostly teenage girls. Being able to hear The Beatles play and sing was impossible so I concentrated on filming with my 8mm Brownie.

Then suddenly, as if on cue, with arms flailing in the air, heads bobbing and shaking from side to side, pulling at their own hair, with tears streaming down their faces and spittle flying from their mouths, 10,000 fans rose from their seats to stand and cheer and jump and shout so that I was also forced up out of my seat in order to be able to see and continue filming. I didn't think that the decibel level of the noise could go any higher but it did.

As The Beatles finished their first song and did their famous Beatle bow, bending over deeply at the waist, the shrieks increased in volume to a crescendo that can only be produced by the frantic, fanatic fervour of fans who are half out of their minds. Then, as The Beatles began their next song, everyone began climbing and leaping up to stand in their chairs. My little sister leapt onto her chair and, with tears streaming down her contorted face, screamed 'Ringo! Ringo!' over and over, pounding me on the head with her right hand, totally unaware of what she was doing and totally out of her mind.

In self-defence, and in order to continue filming, I climbed up onto my chair. I balanced myself as best I could on the folding chair and watched most of the rest of the concert through the 1/2-inch viewfinder of my camera, doing so even after running out of film. I just kept winding and shooting, ending up with only about a minute-and-a-half of decent footage out of a five-minute reel of film. My ears were ringing and my head was spinning as I tried to scream along with the rest. I was a little out of control myself. At the time, I wasn't sure what songs The Beatles performed. I think their big hits, 'She Loves You' and 'I Saw Her Standing There', were included and I think I caught snatches of 'Twist and Shout', but I could not with any certainty have named all the songs performed if my life had depended on it.

From the opening note, the noise level was deafening, something I could never have imagined, even after watching the shots of the screaming fans on *The Ed Sullivan Show*. Except for the random word or phrase, it was simply not possible to hear The Beatles. It was so loud I could not get my sister to quit pounding on me. Then it was over; a final tidal wave of shrieks and screams burst from 10,000 sets of lungs concussing the eardrums as The Beatles made their final bow and exited the stage.

The noise level held for a few remaining minutes, then just as suddenly dropped off to near silence, punctuated by the sounds of hundreds of girls sobbing, plaintive last cries of 'Ringo' or 'Paul' and the clatter of 10,000 fans climbing down and untangling themselves from their chairs and heading for the exits. Out of the blue, I was accosted by a number of girls thrusting their programmes at me, asking in rapid fire 'Are you in a band? Do you play the guitar? What's your band's name? Can I have your autograph?' I was a little taken aback, but pleased that my Beatle outfit had attracted this attention.

LATE 1964:
ON THE ROAD AGAIN

The Beatles returned to England from
the USA in late September 1964. By early
October, they were out on the road again.

ODEON THEATRE

11 OCTOBER 1964, BIRMINGHAM

One of my mates' mums had queued half the night to get us three girls
tickets for the Fab Four. We were huge fans and had a daily running
commentary on our imagined relationship with each of The Beatles. We
spent our breaks and the walk home fantasising about them as though we
were their girlfriends. Imagine!

When we went to the show we promised each other we would not
scream. Well that didn't last long. Call it mass hysteria or whatever but we
screamed our heads off. I am happy to tell you, though, that we didn't wet
our knickers! At one point I was convinced Ringo was looking directly at

*Backstage in Birmingham: The Beatles on
11 October 1964*

me. That made me scream even louder and he wasn't even my favourite. For years my mum would tell anyone who would listen that 'When Sue saw The Beatles she didn't walk in the door, she floated in and no one could get any sense out of her for a week.' Well it was a bit like that.

I WAS THERE: JOHN BATES (AGED 12)

I was lucky enough to see them twice in Birmingham. I remember them appearing at the Ritz Ballroom in Kings Heath which was not far from where I lived at the time, but my father would not let me go as I was considered too young, being 11 years old in 1963. However when they announced they were coming to the Odeon in 1964 my father not only queued up with me overnight when the tickets went on sale but accompanied me to the show along

John Bates, whose father queued up with him overnight for tickets

with my mother. They did two shows that night. I went to the early show, but although the atmosphere was terrific you couldn't hear much of them above the screaming. I was upstairs and many were standing up and leaning over the balcony, giving the Odeon staff on duty cause for concern.

For me, though, it did not detract from a memorable occasion. They were the last act on of many acts, and were touring with Sounds Incorporated, Mary Wells and The Remo Four.

I WAS THERE: SYLVIA ELLIS (AGED 13)

I feel privileged to have seen The Beatles live twice at the Birmingham Odeon, once following the release of their *A Hard Day's Night* album, and then in 1965. I went with my friend Pat Banneville to queue at the box office early in the morning, about 7 a.m., and got row M. It was all very exciting.

I WAS THERE: LIZ WOLSEY (AGED 12)

My friend Julia and I were 12 and queued from 5 a.m. to get tickets. There were hundreds of us, mostly females. The queue snaked round the streets and the back of the Odeon. At one point there was a big surge, which was frightening as we were all squashed together. Julia remembers an ambulance had to come when we were queuing for tickets as people fainted in the crush. But eventually we got our tickets. Julia knitted a black polo neck jumper to wear to the concert, just like The Beatles wore sometimes. The atmosphere was electric at the concert. Girls were screaming so much you couldn't hear very much. Everyone at the concert had to stand up, as you couldn't see anything, because those at the front stood up first. I can't remember what they played, but it was a wonderful night!

I WASN'T THERE: DEAN WALL

ABC CINEMA

13 OCTOBER 1964, WIGAN

My mum, Elizabeth, saw them at the ABC, which had been known as the Ritz until 1962 and became the Ritz again in 1985. She said they were crap! My dad, Alan, remembers them playing Leigh Casino on Lord Street the previous year. Dad said Mrs Brierley, who owned the Casino, had booked The Beatles for two shows, but when they made it big they cancelled their second show. She tried to sue them but was unsuccessful. It's a furniture shop now.

I WAS THERE: SANDY MCGREGOR

CAIRD HALL

20 OCTOBER 1964, DUNDEE

As a young reporter with the *Dundee Courier* newspaper I attended the concert with the then Countess of Strathmore, the late Queen Mother's family, who had called our office asking if we could arrange for her to meet the group. The original idea had been for them to go to Glamis Castle, about 15 miles from Dundee, where she lived. This proved unviable and I then worked on getting them all together for afternoon tea in the home of my then fiancée, my thoughts being that it would make a great yarn for the paper along the lines of 'Countess Dines with Beatles in Council House'. That plan failed

Sandy McGregor is the self-described 'callow youth in the sports jacket', second from right

because of time difficulties, which didn't go down well with my fiancée's mother who had used most of that week's family allowance on boiled ham for the sandwiches! The final proposal, which worked, was for me to take the Countess to the Caird Hall – the concert venue – where they could all meet for tea in a private room. Things went well and the Countess, in pearl necklace and expensive fur coat, stayed on to watch the concert from a special seat organised for her in the wings. All very strange!

In the photograph taken at the time [reproduced above], I am the callow youth in the sports jacket second from the end on the right. The girl next to me in the white dress was my then girlfriend; the bloke at the rear between John and Paul is Eddy McLaren, another *Courier* journalist. The older gent at the back is the Countess' chauffeur and the woman immediately in front of him is the Countess' lady-in-waiting (or companion). The bearded bloke at the far right is an American writer from *Playboy* magazine who was touring with The Beatles for an article he was writing.

I WAS THERE: DONALD STUART

My group Tommy Dene and The Tremors supported The Beatles at Dundee's Caird Hall in 1964 and, after playing, we had to act as stewards at the foot of the stage. I was in front of John Lennon and had a good view of them. I heard their playing, despite the screaming! I saw them again at the Ernst-Merck Halle in Hamburg in 1966 and, again, they were as good live as on record.

I WAS THERE: ALISTAIR FYFFE (AGED 17)

I went with a few friends, one of whom – Bill Russell – organised the tickets. I had only started working some eight weeks beforehand. We lived in Cupar and travelled to Dundee by train. My parents had nothing to say about attending such events. Myself and a group of friends had been attending the Raith Ballroom in Kirkcaldy regularly, something I did most Friday and Saturday evenings until around 1969, and these events were much more likely to expose attendees to fights and assaults. My parents were more concerned for my safety on those nights out.

Above: the young Alistair Fyffe, who remembers seeing The Beatles, despite being more of a Stones fan. Below: his near-mint ticket (both halves still intact)

THE CAIRD HALL DUNDEE	THE CAIRD HALL DUNDEE
Arthur Howes and Brian Epstein present **THE BEATLES SHOW**	Arthur Howes and Brian Epstein present **THE BEATLES SHOW**
Back Stalls 10/-	**Back Stalls 10/-**
A 15	**A 15**
TUES., OCT. 20th 6-30 p.m.	TUES., OCT. 20th 6-30 p.m.

We were at the 6.30 p.m. session and my seat was Back Stalls A 15. The seat cost 10/- [50p]. Somehow I managed to retain both parts of my ticket unseparated and, while no longer in mint condition, it is still presentable.

Two things stand out in my memory. The noise from the audience came close to completely drowning out The Beatles, although where we were sitting may have exaggerated this. And also that people were throwing items onto the stage. I have a vague memory that these were sweets. My wife believes they would have been jelly babies as it was known that Ringo liked them.

I have no memory at all of the supporting acts. My wife was a Beatles fan but she never saw them. It has always been a bit of an amusement in our house that I have, as I was never a great Beatles fan and was more a fan of The Rolling Stones, who I also saw at the Caird Hall.

I WAS THERE: BRIAN MECHAN

We were on the balcony looking down. The four of us went. I got a Beatles jacket, made to measure, in brown corduroy. It cost £68, which in those days was a lot of money. It was a week before they were coming to Dundee. I'd gone to the J.M. ballroom in Dundee, which was one of the biggest ballrooms, and they refused me entry because my hair was longer than most people's, and because I didn't have a collar on my jacket. I was so incensed by this that I wrote a letter to the *Dundee Courier* saying, 'I wonder what would have happened if The Beatles had turned up at the door?' And they published my letter.

I WAS THERE: MORAG THOMPSON

I was at the Caird Hall when The Beatles returned to Dundee but not in the front row as I had been the previous year. I had already bought tickets – then I won two tickets in a *Daily Express* caption competition. The first I knew was when someone at school spotted my name as a winner in the paper. Great excitement, as my new friend from school and I were able to give the spare tickets to our younger sisters – after checking which were the better seats for us! After the show our wee sisters went running after a decoy van, thinking The Beatles were aboard, and in spite of our trying to stop them. Happy times.

I WAS THERE: MOIRA WALLACE (AGED 13)

I was there in the front row. What a night! I was nearly 14 at the time as was my pal Barbara Davidson. Barbara's father Wullie Davidson owned the famous Fort Bar in Broughty Ferry, Dundee. There were many famous regulars at the pub at that time including the Dundee FC team. Wullie Davidson knew Andy Lothian, another regular, who was a famous dance

The view from above, at the Caird Hall: Moira Wallace is the girl in the front row in the white shirt with photos on it, with raised arm

band leader and who brought The Beatles to Dundee through his agency, hence Barbara acquiring the front-row tickets. I can't remember the songs sung but everyone was screaming. Some people passed out and were carried out and then had to be brought back into the hall. All girls of course.

After my husband and I got married in 1980, we used to frequent the Brax Hotel in Carnoustie. One of the guys my husband had a drink and a right good craic with was Ian McMillan, who took the famous *Abbey Road* photograph. One night in the early 1980s, Ian never appeared. My husband asked where he was, to be told Ian had to go to London to photograph Paul McCartney walking over the zebra crossing with his dog for the cover for a new album.

I WAS THERE: SUSAN BROWN

ODEON THEATRE

22 OCTOBER 1964, LEEDS

We managed to get tickets for the Beatles/Mary Wells concert. I think this was as you could only apply by post as opposed to hours of queuing. The tickets we got were seven rows from the front in the stalls – brilliant! Except that the compère, comedian Bob Bain, wound up the audience to such a pitch that when The Beatles arrived on stage, all the people at the back surged to the front of the auditorium. We had to stand for the whole of the rest of the concert! I remember one of the girls trying to get up onto the stage fell down into the orchestra pit. Someone threw a cigarette lighter onto the stage and hit Paul on the head. The look on his face showed he wasn't amused. I think the price for the tickets for this concert was 10/6d [53p] each. I have the programmes for both the June 1963 and this concert. I can't remember how much they cost.

I WAS THERE: CAROLINE FIELDS (AGED 17)

I remember going to see them at the Odeon on their very last visit to Leeds. I went with a friend from work and we had good seats in the centre of stalls, but I was appalled that, not only couldn't we hear anything because of all the screaming, but suddenly everyone began standing on their seats so we couldn't see the stage either. I am a variety artiste and was, in October, in-between summer season and panto, so I used to temp in the same office whenever I was available. As a professional singer, I remember thinking how awful it was that the seats would be spoilt – I had sung on that very same stage myself with Leeds Girls' Choir for their annual 'Tunes for Toys' concerts supported by the *Yorkshire Evening Post* and hated to see the Odeon being spoilt. The audience of mainly girls waved frantic arms about, stamped their feet, screamed the name of their favourite Beatle, bounced up and down on the seats, threw sweet wrappers everywhere and even stubbed their cigarettes out on the back of the seats. In fact, I had worked with the girl I was with for over three years on and off and never knew she herself smoked. However, that night she went through a packet of ten!

Yet I will be eternally grateful that I got to see The Beatles play live.

Caroline Fields, a professional singer, thought the damage to the theatre seats was a real shame...

Their music was new, alive, vibrant and easy to learn and sing along to and all I wanted to do was dance whenever I heard one of their songs.

My hero was Paul and I thought he was the best thing since sliced bread – I still admire him today! That night was great and, despite being deaf for the next few hours (due to all the screaming and the volume of the band) I count myself lucky that I was there. I wouldn't have missed it for the world. At work the following day, my friend and I had a smugness about us as we knew we had witnessed something special. The biggest band in the world had played for us!

I WASN'T THERE: BARBARA MARSDEN

I was unable to go to the concert although I had a ticket. My auntie arrived one day at my home and announced that she had managed to get two tickets for my cousin and myself to go to the concert. However, my dad, who was a special constable at the time and had been on duty for the previous concert and seen all the pushing crowds of screaming fans, made the decision that I couldn't go and no amount of pleading from his sister made any difference. He was adamant that I couldn't go. I can still remember feeling angry at his decision and even now, all these years later, whenever I mention it to my cousin, he

Barbara Marsden wasn't allowed to go and see The Beatles even though her aunt had bought her a ticket. Her dad had seen the excited crowds at a previous concert and decided it wasn't safe

just laughs and I get the feeling he doesn't even remember going to the event. Which, of course, I would have done as I can very clearly remember going to another concert not long afterwards to see Cliff Richard and The Shadows and Lulu.

I WAS THERE: RITA HEWETT (AGED 17)

HIPPODROME

25 OCTOBER 1964, BRIGHTON

I was at the Hippodrome in October 1964 when The Beatles appeared. It was the start of Beatlemania. The Hippodrome was full of screaming girls, making it impossible to hear the boys singing. I went with my boyfriend at the time, who kept questioning me as to which one I most fancied. I told him it was Paul, which led to him going into a mega strop, which caused a breakdown in the relationship. I didn't fancy him much anyway, as he was a rocker and I was a mod.

Rita Hewett: her fancying Paul ended up with her splitting up with her boyfrlend

My parents did not really understand what all the fuss was about when you had such "good music" as The Black and White Minstrels and Billy Cotton. They really had a great taste for music!

I WAS THERE: MARY JONES (AGED 13)

ABC CINEMA

28 OCTOBER 1964, EXETER

I had to beg my parents to let me go. I will never ever forget that night. My friend and I came out of the venue soaking wet with sweat and hardly able to move or speak, utterly drained. My parents were waiting for us. When we got in the car neither of us could say a word. During the drive home my mum got angry with us as she thought we were being awkward, but we were both dumbstruck and in total shock. Wow – what a night!

I WAS THERE: PETER VICKERY

They were promoting *A Hard Day's Night*. The Rustiks opened the show, followed by a solo artist named Michael Haslam. Next was Sounds Incorporated, who stayed on stage to back Tamla Motown's Mary Wells. The Remo Four opened the second half, followed by Tommy Quickly and finally The Beatles. The show was compered by Bob Bain. All I can remember about The Beatles' performance is that you could hardly hear a thing for the screaming but at least I was there, and I still have the official programme.

Peter Vickery still has his official Beatles programme from 1964

I WAS THERE: PAUL WALTERS (AGED 14)

My father owned the hairdressers in Princesshay, a gents hairdressers, and he'd had it for years. My father was a referee, he was a cricketer, and he did loads and loads of sports things. So he knew thousands of people in Exeter and the owner of the ABC, Bob Parker, came across to him and said, 'We had The Beatles here the year before and it cost us a fortune in policing. You know so many people. Would you like to get maybe forty people together and come across and stand across the front of the stage and just stop people getting onto the stage? Like a human barrier.'

And he said 'Well, I'll do it as long as my son can come and possibly get to meet The Beatles. Or at least be there and stood by the stage where he gets a good view.' I was learning guitar at that time. So they stood around the front of the stage.

Afterwards, we went up to the manager's office and he gave everybody a bottle of beer. The Beatles were late because they were staying at the Rougemont Hotel. Liverpool won at home that afternoon and they were involved in that. And they turned up a little bit later and they came in the side door of the ABC. And I held the door open for them. Somebody was filming us. I think it was Keith Fordyce and his crew, and I got on TV. They did two shows and in between I managed to wander into their dressing room.

I said to Lennon, 'I'm playing guitar. Are there any tips you could give me?' So he picked up his guitar and said 'Here's a good chord.' So I sat down between Lennon and McCartney and he gave me the guitar and he said, 'This is the end chord for 'Can't Buy Me Love'. I think it was C diminished 7th. And I said, 'Oh right, that's very useful that.' And Lennon took the guitar away and he said, 'Well, it's not how you start, it's how you finish is the most important thing.'

And Ringo came across as he was washing his hair, and he said 'No, you don't want to play guitar. You want to play drums.' And I said 'Okay, that sounds good.' He then gave me a pair of his drum sticks, which I've still got. They actually had Ringo Starr imprinted on them. Neil Aspinall then said 'Can anybody get some fish and chips for the lads because we've been watching Liverpool and we haven't actually eaten?

They were so carried away.' So myself and Charlie, an ambulance driver who was actually helping my father, said 'Yes, we'll go.'

So we went down to Cables and they did the fish and chips. Being 14 years old and meeting your idols, and knowing you were getting food to take back to them, I said to the woman behind the counter, 'You won't believe it but these are for The Beatles.' She said 'I don't care who they're for, love. You're not getting any more!'

Paul Walters was a lucky boy: he didn't only meet The Beatles, but Lulu as well

I WAS THERE: GLORIA ROODE (NÉE WILSON, AGED 16)

GAUMONT THEATRE

31 OCTOBER 1964, IPSWICH

My friend Carol and I were chambermaids at the Crown & Anchor Hotel in Ipswich. We made sure we booked our tickets for all the shows at the Gaumont Theatre. The first time was in October 1964 to see The Rolling Stones, where we were caught up in the crowd rushing the stage. They called it 'mayhem' in the local paper.

So when The Beatles came not long after, they had the orchestra pit filled with policemen so that events didn't repeat themselves. Halfway through the show, I noticed Carol was missing and then I saw the policemen making a move and then

Gloria Roode witnessed a particularly manic Beatles show: her friend was carried out by one of the officers from the policemen-packed orchestra pit

flailing arms and legs. It was her being carried out. I had a split second of thinking, 'Should I go to her?' but didn't. Afterwards we all filed out and there she was, with the St. John's Ambulance brigade. She was soaking wet. She sobbed, 'They chucked a bucket of water over my head!' We laugh about it now, but it was a crazy time.

What a great time to be a teenager. We couldn't wait to book up for the next concert. Tom Jones singing 'It's Not Unusual', Roy Orbison, and many others... I remember smoking cigarettes round my friends' houses at school lunchtimes and listening to the latest Beatles records. Paul was my favourite.

CHRISTMAS SHOWS, 1964

On 9 December 1964, 'I Feel Fine' was released. The Beatles ended the year and began 1965 with another series of Christmas shows, this time at the Hammersmith Odeon in London.

I WAS THERE: SUE CORNELL (AGED 16)

HAMMERSMITH ODEON

24 DECEMBER 1964–16 JANUARY 1965, LONDON

I went to see them with a friend from college. Her parents worked for Marconi in Chelmsford at the time and their social club arranged for a coach trip to see The Beatles in concert at Hammersmith Odeon, London. The line-up was The Beatles, Freddie and The Dreamers and The Yardbirds. I was not a fan of The Beatles but a fan of The Rolling Stones, who I would

Sue Cornell: on the night, she preferred The Yardbirds and Freddie and The Dreamers

have loved to see live but never had the opportunity. My friend persuaded me to go with her as she liked The Beatles and from what I can remember her parents paid for my ticket. I remember The Yardbirds and how good they were – I felt they were far more talented than The Beatles. Freddie and The Dreamers were okay, with a taste of comedy as well.

However, when The Beatles came on the stage I could only hear screams from the fans in the audience, which went on continuously throughout their performance, making it so difficult to hear a word they sang. I was not impressed and even if there had been no

George Harrison, at the Hammersmith Odeon,
shortly before a Beatles Christmas concert, 1964

screaming and The Beatles could have been heard, it would have not made any difference in my opinion. There was an interval in the performance and my friend and I, along with her parents, went to a pub next to the Hammersmith Odeon, and in there were Freddie and The Dreamers, who spoke to us and gave us their autographs. They were extremely friendly. The whole experience of the evening is something I shall never forget and I can still remember seeing The Beatles with their sort of pudding-basin haircuts, wearing round-necked jackets and trousers to match. But I still prefer the Rolling Stones and their music any day.

Pamela and her husband – he went for a pint
rather than watch The Beatles

I WAS THERE: PAMELA HOUGHTON (NÉE BLENCO, AGED 26)

I went to Hammersmith with my sister Pauline and my niece Karen to see The Beatles' Christmas show. It was introduced by Jimmy Savile and it was very noisy. You could hardly hear the singing because of the teenagers screaming and shouting. Everybody was shouting, but mainly girls. We were downstairs in the first row of the back stalls. My husband drove us down in his Wolseley 6/90 but he didn't come in to see the show. He went for a pint.

Either Karen or Pauline got the tickets. In those days you wrote to a box office and sent the cheque, even an open cheque, if you wanted to get tickets. If the show was on and was going to be a sell-out you put your self-addressed envelope in and wrote to the box office in the hope you'd get tickets. They did 'She Loves You'. They were wearing collarless suits. Karen was a great Ringo Starr fan.

I WAS THERE: KAREN SMITH (AGED 13)

It was The Beatles Christmas show. I think it had either Rolf Harris or Jimmy Savile in. The Yardbirds were the co-stars. It was very noisy. A girl fainted near us.

We were in the stalls, on the end of the row; we weren't that far back. All I can remember is the hysteria really. I couldn't say what they played or anything. They did some sketches and I think George wore a red-and-white spotted headscarf. They did a little panto.

❝ We stood at passport control... I thought 'I know that voice.' I turned around and it was Ringo ❞

Beatles memorabilia from Dena Hubbard: her Fab Four cartoon (above) and her prized Beatles rosette (below)

I WAS THERE: DENA HUBBARD

I first saw The Beatles at the ABC Cinema in Northampton. The next time I saw them was on 28 December 1964 at the Odeon in Hammersmith. We sat in the circle and paid £1. I remember Jimmy Savile was compere and The Mike Cotton Sound, The Yardbirds, Elkie Brooks, Freddie and The Dreamers and Sounds Incorporated were on the bill. I saw them a couple of times after that.

The four times I saw them I didn't hear a note because of the screaming, but I can remember that they always looked smart. Three years ago, we were flying back from New Zealand to Los Angeles. We stood at passport control and we heard a voice say, 'Come on, girls, keep up.' I thought, 'I know that voice.' I turned around and it was Ringo, stood right next to me!

1965 CONCERTS

In the year that The Beatles were awarded MBEs by Her Majesty, they also made the album and movie *Help!*, met Elvis Presley and recorded *Rubber Soul*.

I WAS THERE: KAREN SMITH

EMPIRE POOL

11 APRIL 1965, WEMBLEY

I saw them at an *NME* poll-winner's concert, which was 1965. You booked your tickets before the results came out so you didn't know who would be appearing but they weren't a surprise. They had topped pretty much every poll going apart from female vocalist! They used to be fantastic, those concerts. It used to be a Sunday afternoon. There weren't so many things happening or places open.

MAURICE KINN
presents the

new

MUSICAL EXPRESS

1964-65 ANNUAL
POLL-WINNERS
ALL-STAR
CONCERT

SUNDAY, APRIL 11th, 1965
EMPIRE POOL, WEMBLEY

OFFICIAL PROGRAMME   PRICE 1/6

20 Pages

I WAS THERE: JEAN DEVINE (AGED 16)

ANTROBUS ARMS

6 MAY 1965, AMESBURY, WILTSHIRE

When they were filming *Help*, on Salisbury Plain, The Beatles stayed in the hotel in Amesbury called the Antrobus Arms. And we heard that they were staying there – 'we' being a bunch of schoolgirls. We just decided to go down into the village and hang around the hotel in the hopes that we would glimpse them. We were in the foyer, probably surprised that we hadn't been chucked out. There was no security. There was nobody around. And there was about five of us. And in the foyer there's a staircase that goes up to the rooms. And as we were standing there in they walked in a straight line, like they were walking across Abbey Road, one behind the other. And they had the suits on as well. Paul gave me a cigarette – a Peter Styuvesant. At the age of 16, I declined the offer.

'Hello girls,' they all said. They were all chirpy and then they walked up the staircase. Paul was the last one up and when they got to the landing, he turned round and he beckoned to me to go up. I was just much too scared to do that. So I didn't.

I WAS THERE: DIANA EVEREX (NÉE WORT)

I have memories, like it was yesterday, of The Beatles filming a section of *Help!* on Salisbury Plain. At the time I was living with my family at Shrewton Lodge, a lovely house and large farm off the Shrewton-Larkhill road, bordering the road to a remote pub, the Bustard.

Remember the scene in the film where they drove a tank through a straw stack? The stack was specially built by our farm workers and constructed with a hollow centre, strong walls and a single bale full height wall at each end. Of course, we went up to watch the scene being shot, luckily done in one

Diana watched the Fab Four driving a tank on Salisbury Plain

take. So many times I've kicked myself for not getting their autographs at the time.

I WAS THERE: MAGGIE MAYBERRY (NÉE DIMMER, AGED 18)

I met the group briefly whilst they were staying at the Antrobus Hotel in Amesbury in early May 1965, whilst they were filming *Help!* on Salisbury Plain, and was able to get their autographs. Amesbury was only a village at that time and although we had the usual cafes with jukeboxes, pubs

Maggie Mayberry's Beatles autographs, including that of George 'So and So' Harrison

and dances where live groups played, Salisbury and Andover were the next biggest towns to us. My friend, Sue Dimer, and I were going out and thought that we would have a walk down to the hotel where The Beatles were staying in just to see whether we might see them. It was just a spur of the moment thing and certainly not planned, as we never ever really thought that we would see The Beatles.

When we reached the hotel, it was quite quiet and I cannot really recall much, if any, activity outside the hotel – *if* anyone else was there, it would only have been one or two girls but certainly not a crowd. It was early evening and we discussed whether or not to go into the bar in the hotel and have a drink. I think my friend was a bit unsure. In the end, we went in a bit sheepishly, bought a drink and sat down. There was no one else in the bar at all. We sat and waited, never really thinking that we would see The Beatles at all.

Then after a while they all came into the bar – seemingly to get a drink and take it into the dining room to eat. I scratched around in my bag and only found a scrap of paper – I was not prepared in any way to get autographs – and went up to the bar where they were standing. Strangely, what I do remember, quite vividly, was the dandruff on their reefer jackets – not something I expected to see or even recall but it was so noticeable against the dark colour!

They did not appear to be hanging around – just getting their drink and going – so I had to hurry or they would be gone. I managed to get John, Ringo and Paul and then asked George for his. He wrote Walter Shenson (who was the producer of their film), so I challenged him and asked him for his own name. He then wrote George 'So and So' Harrison. John, Ringo and George left the bar and Paul began to chat briefly with me.

He asked me if I was resident there. I said 'No' and so he asked if my father owned the hotel. I laughed, said 'No' and that I just lived locally. It all seemed a bit surreal to me and so I could never recall anything else Paul said beyond that but it must have only been brief and then I think he probably realised that he needed to catch the others up and just said goodbye and left the bar. My friend had just sat there and watched us all through that!

I WAS THERE: BETH KAPLAN

PALAIS DES SPORTS

20 JUNE 1965, PARIS

I woke up early, set my hair and put on my best dress, the baby-blue shift with the teardrop cutout at the front that would have shown off my cleavage if I'd had any. The rest of the family were driving to the country for the entire day, much nagging, be careful, don't be late, blah blah blah. I could hardly see, let alone hear. The matinee was at 3 p.m. so I got to the Palais des Sports at 2 p.m. Maybe we'd see them arrive, I thought, but no such luck. At 2.30 p.m. they let us in. I bought the big souvenir program and turned it to the picture of Paul; I was ready.

Beth heard Paul McCartney's (moderately) successful attempts to introduce songs in French

The Palais was round and gigantic – 4,500 seats! – and at 2.30 p.m. it was almost empty. In half an hour it was entirely full. For some reason the audience all around me was mostly boys, a wall of boys. We all clapped our hands '1,2 … 1,2, 3 … 1 2 3 4, let's go!' I wasn't as close to the stage as I'd have liked, but the eighth-row centre was not bad. A loudspeaker warned us not to use the flashes on our cameras or they would be taken away and to stay in our seats, that any troublemakers would be removed. Welcome to friendly France, Beatles. Finally it started. The first hour-and-a-half featured some lousy groups, lots of noise and some booing. The best known were The Yardbirds. I'd heard of them but they were awful – just not The Beatles!

The Beatles' blue amplifiers were on stage and at one point they brought on Ringo's drums. There was lots of clapping. When they all filed in we applauded, so I didn't expect that there would be any screaming. French kids were so obedient. An intermission was announced but I was trembling so much I didn't budge. Finally everybody was in their seats, stamping and howling. I was

The Beatles arriving at the Palais des Sports

holding the picture of Paul and my Brownie camera with the flash off. The announcer came out and got us ready, then counted down: 'Dix, neuf, huit, sept, six, cinq, quatre, trois, deux, un, zero – Les Beatles!' He stepped back, a hand pushed aside the curtain and the screams went up to the roof. Screams, yells, sobs, cries, adoration.

There they were, tall and handsome in sober dark grey suits. They smiled at us all screaming and calmly put on their guitars. Paul came to the microphone and said something, but the screams were so loud that no one heard it. I was waving my picture of Paul – shaking, screaming, stamping my feet, clapping my hands, trying to take a photo and getting ready to pass out, all at the same time. They left the house lights on quite brightly so I was sure they could see us. They opened their gorgeous mouths and sang 'Words of Love'. We calmed down and were quiet during the song but when it was over and the four heads went down up went the yells again.

Paul, even more handsome and cheerful than I'd ever imagined, spoke French with a Liverpool accent. 'Saloo. Mane-tenn-ante notre prochane chawnsown... chawnsin... chinsown...' He stopped and scratched his head as he tried to figure out how to say 'Now our next song'. The audience all shouted 'Oui, oui' so he went on '...s'appaile 'She's a Woman''. He leaned forward the way he does, to begin to sing; his teeth gleamed, his eyes twinkled. It was at this point that, as I waved his photo, I was absolutely sure that he looked down and saw the girl in the eighth row in the baby-blue shift with a teardrop cutout. He saw me, waving that big picture of his face and he grinned at me – right at me – inclining his head a bit. If I had died at that moment, it would have been at the pinnacle of my fine, short life.

Meanwhile, George was standing lost in the middle, looking at the floor, while John was planted firmly, his feet wide apart, surveying the audience. They sang 'I'm a Loser', 'Can't Buy Me Love' and 'Baby's in Black', during which we all swayed back and forth, stamping, clapping, singing and screaming. Then Paul announced Ringo, who sang 'I Wanna Be Your Man', which was the only time in the whole evening I glanced at him. He just sat there at the back, bashing away. His hair was too long anyway.

John's sideburns were a mess, George's was curly at the neck and Paul's was perfect, gleaming, shining. I'd always thought his hair was really dark but it wasn't that much darker than the others. Then 'A Hard Day's Night', introduced by John, who only said 'Merci' and then spoke in English. George sang 'Everybody's Trying To Be My Baby', which was just about the only time I ever looked at him. Then 'Rock 'N' Roll Music', 'I Feel Fine', 'Ticket to Ride' and then Paul said, 'Main-ten-ant our last song'. I screamed, 'No, no!', but they heartlessly sang 'Long Tall Sally', bowed, did a little dance, took off their instruments and left. We howled, screamed, cried.

They came back, bowed once more and dashed off. I didn't want to leave the auditorium, but even more, I didn't want my father to be mad. So I rushed out, and there he was. As I got into the car, croaking, sweaty, nearly blind, I was dreading his usual sarcastic commentary; he hated The Beatles. But dad was silent. He just sat, looking at the thousands of ecstatic kids pouring past the car. 'Daddy,' I said, 'it was just the best, the best. I'll never have an experience like that as long as I live. They played all the best songs and they're so beautiful, so handsome and fun and they tried to speak French.' On the ride home, as I babbled, he didn't make fun or yodel 'Yeah yeah yeah!' I kept expecting him to, but he didn't. Not once.

I WAS THERE: DERRY JACKSON (AGED 14)

ABC THEATRE

1 AUGUST 1965, BLACKPOOL

I believe it was the first time they sang 'Yesterday', after which John walked on stage with a bunch of flowers. As John turned to walk away, he kept the tops of the flowers and Paul was left just holding the stems! What made the day very special was that I was in the theatre all day watching them rehearse. For some reason Bob Monkhouse was there.

I saw them during rehearsal do a very funny and slightly cruel send-up of The Rolling Stones. I watched them laugh and joke together which proved they were very close, not just musically, but also as friends.

I WAS THERE: MAUREEN GROGAN (AGED 15)

SHEA STADIUM

15 AUGUST 1965, NEW YORK

I was 14 in 1964 when The Beatles came on Ed Sullivan and, along with my 12-year-old sister Kathy, became obsessive Beatles fans. We were obsessed with the entire British Invasion, which brought us to the Rolling Stones show and Herman's Hermits and others who came to town. But we pretty much lived and died for The Beatles. I used to get a teen magazine every week called *16*.

Maureen Grogan, who became an obsessive Beatles fan

One week in the spring of 1965, I saw an ad for Sid Bernstein Enterprises with a PO box, ticket prices, etc. for The Beatles' Shea Stadium show, to be held on 15 August 1965. I immediately freaked out and, naturally, then started asking my mother if I could go... if I could go... if I could go! My job was babysitting but I got a lot of it, so I was able to tell her that I would have the money. The tickets cost $5.65. We lived in central Massachusetts, which was close to a four-hour drive to New York City at that time, but she said 'If you get the tickets, your father and I will drive you down.' The key there is she never thought in one million years I would get the tickets. Well ha ha for her!

Myself, my sister, my two best friends Darlene and Lynn all got our money together and I went and got a money order at the bank and mailed it off to Sid Bernstein. A few weeks passed and one day I went to the mailbox, which was outside our front door on the porch and pulled out the envelope with the tickets. The screaming, the crying, the jumping up and down and the hysteria was heard all over the neighbourhood. Some of the neighbors even joined in – the younger ones! My dad agreed to drive, so he, my mother and my grandmother all got into a three-seat station wagon with four semi-hysterical girls ranging from 13 to 15 years old. Very brave of them. We made it to New York City on a record-breaking hot day in a non-air-conditioned car. That can't have been fun, but it wasn't really important to us. My parents dropped us off outside Shea Stadium, set up a place where we would meet after the show, and four little girls from a very small city went off into the bowels of this huge stadium in the largest city on earth without a thought in our heads but 'Beatles! Beatles! Beatles!'

My parents' thoughts were a little more stressful. The outfits were all important and we had shopped to find the most mod outfits that we could possibly come up with in Worcester. Not quite as good as Carnaby Street, but we tried. And the whole stadium looked the same. There were boys there by the way; in fact a young boy and his father were sitting right in front of us. The things I remember most about the concert are that we were on the very top level, sort of in the corner, and even there we recognised every single song they sang. The myth that no one could hear them has been out there for so long and it's always frustrated me. We wrote down a list of the songs they played in order and it's absolutely correct. All that we have lost is the handwritten list. According to the note I wrote inside my programme cover, The Beatles came on stage at 9.15 p.m. and I know it was about a 35-minute show. We jumped up and down, we screamed, we sweated, we cried, we threw confetti, and we almost fell on top of the people in the row in front of us.

We jumped up and down. We screamed and we screamed some more. We had binoculars that we had borrowed from a relative and I tried to put the binoculars up to the little box camera to see if I could get pictures. But all we got was black film. I'm sure my hands were none too steady. I was then, as always, madly in love with John and went crazy when he was playing the keyboard with his elbow. It just seemed like typical John Lennon smart-ass kind of stuff to me. I didn't know until later on that he was doing it partly because they couldn't hear themselves play, and they thought no one could hear what they were doing either. We could hear! It was 35 minutes of the most manic hysteria that teenage girls could ever withstand. Why none of us passed out considering that heat is a miracle. All of us being girl scouts, or former girl scouts, we were prepared with smelling salts.

The good thing about being on the top level turned out to be that

The Beatles take to the stage at Shea Stadium

when The Beatles came into the stadium they came by helicopter. The helicopter was flying around, more or less buzzing the stadium, although I did hear years later that The Beatles were taking a look at the size of the crowd and were just overwhelmed. But we could see them flying back and forth over our heads and we could see them in the doorways waving and peering out the windows.

So, long before the show started, we were all standing up on our seats stretching, screaming and reaching up to the sky, trying to figure out which Beatle was looking out which door. Again, how we didn't fall off the chairs and split our heads open is beyond me. I am now thinking as a mother not a 15-year-old hysteric. When the show ended came the most severe mood crash probably ever seen outside a medical setting. From the highest high to the depths of despair in seconds.

By the time we got outside to meet up with our folks, we were all crying hysterically. We had passed by the driveway where the Wells Fargo truck had driven The Beatles out of the stadium. It was now locked but we, and many other girls, were down on the ground touching the pavement – kissing it, crying and moaning 'They're gone, they're gone!' over and over. This is what my mother came upon. She was not too happy that we were crying when she thought we would be so happy and grateful that they had brought us all the way to New York to see our idols. She had no concept of the emotional rollercoaster that goes into something like this. She was a bit angry at first. But, in order to make us more happy she, dad, and gram said they would drive us over to the marina and show us something that would cheer us up. It was just across the road.

We go over, get out of the car, stand along the railing on Flushing Bay and there's a big yacht. And they informed us, 'The Rolling Stones are on that yacht.' Well guess who started crying and screaming all over again? You'd be correct. It turned out that while we were at the concert the yacht with the Stones' and The Beatles' girlfriends and wives had pulled in. They had all gotten into a limo and driven over to the stadium, passing right in front of my family standing on the sidewalk. They literally saw Cynthia Lennon, Patti Boyd and others sitting in the car. One of the guys working on the boat ran into my grandmother and told her that The Beatles were coming back over there after the show to party with the Stones.

My grandmother, who was terrified of the water her whole life, asked this gentleman if there was any way she could get an autograph for her granddaughters who were over at the show. He walked her out on a fairly rickety pier to wait while he went in to find Mick, who, he said, was a really nice guy. He came out with Mick Jagger's ballpoint pen autograph on a little piece of paper from my grandmother's purse. Now if we promised to stop crying and acting crazy my grandmother was going to give me a surprise.

We did, she gave me the surprise and explained it – and we all went hysterical all over again. So for a couple of years I had an authentic partial Mick Jagger autograph with unassailable provenance. However, I eventually cut it in half with my most best friend who had been there. One year later, I traded most of the first name to a girl who had a double Beatles album that I wanted and had no money for. I retain a portion of the M in blue ballpoint ink and I know it's Mick's, but no one else ever would. Of course we did not know then that it would become the most famous concert probably ever held in the world. We just went because we adored The Beatles; they were miraculously within an area that my parents were kind enough to be willing to drive to; and I saw an address that I could mail for the tickets. Thank you, Sid Bernstein Enterprises and *16* magazine!

I WAS THERE: KAREN WALZ

The whole night is somewhat of a blur for me; I was not yet in my teens. My mom had surprised me (to say the least!) with tickets for her, myself and two friends to see the Fab Four at Shea Stadium. I remember dressing up a bit – as though they would see me — for the special occasion. Weather history says it was only in the 80s, but maybe because of the crowd, it seemed like such a hot night. We pretty much sat in the nosebleed section, but luckily facing the stage.

I don't remember the opening acts, but do remember The Beatles being introduced and the ensuing joyful pandemonium. No sophisticated sound system, no Jumbotron. I have a vague recollection of briefly borrowing binoculars, but otherwise, from where we sat, they looked more like (as the old joke goes) The Ants. It was all but impossible to hear them, but my most distinct aural memory is discerning 'Can't Buy Me Love'. It was such a thrill to know that I was hearing their voices live! I really didn't want to be a screamer, as I was more intent on being a listener, knowing that this was probably a once-in-a-lifetime event for me – it was. My mom took some photos, and I can picture the one of me looking near hysterical, but I haven't been able to find them for a while. On the way home, Mom good-naturedly said she couldn't hear a thing but the screaming. I was happy to tell her that I could hear some vocals, as did my friends. It was, of course, a super night to remember; probably the coolest thing my Mom had ever done. My friends were so appreciative, as I've always been ever after. Mom's gone now, but I know in her own way she dug it as much as we did. Simply unforgettable.

I WAS THERE: JOANN GRUBBS (AGED 14)

I saw The Beatles at Shea Stadium in 1965. I was in the press box seats so didn't experience as much of the craziness – and I actually heard them. I was almost 15 years old and it is etched in my memory forever. I remember the excitement of the helicopters circling overhead. I had binoculars and my cousin almost ripped them off my throat when they ran on the field. I remember asking my cousins at one point during the concert, 'What did Paul just say?' In watching films of that day I noted that Paul and John were speaking gibberish at points because no one could hear what they said anyway. No matter what they said, I was in awe of just breathing the same air as The Beatles.

JoAnn Grubbs, one of the few audience members that actually heard the band

I could never have imagined what an impact they would have on musical history. I just knew that I loved their music, their beautiful vocal harmonies and their haircuts and suits and I adored Paul the most. He just oozed joy and enthusiasm and was so darn cute. I was smitten. I have seen Paul and Ringo since and love them as much as I did as a teenager. They are incredible!

I WAS THERE: ELIZABETH COLEMAN

Being a small-town girl in the 1960s, seeing The Beatles in concert was just a dream. But it was every 13-year-old girl's dream. And that dream came true for me thanks to a local radio station. They sponsored a contest to see The Beatles at Shea Stadium and I was a winner. The bus ride to the stadium seemed never ending. Singing our favorite Beatles songs helped. Finally, we arrived and my eyes lit up with amazement. Never had I experienced anything like this. Inside, we had our seats and nothing could be heard except our shrill screams. And the show hadn't even started yet!

There was an older lady trying to give us candy to stop us screaming. Forget about it! When Ed Sullivan appeared on stage, we knew it was time and time stood still. When introduced, The Beatles appeared running out to the stage. This was really happening. The screams didn't stop and I can still see John running his elbow across that keyboard. We screamed every word to whatever song was being sung. I never cried during the concert but as soon as we were on the bus after the show the tears came. I didn't want this to end. And it didn't – these moments live on in my heart forever. Thank you John, Paul, George and Ringo for making this young girl's dream a reality.

I WAS THERE: JANIS PRATT

My sister Donna and I were fortunate to attend two Beatles concerts. The first was in our hometown of Baltimore in September 1964 and the second, and most memorable, was at Shea Stadium in New York. We travelled to New York on a charter bus sponsored by a Baltimore radio station with a trip that included a day at the 1965 World's Fair. We very proudly wore our BBII (Beatle Bobbies International Incorporated) uniforms, consisting of a long-sleeve white shirt, black tie, black skirt, and black arm band with white BBII lettering.

I remember that the sun was shining, the sky was blue and there was a sense of anticipation building in the air. Upon entering Shea Stadium, the sheer size of the stadium and the sea of people pouring in was mindblowing and increased our anticipation and giddiness. We were then filled with anxiety upon arriving at our seats in the nosebleed section and behind the net, realising that our view of the Fab Four was not going to be very good. So we immediately scoped the lower bowl to find seats with a better view. Suddenly, everyone was standing and screaming – the roar was deafening! Every now and then we could catch a glimpse of The Beatles and heard a few notes and lyrics, but mostly it was a sea of jumping, crying, screaming teenage girls.

We couldn't help but get caught up in the frenzy. Many girls tried to climb the barriers and one girl finally got out onto the field and began running towards the stage. This caught John Lennon's attention and he waved, encouraging her to 'Come on!' Unfortunately, she was intercepted by one of New York's finest, who promptly escorted her away. As the concert came to a close and The Beatles were whisked away, euphoria and exhaustion swallowed me, but the deafening roar followed me all the way back home to Baltimore. I left Shea loving George.

I WAS THERE: SHAMO JANIE BISHOP

In 1965 they did not have a concert in Boston. So all my Year Two friends and I schemed on going to the concert at Shea Stadium in

NYC. Us three high school girls found out the dates and reserved hotel rooms at over 220 NYC hotels. Of course, we lucked out with the Warwick, where The Beatles stayed. We were in the lobby but weren't allowed to check in. We even asked an elderly lady to help but we were turned away so we stayed on the street corner, looking up at the rooms and waiting for them to exit. We met a lot of other fans and there was even a fight, with bubblegum, of Beatles versus Stones fans. The Stones were at the Plaza Hotel at the time.

We only went to our room at another hotel when we needed to get ready for Shea. It was an awesome concert, with The Beatles on a stage at second base. I left before the end and was at the exit when they came out in a Wells Fargo truck. I put my hand on the window and Paul put his hand up and winked. That was over the top for this 17-year-old fan.

I WAS THERE: DAVID BRYANT

ATLANTA STADIUM

18 AUGUST 1965, ATLANTA

My mother worked at the Bell record shop in High Point, NC and actually introduced me to The Beatles' music. I still have in its sleeve the first record she brought home to me, the 45 of 'I Want to Hold Your Hand'. At first listen I was smitten. This was the best thing I had ever heard, and from that moment on I was as big of a fan of The Beatles as she was. To say The Beatles had an impact on my life is an understatement. My mother continued to bring home all the Beatles records to me the day they arrived at her store. I'm sure I had the best collection in town.

Shortly after becoming a Beatle fan, some of my buddies and I decided to learn how to play guitar – rhythm guitar for me – and drums and start a band. It was called The Morlocks. We covered a lot of different bands, including The Beatles and enjoyed a few years of local success playing the County Fair, State Fair, local dance clubs, parties, and even a local TV dance show. Music became my life and it was largely inspired by The Beatles! The store where my mother worked also sold tickets to all the rock concerts that came through Greensboro and I did not miss a show.

The Morlocks, David Bryant's Beatles-inspired band. David is on the right, wearing a top hat

I saw The Rolling Stones, The Dave Clark Five, The Beach Boys, Herman's Hermits, The Monkees, Jimi Hendrix and just about all the rest at Greensboro Coliseum, but The Beatles never came. I listened to our local High Point radio station faithfully because they played Beatle music and one morning heard my favourite DJ, John Ferree, announce that he and his wife had put together a bus trip to see The Beatles in Atlanta, Georgia. Wow oh wow! When my mother heard about this she immediately said, 'Well, David, you have to go and I'll pay for you to go!' She did, and I think the whole trip including the ticket cost $50.

I will never forget the excitement I felt as I boarded the bus early that morning and headed to Atlanta to see The Beatles. We got there that afternoon, stopped at a YMCA, freshened up and changed clothes and then grabbed a bite to eat before heading to the baseball stadium. The stadium was filling up quickly with mostly teenage boys and girls, beyond excited knowing that shortly they would be seeing and hearing the greatest band in the world!

It was amazing. It was hard to believe; quite surreal. Everyone was scanning the stadium, some standing, to see if The Beatles were to be seen anywhere, perhaps in a dugout or 'look over there!' Sometimes screams would go up in certain sections as they thought they had got a glimpse of them. The atmosphere in that stadium was electric! I had never experienced anything like that before. I can't remember who the opening act was but my feeling was most did not care – let's just get on to The Beatles. Then they were announced and I heard the loudest roar I had ever heard.

They walked out to the stage and began to plug in their guitars and get things adjusted. Then they began to play 'Twist and Shout' and the screaming was so loud you really could not hear much music. The PA system was bad, but to be honest nobody cared. It was the experience! The incredible experience of being in that stadium at that moment, being a part of something historical that you would never forget. Seeing The Beatles live and in person!

I WAS THERE: RODGER BROWNLEE

SAM HOUSTON COLISEUM

19 AUGUST 1965, HOUSTON

I had previously seen The Beatles in Dallas, but over the course of a year they had grown in popularity beyond anyone's wildest expectations, their music becoming more popular, more sophisticated and more influential. The British Invasion and The Beatles were not fading away into obscurity and practically everyone in the music and entertainment business wanted to be a part of the scene and was carried along on that wave.

I was a member of The Elite, one of the most popular and successful bands in the north Texas area. Our British sound and style led KFJZ radio disc jockey Mark Stevens to introduce us as 'the band that looks and sounds like they just stepped off the boat from Liverpool'. We reveled in the popularity and attention and became the house band at Teen A Go Go, the largest live music venue for teens in Fort Worth, sponsored by KFJZ. Little did we know that how we looked was going to lead us into trouble. Eddie Deaton, Bob Barnes, Bruce Lair and myself loaded into Eddie's '62 Chevy Impala and headed to Houston for the Beatles show. KFJZ had provided us with great tickets for the show but hadn't booked us a motel room. So we had to make the 50-mile drive to Galveston to get a hotel room.

In the morning, we drove to Houston to do a reconnaissance; we wanted to see the layout, parking and entrances at the Sam Houston Coliseum. It was only mid morning and there were already lines forming for the early afternoon show. Having been to The Beatles concert in Dallas the year

The view from the crowd at the Sam Houston Coliseum

before, I knew a little of what to expect, but hadn't witnessed anything like this. As we slowed to a crawl, with the windows down, someone spotted us and let out a yell.

Suddenly fans broke from the lines and came running towards our car, screaming and yelling all the way. Just as quickly, cops at the scene ran to intercept the runaways, while one of their number took to a bull horn to announce, 'It's not The Beatles. I repeat, it is not The Beatles.' Returning to the Sam Houston Coliseum in the afternoon, we were again spotted by the crowd who again mistook us for The Beatles. A cry went up, the crowd broke ranks and it was like a chase scene right out of the movies.

Thankfully, the alert Houston PD cops noticed our plight and began yelling and frantically waving us towards them. We made it just as the mob was closing on our heels. The cops shoved us through a side door and slammed it shut behind us. We blinked and looked around. The area was cavernous and empty except for a couple of janitor-looking types. It took a minute and then it hit us – we were backstage at The Beatles concert. We began exploring, sticking our noses through every door, and checking every alcove. We failed to locate any of the dressing rooms; our best find was a restroom, which we desperately needed by this time. Finished with our business we finally came to a set of stairs that led up. Looking at each other and shrugging our shoulders, we started climbing. At the first landing, we could hear the noise and rumble coming from the gathering storm of fans. At the top of the next flight, we stepped out on to a balcony bathed in the brilliance of spot- and floodlights. As soon as our eyes adjusted, we could see that we were in the balcony row right above and behind the stage.

It only took seconds for the crowd below to spot us, and in one body they rose to their feet with a cheer that rattled the ceiling. At the distance we were from them, they had no idea who we were. Then all the cops located around the front of the stage turned, and looking up, began pointing in our direction and shouting orders. In a matter of a few seconds cops were closing in on us from all directions. One angry cop, thinking we were part of the show, demanded to know why we were not backstage where we belonged, and instead up here causing all this disruption. Surrounded and intimidated by a ring of angry, scowling faces with badges, we meekly showed them our tickets and told them we were lost. With barked orders and a flurry of activity, we were hastily escorted to our seats and told to stay put.

The seats were great; only a few rows above and on the left side of the stage. The lights were down, and we remained cloaked in darkness and unobserved for a time. Then the master of ceremonies came out, introduced the opening act and the lights came up. Before we knew it, hundreds of girls were surrounding us. The opening act, Sounds Incorporated, was largely ignored by the fans around us as they jostled to hand us things to autograph, most of which were Beatles album covers. They didn't care at all that we weren't The Beatles or that we weren't even in the show; they thought we were a band, any band, and that's all that seemed to matter. It was too chaotic for questions and answers, so they kept jostling, handing us anything that came to hand and we kept signing.

I don't recall much of the concert up to the time that The Beatles came on. It was impossible to see through the wall of young female bodies and flailing arms. The crush of autograph-seekers abated somewhat only when the imminent presence of The Beatles caused them to scurry back to their own seats. Then The Beatles were introduced and pandemonium erupted. The noise, as in 1964, was deafening, unbelievably loud. Only this time it came from two or three times more sets of lungs than the 10,000 I had witnessed the year before. Even with their new special made Vox Super Beatle amplifiers, each with 100 watts of power, the music hardly made a dent in the impenetrable wall of noise – the shrieks, screams, sobs and yells of the crowd.

It was a little better for us. With the location and close proximity of our seats to the stage, we were able to catch snatches and sometimes entire phrases of 'Twist and Shout', 'Dizzy Miss Lizzy', 'Ticket to Ride', 'A Hard Day's Night' and 'Help' amongst others. And of course McCartney's show stopper 'I'm Down'. Our seats also gave us a decent view of the stage, despite the obstructions. And as always, I had along my trusty Kodak Brownie 8mm movie camera and started filming as soon as The Beatles came on stage; and kept it up until the film ran out.

The goosebumps were crawling and the adrenaline was rushing as George, John, Paul and Ringo played the hits that we had come to hear. And then, after 10 or 12 songs, it was over. The girls continued to scream and shriek and sob and call out the names of their favorite Beatle, even after they had left the stage and the lights came up.

But the show was over, and fans began making their way to the exits. As we tried to rise up out of our seats, we were once again beset by die-hard autograph-seekers, who pulled and tugged at us relentlessly until once again we were saved by the Houston PD. They took us to a side door and turned us loose. We made it to our car a few blocks away without further incident and took stock. Other than a few bumps and a few missing tufts of hair, we were intact.

I WAS THERE: ELAINE MCAFEE BENDER

I ran a local North Texas chapter of the official Beatles Fan Club and did live readings of Beatles News on KFJZ Fort Worth, sister radio station to KILT Houston. I saw them at the Memorial Auditorium in Dallas in September 1964 and got complimentary tickets to both shows in Houston [in 1965]. KILT had me stop by for a live interview. I met the Fab Four and gave each one a cowboy shirt.

I became a Mary Quant model and a professional go-go girl. I'm in the documentary film *Teen A Go Go* and the book "Fort Worth's Rock and Roll Roots." It was an awesome time. There was nothing like the Sixties and there was nobody like The Beatles!

Elaine was a Mary Quant model, a go-go girl and a "Beatles newsreader" – truly living the Sixties dream!

I WAS THERE: DOROTHY GIBSON (AGED 13)

My parents allowed me to fly Braniff Air with my good friend to Houston for the Beatles concert. At that moment, I could imagine myself dressed as a classy hostess serving my beloved Beatles on a flight to where all my dreams came true. We were picked up by other parents at the Houston airport and taken to an all-night slumber party in preparation for the next day's event. We filled ourselves with tuna sandwiches and chocolate-chip cookies. In 1965, kids were pretty much safe everywhere. About six of us well-dressed young ladies – in very mod navy top and mod dress that I kept for years and never wore again – were dropped off at 4 a.m. for the Back to School Beatles concert to be given at 3 p.m. that afternoon.

Believe me, we were at the head of the line to get in. It was, after all, a 'run for your seat' event. Nothing could drag me away from my front-line position. At least, not until I got sick. Remember those tuna sandwiches? They don't mix with a young girl's emotions. A very nice officer escorted me from the line and I remained in his cruiser until 15 minutes before the doors opened. Yes, he made sure my place was secured and I was back in front. I can't remember if I held on to my friend's hand when we charged forward or if we were equally ached for speed. We made it though, eighth row center.

Oh, it was so hard to get through those opening acts. We, the entire crowd, were on edge and many times thought we spied our favorite peeking through the side curtains. It must have been worse for those performers. They never had the crowd and they never had a chance. Then there they were – John, Paul, George and Ringo. I still remember that first chord. It may have been the only one I truly heard, as most everything else was drowned out by our cries of utter abandonment. We stood not on the seats of our chairs but somehow were balanced up on the backs of the metal folding chairs. And before it even registered it was over.

Of course, I can tell you how I bragged about how I knew George looked directly at me and we connected. He was truly magical, as I later found out he was able to do that with other girls too! Still, I knew then his look at me was personal. A friend, much braver than I, was able to sneak into the Sheridan Hilton hotel and got a picture of George walking the hallway. I still love my copy of that photo. I told a few lies over the next two years or so about who took the picture. I had it and it was proof enough.

My children celebrated 19 August with me for many years. My middle son found a video recording of the Houston 3 p.m. concert and gave it to me one Christmas. Then, when we attended his college graduation in Iowa, we returned to Texas via Memphis. In a little souvenir shop across from Graceland, my husband found a memory book with

Dorothy Gibson: her parents allowed her to take a flight to Houston for the Beatles gig

photos from the same concert. There are pictures looking out at the crowd. You really can't identify who's who, but I still think I see me right there in that eighth row with a shout on my lips and tears in my eyes. Wow, I surely was blessed. What an experience! When we returned to San Antonio, we started a club of girls – the FLMC. This stood for Father Lennon Many Children. We disbanded when other boys became real.

I WAS THERE: ALBERT HERNANDEZ DE LEON (AGED 16)

COMISKEY PARK

20 AUGUST 1965, CHICAGO

When my mom and I arrived in Florida from Cuba on one of Pan Am's last flights, just a week before the October missile crisis in 1962, all we had was the clothes on our back, two small suitcases and an enormous relief to have at last got out of that proletarian hell. And a small list of all the vinyl LPs I was going to buy on arrival.

It was the manager of the building where we lived who gave me a small record player that Christmas, which I kept for the next three years. The number one song in the *Billboard* charts was The Four Seasons' 'Big Girls

Don't Cry'. I proved to be a hardcore pop fan the moment I got off the plane on that fateful September day in Miami, and in high school in Chicago I nearly spent all my lunch money and allowance on 45s.

First it was The Four Seasons – the first group I ever saw on stage in 1963 – and then Leslie Gore, The Beach Boys, Gene Pitney, Connie Francis and more. It was during my world history class in February 1964 that someone had a copy of a newspaper with the Fab Four on the front page. My first impression was not favourable. I thought they all looked like Moe from *The Three Stooges*.

Albert Hernandez de Leon became pop mad when he arrived in the US from Cuba. At school, he was called 'The Fifth Beatle'

All that changed a week later when I heard 'I Want to Hold Your Hand'. In my music class we listened to light fare like the music from *Breakfast at Tiffany's*, *The Sound of Music* and *West Side Story* and my teacher was not crazy about The Beatles. As an assignment, we had to do an essay explaining whether we thought the Fabs were a social phenomenon or just a passing fad. I got an 'A' on mine, and she told me it was by far the best and most convincing one she had graded. There were roughly 3,000 students at Waller High in Chicago in the spring of 1964, and only three guys had their hair 'long', which Beatle styles were! At one point, the principal threatened to suspend us unless we cut our hair.

Then my French teacher Mme Ivoire intervened. She started a petition and we gathered over 1,000 signatures, so the old fart gave up and left us alone. That summer The Beatles came to town and tickets were gone within an hour. I was shattered. But I did not totally despair. Between my oodles of mags and singles and outings to the local radio station lobby with mod friends with fake Liverpool accents on Saturday afternoon, life went on.

The following year I saw The Hollies, The Yardbirds, Herman's Hermits, The Rolling Stones, The Animals, The Dave Clark Five and two dozen other bands. Me and my friends combed every hotel in town until we finally would somehow find the band. Then the pics, autographs and parties would follow. But we were just biding our time for the return of the Fab Four. Finally, the big day was announced. By then people in school were calling me the fifth

Fans watching The Beatles at
Comiskey Park, Chicago, 1965

Beatle. We were the envy of those unlucky ones who did not get tickets.

On the morning of 20 August, a friend whose aunt worked at the Sahara
Inn by the airport called to tell me they were staying there. I was sworn to
secrecy, but by the time we got there at noon, there must have been 500
frenzied teenagers in the parking lot screaming at the top of their lungs. A
hundred police and security guards firmly stood between the crowd and the
entrance. It was absolute pandemonium. I started scheming with my friend
Christopher on how we could get in through the back and we sneaked away
from the crowd and forced our way through a side door service entrance.

We moved stealthily but cautiously, not knowing where the hell we were
going. We heard women's voices and hid in a laundry closet until they
had gone. A few feet ahead there was a staircase, so we decided to take it
all the way up to the top, while carefully scrutinising for any movement
– or British accents – on every floor. When we reached the top floor,
two security guards saw us and gave chase. We scrambled up to the roof
and started running. The crowd down below saw the chaos and started
cheering for us. They were hysterical as we outran the guards.

We went to the far side of the hotel and proceeded down the opposite
staircase when suddenly – British accents! We hid in a broom closet as
the two guards continued speeding down the stairs, passing us. We then
emerged, thrust the hallway door open and saw a dozen men in suits. And
George, walking from one room into another! Obviously, some of these
men were roadies and guards protecting them. Like idiots, we screamed
'George!' He turned around and said 'Hello' but by then we were already in
the arms of two gorillas handing us over to the two security guards. We were

unceremoniously marched downstairs and thrown out into the cheering crowd. We were almost crushed by the inquisitive multitude.

In the next issue of *Fab* (208), the Chicago correspondent who happened to be present went on to describe this madness in her weekly column: 'Suddenly, two blokes wearing matching lavender shirts with black ruffles down the middle were being chased by security guards on the roof, and the crowd went wild with cheers and yells of encouragement, as they soon disappeared into the hotel below.' I was famous! Britain would read about me and Chris! What a morning!

We arrived at Comiskey Park Stadium shortly after noon. Ticket purchase had been mail-order only, with no lines at the box office. Luckily myself and my two best friends, Linda and Rhonda, got tickets to both afternoon and evening shows. We were within the first five rows, but what difference did it make? The stage was almost an entire city block in the distance. We had binoculars and cheap Instamatic cameras, but these could not even begin to capture the four figures which soon broke into song. I did not hear a note. It was just screams and more screams. Looking back on it, I would have loved to hear them as well as seeing them. But, hey, who was complaining?

The scenes of total madness and pandemonium were repeated that evening at 8 p.m.. It was more exhilarating at night than in the afternoon! My diary could not hold all the emotions I experienced that day. I was hoarse and exhausted the next day, as if I had run a marathon. I think half of the 35,000 fans that saw the performances either slept all day Saturday or spoke on the phone. Mom was just beside herself as that's all I talked about for the next month.

I WAS THERE: RICH PINE (AGED 11)

I had seen them for the first time on the *The Ed Sullivan Show* three days prior to my tenth birthday, so by the time I saw them live, I had been a rabid fan for a year and a half. Besides my wedding and the birth of my children, this was one of the most unforgettable days of my life. How many people can say their first ever concert was The Beatles?

They played at old Comiskey Park, a baseball stadium and home to the Chicago White Sox baseball team. A raised platform had been constructed in the vicinity of second base and The Beatles and their opening acts – Brenda Holloway and the King Curtis Band, Cannibal

The Fab Four rocking and rolling at Comiskey Park

and The Headhunters, Sounds Incorporated – performed from there. There was no audience seating on the field itself, only in the stands where one would normally be during a ball game.

There were two shows that day – one at 3 p.m. and another at 8 p.m.. I was at the three o'clock show with my nine year old sister and my aunt's roommate, the person who took us. She was in her early to mid 30s at the time, but was head of the steno pool at the Wrigley Gum Co. and had a number of late-teen and 20-something women who worked under her. Their enthusiasm for The Beatles had rubbed off on her and, knowing my sister and I were crazy about them, asked my parents if she could take us.

Thankfully they agreed, otherwise it never would have happened. It was a beautiful sunny day and August can be very hot in Chicago. My recollection is that it was warm but not overly so. I do recall that it seemed to take forever until The Beatles came out – I knew Cannibal and The Headhunters, not so much the other bands. But all I cared about was seeing the Fab Four.

When they finally did come out, they had to run across the field from one of the dugouts to the platform and the audience went bananas. The screaming began full force and everyone was on their feet. When they began playing it was difficult to hear, but you could tell what songs they were playing. I clearly remember John doing runs on the keyboard with his elbow during 'I'm Down' and George at one point turning from his position on the stage and running toward the edge of the platform, facing one part of the audience with his arms open.

You could physically see that part of the crowd react as though they'd all been hit by lightning at the same time. They played 'Help!', 'She's a Woman', 'Ticket to Ride' and 'Dizzy Miss Lizzy'. When it was over and they were gone, I remember looking back over my shoulder up into the stands. Here and there were scattered groups of girls – most of them older than me – sitting in their seats and crying. The Beatles made a huge impact on my life. I started playing drums because of Ringo and just two years ago realized my dream of owning a new black oyster Pearl Ludwig kit, built to the same specifications as one of the kits he used while a Beatle. In high school, I made an animated film with another student using 'You Know My Name, Look Up The Number' that got us an honorable mention in the Kodak Student Film Awards Contest in 1973. I will die a Beatles fan....

I WAS THERE: CATHY SANCHEZ

HOLLYWOOD BOWL

29–30 AUGUST 1965, LOS ANGELES

I remember when they first appeared on *The Ed Sullivan Show.* At the time I hadn't heard of them as I was into The Beach Boys and surfer songs. The next day at school, all us girls were talking about The Beatles and who was the cutest. George was mine. I, along with my friends, went out to buy their records. In 1965, two of my good friends and I went to the Hollywood Bowl and saw The Beatles live.

We had pinstriped pants made especially for the concert, and our black turtleneck tops and boots. I remember all the screaming and crying all around us. One friend, Nancy, was crying and saying how much she loved John. The very next day we went to the movie theater and

For Cathy Sanchez, the Ed Sullivan Show appearance was an epiphany

336

watched *Help!* We even took binoculars to get a real up-close shot. I have a sweatshirt now that I wear out sometimes that says 'Yes I am old but I saw The Beatles on stage.' People will come up to me when I'm wearing the sweatshirt and ask me, 'Did you really see The Beatles?'

I WAS THERE: ANNE STASKEWICZ

I attended back-to-back Beatle shows at the Bowl and remember hearing them play. I even wrote down the playlist. They were much less formal than on their first visit to the Bowl the previous year, joking with the audience and skipping around on stage. In those days, there was a water-filled moat in front of the stage and John spat into it several times and nearly fell in at one point. Opening for The Beatles on the first night, which was a Sunday, were The Discotheque Dancers, Sounds Incorporated and others.

Our seats were stage-right again and even better than the previous year – in the boxes! I recall the celebs who were around and in front of us: Sonny and Cher, Dino Martin, Joey Paige, a Beach Boy or two, Joan Baez, a few Byrds and Shindogs, even Debbie Reynolds. Were we old enough to drive, we'd probably have driven up after the concert to Benedict Canyon, where they were staying.

It was after show number two at the Hollywood Bowl, on the Monday night, that I came closest to The Beatles. When Paul announced that 'I'm Down' would be the last song, the whole audience surged toward the stage. John pointed for someone to jump into the moat and several girls did. By 1965, my friends and I were already veteran groupies and, as all knowledgeable groupies do, we staked out the stage exit and were caught up in the surge of fans surrounding the armored truck that ferried them out of the Bowl. I somehow got wedged between a policeman and the rear window of the truck and suddenly was face to face with George. That was the closest I ever came to a Beatle!

I WAS THERE: MICHAEL SCOTT (AGED 16)

COW PALACE

31 AUGUST 1965, SAN FRANCISCO

I went to see The Beatles on their second tour of the US with three buddies from high school. I remember very little about anything that preceded The Beatles taking the stage. When the band began, pandemonium broke out. We left our seats and inched our way towards the stage through a sea of hysterical young girls, winding up three back from the barricade on Paul's side of the stage, with security lined up between it and the stage. There was no air and very few boys up front, just bat-shit crazy young females! One actually bit my ear lobe and said 'Boys shouldn't be up front.' 'OK,' I said, 'but I ain't moving.' The Beatles were dressed in camel tan military-style jackets and black slacks. Paul and John looked amused by it all. George looked freaked out, maybe scared. There was a cymbal in front of Ringo's face so I don't know how he looked. The screaming was as loud as their playing. It never stopped!

The lack of breathable air started causing girls to pass out. There was no way to get them out of the fracas so the security behind the barricades started passing them up to the roadies who were crawling around The Beatles and would pull them to the back of the stage. Some girls got the idea of faking passing out, and once they were pulled on

Lennon looks on as security remove a fainting fan at The Cow Palace

stage they would come to life and go after a Beatle. Just frigging crazy. Paul, who was about ten feet from me, was doing his thing whilst keeping an eye on the zombie girls being dragged across the stage. He looked a bit bewildered and amused. In front of me was a very petite girl with a bigger one in front of her and then the barricade.

Then the security cops, then the stage and Paul. I noticed that the little girl seemed to be getting smaller. She was supported by the girl in front and by me from behind. I tried to bring her to with no success. Alerting the security I passed the little zombie to him. The whole while, Paul was watching what was happening. The security passed her up to a roadie crawling around Paul's feet. This little zombie was out and didn't return to the living.

Looking at the floor I saw a coat where the girl had been. I grabbed it and held it aloft, yelling to get anyone's attention. The roadie was right behind Paul dragging the little zombie. Paul was taking it all in, seemingly concerned. I threw the coat at the stage. Paul caught it with the neck end of his Höfner and pitched it back to the roadie. When he turned back to us, Paul smiled and gave me a wink. It was kind of like 'We got it done!' This shall forever be embedded in my memory.

I WAS THERE: JOHN BATES

ODEON THEATRE

9 DECEMBER 1965, BIRMINGHAM

I went with a friend but, as in the previous year, my father and I queued up for most of the night a few weeks before to get the tickets. In those days the tickets were nothing special like they are today, but just normal cinema stubs typical of that era. Sadly I no longer have the tickets but I do have the programmes and newspaper cuttings about the concert. They only performed for about 30 minutes and were accompanied by The Paramounts and The Moody Blues.

I WAS THERE: SYLVIA ELLIS

By the second time I saw them they were even more famous. My friend Liz Russell and I decided that in order to get decent seats we should stay out all

The Beatles in Birmingham and in black, 1965

night. We both fibbed to our moms and said we were staying at each other's homes and setting out early. Problem being we had no creature comforts like hot drinks and blankets and it was very cold! We struck up friendships with some girls from Wolverhampton who shared tea with us. I remember one of them was a girl called Margaret from Penn, Wolverhampton, who afterwards sent me autographed photos she had obtained plus a photo of George's parents on a visit she made to Liverpool. We were so excited and a cheer went up when the box office opened after a long chilly night. We got two end of row seats on Row L and we were elated to go home with our precious tickets. Roll on 11 October!

When the day came, the excitement was overwhelming and off I went with my sequined sash with 'Paul' carefully sewn on it but unfortunately it was stolen from me by a steward when I waved it in the air when the band came on. I was gutted about that. The poor supporting act, which I cannot recall, had no chance as we all wanted the boys to appear. I will never forget being in the darkness and the anticipation and then the twang of the first note of 'I Feel Fine'.

That was practically all I heard as the screams were deafening and this continued throughout. I remember Paul taking a position on his own and we assumed it was for 'Yesterday', but we couldn't hear that much! It went by so quickly, like a dream. Then they were gone, and girls were crying. Next day I couldn't speak through screaming. I had decided, at the concert, that I may as well join in. And I thought I had gone deaf. Despite this, I would not have missed it for the world. I think the lads had on grey, or electric blue, mohair suits. They looked great anyway, even if we could not hear them!

I WAS THERE: SANDRA LONGMIRE

Fast-forward to 1965 and we heard that The Beatles would be appearing at the Odeon Birmingham in December. By this time they were world-famous so tickets were like gold dust. My recollection is that a very good friend of ours called Bernie went and queued all night to get the tickets for us. Our tickets were in the balcony, but it was good to see our idols again.

We didn't all have cars in those days and we went to Birmingham by train, not thinking to find out what time the last train was. On arrival at Birmingham New Street, after the show had finished, the train had of course long gone, probably at 9 p.m. I think we came home on the milk train (whatever that was) at about 3 a.m. There were no mobile phones in those days so I guess our parents must have been worried. Teenagers, eh?

I WAS THERE: PAUL LUTON (AGED 14)

We queued up all night long to get our tickets for the Beatles show at the Odeon Cinema in New Street. I remember the queue stretching all around the back of the cinema and us being quite a way from the front. We were hoping of course that they wouldn't sell out before it was our turn. Well, after many hours standing in the queue it was our turn. I purchased two tickets, one for me and one for my best mate, and we got the 15 shilling [75p] ones which were the better seats. We were so excited and, looking forward to the show, we soon forgot the long wait the night before.

The main thing I remember about the show itself was that the noise was so loud with the crowd screaming and shouting that you couldn't hear a word that The Beatles were singing. But that didn't really matter as we were seeing the greatest ever band live right in front of our eyes. I can't remember how long they were on but it didn't seem too long compared to today's artists. The set list was: 'I Feel Fine'; 'She's a Woman'; 'If I Needed Someone'; 'Act Naturally'; 'Nowhere Man'; 'Baby's in Black'; 'Help!'; 'We Can Work It Out'; 'Yesterday'; 'Day Tripper'; 'I'm Down'. When you tell people that you have seen The Beatles live they are almost in awe of you, such was the kudos of seeing the greatest band ever actually performing. I can't believe it was 50 years ago.

HAMMERSMITH ODEON

10 DECEMBER 1965, LONDON

In mid-1963, I moved to London and joined the Met Police and after training was transferred to Hammersmith to serve in uniform there. The Beatles played the Hammersmith Odeon to full houses more than once and I was employed with many others on crowd control. Many years later on retirement I had moved to Ham in Surrey and spent quite a bit of time in a local betting shop. In doing so one makes many acquaintances. One guy I regularly chatted to called John had been born and bred in Hammersmith and lived on the same street there as me. He was, shall we say, a rough diamond. But despite him knowing of my time in the Met he was always willing to chat.

One day, talk turned to The Beatles and he volunteered the story that as a young scallywag he had shinned up the drainpipe at the Odeon when The Beatles were playing there one night, got into their dressing room and nicked John Lennon's wallet. On reaching the ground again he stole money from the wallet and then threw the wallet and John Lennon's driving licence down a drain! He bemoaned the fact that he didn't keep the licence. How true his story was I don't know, but he seemed a genuine type of guy who had – perhaps – matured over the years.

1966 GIGS

Between January and June 1966,
The Beatles kept a low profile,
concentrating on recording until performing
a handful of dates in Germany in June and
then one-off shows in Japan and the Philippines.
On 11 August 1966, they flew from
London to Chicago to begin what was to be their
last tour of North America. Or anywhere else...

I WAS THERE: ALBERT HERNANDEZ DE LEON

INTERNATIONAL AMPHITHEATRE

12 AUGUST 1966, CHICAGO

If we were lucky to have seen The Beatles twice in 1965, we were even luckier in 1966, when me and my two girlfriends Lin and Rhon got second row, right in front of Lennon, at the Amphitheatre with only a cordon of policemen and a six-feet stage separating us from them. Both my girlfriends were huge fans of John, while I was rather fonder of George myself.

The scene was even more chaotic in a closed environment. I thought my friends were going to faint, as many gals did. There were many guys in the audience this time around but not as many nor as frenzied as the female fans. First came The Ronettes, then The Cyrkle and finally The Beatles. The roar of the crowd was deafening. Even mothers and their pre-teen daughters were there, as

A much-prized ticket
for the International
Amphitheatre
concert

well as a few grandfathers. The sound was better this time though not ideal. From the second row, it was hard not to catch a few notes.

I WAS THERE: VALERIE H WARD (AGED 15)

OLYMPIA STADIUM

13 AUGUST 1966, DETROIT

The first time I saw them was in 1964. I had just turned 13 years old and was way up in the balcony. The second time I was just one row off the floor but way in the back. I remedied this, though. I caught a glimpse of Paul behind a curtain at the stadium. I remember the shirt he was wearing. It was red. I was a *Datebook* magazine teen interviewer and I wanted to get behind the curtain and do a brief interview. I had my 'press' badge but the police security would not let me through. Hey, I gave it my best shot!

The Beatles wore pinstriped suits for the performance. Even though I sat straight in front of them I was quite far back. There was such commotion. I managed to leave my seat and found my way up to the fourth or fifth row from the stage. No one was in their seats anyway. I found an empty seat and quickly took it. A couple of times I left my camera on the floor next to my seat. At one point I did not even care if I lost the camera. I was too caught up in the moment. All I wanted was to touch them. I never thought that this would be the last time I ever saw them as The Beatles.

Above: Valerie Ward. Left: her idols, on stage at the Olympia Stadium, Detroit

I WAS THERE: SEAN EDDY (AGED 5)

I don't remember it. But my mom says that I asked her to make all the girls stop screaming so that I could hear the music.

I WAS THERE: BONNI GRANATO (AGED 15)

CLEVELAND STADIUM

14 AUGUST 1966, CLEVELAND

Bonni Granato, proudly showing off her Beatles pennant

$5.50 seemed such a bargain for that ticket. I only got $1.00 a week allowance back then, so I had to get a loan from my mom and went for five-and-a-half weeks without so much as a ten-cent cherry coke in all that time. It was the best sacrifice I ever made! I remember The Cyrkle and Bobby Hebb singing 'Sunny' but not any of the other groups, as we were there to see a phenomenon that we had never witnessed before. About ten minutes after The Beatles came on, the chain-link fence that was there for security was broken down and the crowd rushed the stage.

You could barely breathe due to the pushing and shoving. It was mass hysteria. My leg was caught between other fans' legs and kids were actually climbing and standing on our legs for a better view. Some of the guys were grabbing girls' breasts because they could get away with it. The Beatles were taken off stage and would not be brought back out unless everyone returned to their seats. Once the massive frenzied crowd returned to their seats, the fence was erected again. Looking back down on the field was a sea of trampled clothing, crushed umbrellas, broken cameras, shoes, etc. The Beatles returned and began playing. Who knows what song it was because you could never hear them. The fence was broken down again and I made it to the front of the stage. The Beatles were laughing and Paul motioned the girls forward. I jumped up to touch his boot and got hit with a policeman's billy club. I saw stars!

They took The Beatles off stage and the concert was over. The next day at school I was covered with bruises from the frenzied crowd and had a big goose egg on my forehead that I was very proud of. It was the night of my life!

I WAS THERE: NEIL FAUGNO

DC STADIUM

15 AUGUST 1966, WASHINGTON DC

I saw The Beatles during the period where John Lennon had made the statement that 'We are more popular than Jesus' and there was some concern for their safety, especially in the south. There were opening acts, of course, to get the crowd all anxious and excited, and then a limo pulled onto the field behind the stage and of course all eyes were on the car in anticipation of their arrival. Well, nothing was happening and then I heard some cheering and looked down. The Beatles were standing outside one of the dugouts waving at a crowd that mostly thought that they were in the limo. They were then escorted to the stage and started to play.

Of course there was screaming and flashbulbs galore, but the sound

The stadium press conference shortly before the DC gig on 15 August

was poor and as a musical event it kind of fell short. But there was one very interesting happening. A young man got on the field and raced to the stage with police and security in hot pursuit. The band was playing 'Ticket to Ride' with John singing the lead. The man made it to the stage, climbed up and John hit him with the butt of his guitar, sending him into the arms of security. John never missed a beat.

I WAS THERE: BETH KAPLAN

I saw them in Washington, DC in August 1966, just before they stopped touring for good. And for good reason – it was a terrible experience, a vast football stadium and so much noise. It was hideous and deafening, impossible to hear anything. I feel very fortunate that my Paris experience was in a very small venue and so tightly controlled by the French authorities that we could see and hear everything. A great blessing and one of the great memories of my life.

I WAS THERE: JACKI REESE (AGED 11)

By 1966 they were playing stadiums. My sister saw them at DC Coliseum in 1964, which is smaller but still a pretty good size. I wore my first miniskirt to The Beatles' concert at DC Stadium. It was bright orange and came to the middle of my knee, so it really wasn't as 'mini' as I thought it was. Though we were a good 500 feet or more from the stage, my friend Susie and I were convinced that Paul looked at us! I had seen The Rolling Stones the year before. The ticket cost six dollars!

I WAS THERE: DAVID BRYANT

1966 found The Beatles under a cloud of controversy because of John's comments about them being 'more popular than Jesus'. Some in my family encouraged me to destroy my records and never see them again, but on 15 August I went to Washington, DC on that same bus trip to see them one more time. Their last tour!

This time I carried a portable battery operated reel-to-reel tape recorder to try and capture the concert experience on tape. Well I did capture some music and mostly screaming but it was fun to listen to it and let my friends hear it. My girlfriend went with me on this trip and I thought I was going to have to carry her back to the bus after the concert. Once again the experience was incredible and I will never forget it.

Sadly my mom, who was so instrumental in me being a Beatle fan and even paying for my trips to see them, tossed my ticket stubs and tape recordings in the trash while cleaning out the attic one day. Oh well. I still have the memories! As incredible of an experience as it was to see The Beatles twice and love their music so much, as I still do, nothing can begin to compare with the experience I had almost exactly one year from the date I last heard them in Washington, DC, when I accepted Jesus Christ as my Lord and Saviour and became a minister of his gospel. I sing, play the guitar and minister as a missionary evangelist around the world.

I WAS THERE: SUSAN VALLEE (AGED 15)

MAPLE LEAF GARDENS

17 AUGUST 1966, TORONTO

My mom was born in Liverpool, so some of my cousins went to school with them. My cousin Barbara lived next to George Harrison's family. She would bring him to school when he was the new kid on the block. He was 8 or 9 and Barbara was 13. I was hooked on The Beatles since I was 12 in 1963. I saw them in 1964 on *The Ed Sullivan Show* and that was it. In 1964 The Beatles came to Montreal but I couldn't go – my dad was against it. I was too young at 13, and at the time I was living in Quebec. The next year they came to Toronto and two of my best friends won plane tickets to go and see them. I was so sad that I could not go, as all this time I had been in The Beatles fan club.

The next year, 1966, I learnt that they would tour again so I bought a ticket in January to see them in August in Toronto with the fan club and I went with my best friend who saw them the year before and with Rodrigue, who is now my husband. The tickets were $5.50, and the bus to go from the city of Quebec to Toronto took over eight hours and was $50. So we left two days before and the bus was full – it was Beatles songs for all the trip.

We went to the airport hoping to see them but missed them as they had gone before we got there. And then we went to the hotel, the Sheraton, and waited to see them, but no luck. And then we went and sat outside the Maple Leaf Gardens listening to the afternoon gig. I was just so happy knowing that I would see them in the evening. We finally got to the evening show and it was just magical. And the screaming! It blew my mind. I was just in heaven and got back home two or three days later. I was so blessed and lucky because that was their last year of touring. Later on I saw George in Montreal with Ringo and Ravi Shankar, and saw Paul in 2008. And I saw Ringo in October 2014, and Julian Lennon in 1987. And I'm hoping to see Paul again. I just treasure all my beautiful memories. I've been to Liverpool twice to visit my family and to visit Beatles places. I've been to Abbey Road in London. My hubby is a drummer and our life is full of Beatles stuff. I still live by them. They still rock my world.

I WAS THERE: SHAMO JANIE BISHOP

SUFFOLK DOWNS RACETRACK

18 AUGUST 1966, BOSTON

I went to two Beatles concerts in 1966, one in Boston and then back at Shea. I worked at a cookie factory to get enough money that summer for the concerts and for the train fare to NYC. I loved all four of The Beatles. Each of them was so unique and, as they grew, I grew as well. I even ending up at the Concert for Bangladesh and, later, in India. Together they were such magic and the voices for a generation. I was at Ringo's star on the Hollywood Walk of Fame, where he was giving out cupcakes on his birthday and said to post for peace and love.

At Suffolk Downs, many of the audience were seated at the equivalent of an entire football field's distance away from the band

I WAS THERE: PAM GIORDANO (AGED 15)

I was a hopeless Beatlemaniac, as were a few of my friends. We spent every day talking about them and dreaming of meeting them, so when we heard they would be performing in Boston we knew we had to find a way to go. We lived in Maine, about 170 miles away. We saved our money. I even sold my bike to be able to afford to go. We sent off for tickets and drove the postman crazy until they arrived. I think we paid $5.75.

Then came the task of getting there, so we bribed two of the mothers to chaperone and drive us. We all chipped in for gas and paid for their hotel. My parents were not going to let me go, but they finally agreed after many tears! There were eight of us so there were two cars. When the day finally came, we decorated both cars with Beatle posters and signs that said 'Boston or Bust'. We were quite the sight on I-95. We got there only to find out our room was not available because of an airline strike, so they put us up at the Robin Hood Inn. We all stayed in one room and the chaperones in an adjoining room. It turned out to be more fun.

Well, we made it to the stadium. They were nosebleed seats but we were there and the excitement was electric! The Beatles finally took to the stage in dark green suits with pearl buttons to the deafening sound of screaming! Little did we know this would be their last tour together – I believe they ended the show with 'Yellow Submarine' but don't quote me – it's been 50 years! We were all in a daze and we all had laryngitis after the show. Needless to say, none of us slept that night. We bought out every newspaper in the hotel as soon as they were delivered, to the dismay of the other guests. We woke our chaperones at the crack of dawn to take us to the airport to see the Fab Four off – they weren't too happy with us! We climbed fences to get closer but security kept us at a distance. We got our final look – a lot closer than we got at the stadium. They waved as they boarded the plane.

It was a quiet ride home, our eyes red from crying and voices hoarse from screaming, but our dream had come true. I'm still friends with Jane, who was one of the girls who came on that trip. I look back, 50 years later, and realize how important this experience was in my life. I had a rough childhood and I believe if it had not been for these four guys I would not have got out as well. They were my distraction. They shaped me as a person and my love for music.

MID-SOUTH COLISEUM

19 AUGUST 1966, MEMPHIS

I got my best friend Gwen to go with me. I found out they were coming via *Teen* magazine before it was advertised locally and sent my money in to the local ticket office in Memphis and not even sure at that point if my parents would let me go. The tickets were $5.50 each. I was so excited I could hardly stand it. After the tickets came, my mom called my friend's mom to work out the details. We lived in a small town called Cleveland, Mississippi – 110 miles south and two hours away from Memphis. My mother and my friend's mother worked out that we could spend the night at her grandmother's house, which was down the street from the venue in Memphis. There were two shows that day and we were at the night show. The Ku Klux Klan was in the parking lot, as this was right after the statement that Lennon made about Jesus. They were protesting because of that and there were some people who were burning their albums also in protest of his statement. It was a tense time, but I never felt any of that and was oblivious because of my excitement.

Our seats were about the 27th row on the floor of the Coliseum so not too bad, much better than up in the stands. There was so much noise when they came out, you could not really hear the songs. It did not matter though, just being in the same room with them was enough and such a huge thrill. The opening acts were The Cyrkle and Bobby Hebb. They were both good but it was so hard to contain our excitement for The Beatles to come out. When they did come out the roar was almost deafening. It felt like a dream to me. My friend was not quite as into them as I was, and was a little reserved.

A view from the audience: the Fab Four at the Mid-South Coliseum in Memphis

Everybody was screaming around us and we weren't. I guess we were both shy about that but finally I said, 'I am going to count to three and let's scream'. So that is what we did! We did not scream the whole time like most of the girls did, just in bursts every now and then. How funny.

The show passed so quickly and then it was over. Although we did not want to, we left immediately the show was over to meet Gwen's mother, who was picking us up from the venue. As we drove down Southern Avenue by the Coliseum to Gwen's grandmother's house, a white limo passed us. We thought it was them leaving the Coliseum. It really might have been – you did not see limos, much less white ones, in 1966. And they were on the road from the Coliseum out to Memphis airport, which was close by.

I remember when we got to Gwen's grandmother's we went straight to bed with

❝ I remember getting a birthday card from my daddy ... He enclosed a $10 bill and wrote 'Please do not buy Beatle records with this' ❞

The Beatles on stage at the Mid-South Coliseum

visions of Beatles in our heads and it took a while for me to go to sleep. We did not know about it at the time as there was way too much noise and we were too far back to see it, but a cherry bomb was thrown on stage during the show by someone at the front, scaring The Beatles and being one of the reasons they did not tour any more after that. Going to concerts became a hobby for me and still is. Because of The Beatles

I became a huge British Invasion music fan. I loved so many of those groups and still love to listen to the old songs. Music has been a huge part of my life since The Beatles landed and it continues to be so. Our parents thought we were crazy to like those Beatles but they did not understand the joy they brought. I remember getting a birthday card from my daddy and I still have that card. He enclosed a $10 bill and wrote in the card, 'Please do not buy Beatle records with this money.' The girls in my mother's day could scream over Frank Sinatra. Why couldn't we scream over The Beatles?

I WAS THERE: FLETCHER TERRY (AGED 10)

Fletcher Terry, aged 10, in 1966, the year he saw The Beatles

My mother told me that she had heard that The Beatles had been booked to play two concerts at the Mid-South Coliseum. Since my birthday was on 21 August, my mom asked me what I wanted for my present. 'Would tickets to the Beatles concert do, Fletcher?' My immediate answer was, 'Yeah, Mom, that would be fantastic.' She was one of the first people to order tickets by phone. Back in 1966 there was no internet, no pre-sales, no Ticketmaster or any other sort of ticket brokers. She managed to score tickets close to the stage for the then-expensive price of $5.50 each.

As the day got closer, mom made our travel plans. I was in hog heaven counting down the days until I was able to see my favourite band. Finally that day arrived. We left our home in Cleveland, Mississippi, to make the two-hours-plus drive to Memphis on Highway 61. It seemed to take an eternity to get to Memphis, but we finally arrived and secured a parking space right outside the Mid-South Coliseum.

We noticed a couple of Klan kooks with their picket signs on the way to the Coliseum and a couple of random protestors with their 'Beatles Go Home' signs. But we didn't pay them any attention. We made our way to our seats and waited through what seemed like another eternity until The Beatles hit the stage. The Ronettes were the opening act, followed by Boston band The Remains, whose set lasted about 30 minutes. The Remains were followed by the Pennsylvania group The Cyrkle, who had a huge hit that summer called 'Red Rubber Ball'. After their 30-minute set the last warm-up act was Nashville musician Bobby Hebb, whose big hit that summer was the song 'Sunny'.

Finally, after two hours of warm-up acts, the moment was at hand! The Beatles took the stage around 10.30 p.m.. The audience started screaming at the top of their lungs.

I could barely hear the opening number, 'Rock'n'Roll Music'. Back in 1966 there were no sophisticated sound and PA systems. The Beatles would just run their Vox amps through the arena's PA. You would not believe how loud it was. I have never ever seen or heard anything like it since. And it seemed like everyone and their brother was taking pics. I was almost blinded by all the camera flashes. The second number they played was 'She's a Woman', which featured my favourite Beatle, Paul. Paul was the spokesman for the group and made small talk with the crowd after each song.

The next song they played was 'If I Needed Someone'. About a minute into this song I heard a loud explosion. I was intently watching Paul so I didn't actually see that a cherry bomb had landed close to George Harrison. When the bomb went off, Paul took a quick look to his left to make sure that his bandmates were okay. To their credit, The Beatles never missed a beat. The kid who threw the cherry bomb was arrested. Apparently he was trying to impress his date and, needless to say, she wasn't impressed.

The rest of the concert went by very quickly. The only tune I could really hear well was 'Yesterday'. The gals finally shut their mouths for that one. The Beatles ended the concert with the Little Richard standard 'Long Tall Sally'. Their entire set lasted less than 30 minutes. Mom, my sister Sharon and me slowly made our way out to the car, and for the long drive home to Cleveland. Little did we know that we would never have a chance to see them play live again. This show was my first concert experience. It was also one of the highlights of my life.

CROSLEY FIELD

21 AUGUST 1966, CINCINNATI

I suppose organizers felt a larger venue than the small Cincinnati Gardens used for their 1964 show was needed, so Crosley Field – home of the Cincinnati Reds – was selected. I assumed we would all be going again. I was wrong. Mom wasn't going but my sister was and naturally, despite our five-year difference, I thought it was a given she'd be taking me. Nope. She wanted to go with friends. Ohhh! I burst into tears, until my dad told my eldest sister to take me. Her boyfriend drove us to Crosley Field and we presented our tickets and went in. Rain poured down – but did we care? We were going to see The Beatles. Or so we thought. The rain never let up and

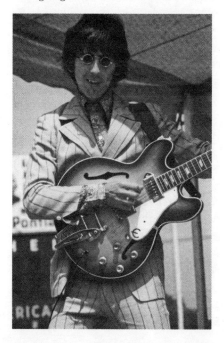

George Harrison, Epiphone semi-acoustic guitar in hand, at the postponed gig at Crosley Field, in August 1966

the show was cancelled. The Beatles never emerged. The concert was called and rescheduled for the following day. An announcement was made that you had to have your ticket stub to re-enter. Many girls were crying because they had thrown theirs away. I was so glad I held on to mine! Off we went to find my sister's boyfriend, happy to know we'd be coming back tomorrow.

I WAS THERE: PAULA BROCK (AGED 13)

I was now a teenager! My parents had bought me and my sister tickets to see The Beatles perform at Crosley Field, the old Cincinnati Reds baseball team's stadium. A few weeks prior to the concert, my sister and I somehow managed to get ourselves grounded. My mom was mad at us and said we couldn't go to the concert. I hid our tickets and was determined to go anyway. We got out of the house somehow and made it to the stadium with some friends. And it rained and rained all day. We knew we were going to be in big trouble for leaving the house, but it all seemed worth it to us. Then something unbelievable happened! They called off the concert due to rain! It was too dangerous for anyone to go on stage.

They told us we could come back the next day with our ticket stubs but I knew I would not be back – that I would be closely watched and forbidden to go since I had snuck out the day before in defiance. Oh, I cried and cried that day. I will never forget the concert I never got to see.

I WAS THERE: DAVE BUTTIG

BUSCH STADIUM

21 AUGUST 1966, ST LOUIS

My dad took my sister and me and the two girls from next door to see The Beatles at Busch Stadium on their last tour in 1966. It was one of the coolest things my dad ever did for me. It was all very spur-of-the-moment. I don't remember if my sister or I asked, or if he offered. It was raining that evening and it seemed like it took the opening acts ages to get on and get off before The Beatles started. And then, before you knew it, they were finished. Tickets were around $6 as opposed to $125.00 to see McCartney in St Louis in 2001 on John Lennon's

Rain couldn't dampen any of the fans' enthusiasm at the Busch Stadium concert

birthday. Anyway, it was a great time. When asked what was the first concert you went to, I can proudly say – The Beatles!

I WAS THERE: VICKIE SCHALL (AGED 15)

SHEA STADIUM

23 AUGUST 1966, NEW YORK

Every single time I told my mother that I wanted to go see The Beatles in concert she would tell me that I couldn't get a ticket until she was ready to get hers. Back then I lived in Newark, New Jersey. My parents were exceptionally strict and there was no way they were about to allow me to travel alone or even with a friend at night. Neither one of my parents drove or even owned a car. By 1966 I got fed up with my mother's continuously putting me off about going to see The Beatles in concert so I took matters into my own hands. Back then, $5.50 for a concert ticket was expensive so I saved my school lunch money and purchased a money order, filled out the form that I found in a magazine and sent for my ticket to see The Beatles at Shea Stadium. I didn't breathe a word of this to anyone, especially not to my father, who was born in Europe and was worse than a dictator when it came to certain things. My mother could be more of a soft touch once in awhile.

When I finally got my ticket in the mail I had to tell my mother and showed her my ticket. She immediately asked me for an order form, which I very happily handed over and she sent for her ticket the same day. There

Ringo and Paul en route to the stage at Shea Stadium, 1966

was no way my parents were going to allow me to take two buses and a subway by myself at night. The #31 bus to downtown Newark; then a one-and-a-half mile walk to the street where the #107 bus would go directly to the Port Authority in New York City; and finally downstairs to look for the subway to Queens, New York, from the subway to Shea. Then the reverse trip back home!

When the big day finally arrived, even though the weather was very warm, I wore a new dress. It was very mod – a bright green Poor Boy top and a skirt of off white, green and blue Tattersall with a bright blue belt. I wore white fishnet stockings and my babydoll shoes that were just like the ones Pattie Boyd wore in photos. I even had my hair done in a flip – I wanted to look stunning for Paul! Oh, the dreams of a teenage Beatle fan.

We finally arrived at Shea and there were vendors hawking all sorts of items. I had saved for months to be able to buy some Beatles souvenirs. I bought the 1966 tour program, a small Beatles diary and a very cheap pair of plastic binoculars. Our seats weren't the greatest – we were in the green section – but who cared? I was breathing the same air as The Beatles! Much to my mother's dismay, her seat was 26 rows away from mine and I was given quite a lecture on not leaving my seat for any reason at all, and especially not to even think of exiting at the end of the concert until she reached the row that I was in. I didn't care. I was finally going to see The Beatles and my beloved Paul in person – live at last! I was surprised to see lots of empty seats. Murray the K was the emcee and I thought he was annoying. I couldn't wait for him to shut up and get off the stage. He introduced his wife, Bobbie The K, and was dancing with her and some other dancers. It was hard to see really well as my seat was pretty high up.

The opening acts were The Ronettes, The Cyrkle, The Remains and Bobby Hebb. No one seemed to care about any of them. We were there to see The Beatles, and when they finally ran out onto the field to the stage, the screaming and girls standing on their seats was endless. My cheap binoculars were, surprisingly, pretty good. I joined the other girls in my row with screaming 'I love you Paul!' with all my heart. An older woman next to me told us, 'Aw shut up, they can't hear you. He can't hear you.' Another girl around my age on the other side of me retorted, 'You shut up! I don't care! Paul can so hear me!' A nice woman in front of me turned around and lent me her high-powered binoculars for a few songs and I had a super view with them. In total they sang 11 songs: 'Paperback Writer', 'I Feel Fine', 'Long Tall Sally', 'I Wanna Be Your Man', 'Yesterday', 'Baby's in Black', 'She's a Woman', 'Nowhere Man', 'Rock and Roll Music', 'Day Tripper' and 'If I Needed Someone'.

It was during 'Day Tripper' that fans started breaking through the barriers and making a run for the stage. A couple of girls got really close before they were grabbed and carried away by the police. Paul egged on John with booing the police and John was like, 'Awww, lookit that.' Paul laughingly told the police, 'Leave 'er alone. I know her!' You could actually hear some of the songs but the rest were muffled by the screaming.

I didn't want that night to end. After the concert, I didn't realize it but I had tears streaming down my face. I was so happy to have finally seen The Beatles and so sad that the concert had ended. My mother met me at the end of my row and, as we left the stadium, told me that a girl was there with her grandmother and that her grandmother had been giving the girl a hard time, telling her 'Stop screaming! You're embarrassing me! Everyone's looking at you!'

No one really cared because all the other girls were screaming too. My mom said she tried to muffle out the noise by sticking tissues in her ears and, if she had known it was going to be a continuous roar of screams, she would've brought ear plugs. In her younger days, mom had gone to see Frank Sinatra in concert and she said seeing The Beatles live in concert and the way all the girls were going bananas made Sinatra's fans look tame in comparison. Then my mom said she doubted if she would ever go to another Beatles concert again. Who knew this would be the last concert tour they ever did! I have the ticket stubs safely tucked away in one of my Beatles scrapbooks. I don't recall exactly which one, as I've got over 100 Beatles scrapbooks!

I WAS THERE: MITCH SILVERSTEIN (AGED 8)

I saw The Beatles with my family in August 1966. My parents surprised my sister and me by getting the tickets mail order. Needless to say we were very excited and we were big Beatles fans. Shea Stadium was constructed at the same time as the New York World's Fair, which ran from 1964 through 1965.

I remember the fanfare when The Beatles played at Shea in 1965 and that they flew in by helicopter to one of the pavilions with a heliport on the roof. I am sure that my parents must have tried to get tickets in 1965 but it sold out. When the day arrived we could not contain ourselves. We got to the stadium and I remember seeing a lot of teenage girls. We made our way to our seats on the mezzanine level, stopping to buy a program of course, and then hunkered in for the evening.

The stage was set up over second base on the baseball field. The field perimeter was lined with security and police. I don't remember the warm-up show too well but I do remember the local NYC radio station WMCA gave the staff a nickname – 'The Good Guys'. They came out in a group and entertained for a bit wearing their yellow shirts with a sketched logo that looked something like a smiley face. Then it was time for The Beatles. They came in through the left-field bull pen in an armoured car. They got out of the back and headed to the stage and the place went wild. Every girl seemed to be screaming as loud as she could. You could barely hear the music!

I remember a couple of attempts by fans darting on the field and quickly being caught and escorted out of the stadium by security. That was fairly exciting for an eight-year-old. They played for about half an hour which, of course, was not long enough – but it was still rather satisfying being part of history.

Mitch, aged just eight when he attended the concert, held onto his Shea Stadium ticket stub

One of their last ever
concerts: The Beatles on
stage at Dodger Stadium, 28
August 1966

As they left in the same armoured car, many fans raced out of the
stands and watched from the open sides of the stadium as the car
made its way out from the stadium grounds and onto the highway.
A subdued quiet fell on the crowd as everyone made their way out.
I also noticed the adjacent fairgrounds were quite far along, in the
demolition of the pavilions.

I sort of felt two great losses at that moment. But also savoured the
enjoyment of these life-changing events.

I WAS THERE: ANNE STASKEWICZ (AGED 15)

DODGER STADIUM

28 AUGUST 1966, LOS ANGELES

By the third and final tour of 1966, the days of small venues and
good seats for The Beatles were over. The stadium tours had begun.
The Beatles were barely visible on the field at Dodger Stadium.
At the grand age of fifteen-and-a-half, I was jaded enough to stop
recording my memories. I still kept mementos like ticket stubs and the
black nylons I wore, even though it was summer in Los Angeles.

By the time I could drive myself to concerts, The Beatles were
done touring the US. My treks to the Hollywood Bowl continued
throughout the Sixties and Seventies. I still attend summer concerts
under the stars, including a recent 50-year anniversary production of
Hair. But I will always remember that first Beatles concert in 1964.

I WAS THERE: JANINE BARNES (AGED 16)

CANDLESTICK PARK

29 AUGUST 1966, SAN FRANCISCO

I went with a few friends. I always wrote the places I heard that they were coming to in the next year, so I got some pretty good seats! I paid $6.50 for my ticket. I took a bus to San Francisco, then another bus to the Park. The show was great! Everyone was waiting for them. An armoured car came out to the field, so everyone thought it was them. But they came out from the dug-out – wow, nobody was expecting that! Girls were running down the field to get to them, but got caught. I had a chance to jump over the fence onto the field but I did promise my dad I'd be good. So I didn't. The Beatles still mean a lot to me. I will always be a Beatles fan!

I WAS THERE: MAUREEN O'REILLY LASLEY (AGED 15)

Whenever I say 'I was at Candlestick' people respond with a look of reverence and a simple 'Oh, wow!' None of us knew it would end up being the final performance of the guys we loved. We had fabulous seats, only seven rows up from the field and straight above the dugout. The stage was set up on second base, as far away from the fans as possible. Memories of the Cow Palace were still fresh in the mind of the authorities. An armoured car was moved onto the field just before they were due to perform, and we all thought they were in there. All eyes were fixed on it but I glanced down at the dugout, a few feet from our seats, just as John appeared followed by the rest. Paul actually looked up at our group and we made brief eye contact. Suddenly I had a life!

Maureen made eye contact with Paul McCartney as The Beatles ran out to play their last ever concert.

The announcer had warned us about staying off the field. They told us how bad the audience had been in Los Angeles and that, if anyone got on the field, they would stop the concert. Naturally, within minutes of the first notes, a group of boys hit the field and began a wild chase around the bases with the police! John quit playing and started taking pictures. During this, the fans began really screaming and crying not to take them away! One of my friends grabbed a policeman and begged 'Don't take them away! It's not us – they are *boys*!' Eventually, boys rounded up, the show went on. We were not blamed – phew! There was a mother with two girls sitting in front of us. I noticed her because she sat and knitted throughout the concert until all the lights went down except for one blue light, firmly planted on Paul, followed by the opening note of 'Yesterday'. She put down her needles and exclaimed 'Now this is what I came for!' Contrary to popular belief, fans knew when to scream and when to weep. There was nothing to be heard except Paul's beautiful voice and the sniffling of fifty-five thousand girls.

Driving the 180 miles home to Red Bluff, California, my friends and I sang. I laughed and cried and drove my friend Laurie's father nuts. But at midnight I turned 15, and I knew I'd had the most magical birthday I would ever experience. The magic of The Beatles is really hard to explain. I spent a career as a teacher and a librarian, but I can still feel that special feeling, a feeling that has never been replicated. In thinking about that night, and remembering 29 August 1966, I know I have memories that most people will never experience. The feelings transcended everything that was wrong with teenage angst and political America. The Beatles understood me completely. They helped me grow up, to become a critical thinker and to care about the world. That's a lot for a group of musicians.

I WAS THERE: DIANNE HICKS (NÉE WINGERT, AGED 16)

I was in love with Paul from the first time I saw him on the *Ed Sullivan Show*. He was my first love, at the age of 13, and I imagined all kinds of ways I could meet him and imagined kissing him with my pillow. This was real teenage-girl stuff, I hate to admit. Unfortunately, I never got to meet him. I still hope I am at the right time and place for it to happen some day! I would go to my middle school with my turquoise transistor radio and listen to the local radio station play Beatles songs while I had recess and would sneak it into my lift-up desk and hide it from the teacher. I even wrote a letter to Paul when I was 14, but it got intercepted by the teacher and it got sent to the principal's office. I ended up being called

Dianne survived peltings of jelly beens ringing ears and a bloody nose to see The Beatles three times

into the office to explain the letter that disrupted the class. I was humiliated and never got the letter back. It wasn't until about ten years ago that I decided to finally write and send a letter to Paul. I got his LA address on a website and sent the letter. I told no one – not even my husband. Two days later, I got a phone call from James McCartney (Paul's son who was living in the Pasadena home). That was a shocker, that's for sure. I don't know if Paul ever got my letter but James said he would give it to him. I never heard.

I saw The Beatles three times and I feel so lucky. Each time was different, each time so special. I had just turned 14 when the Beatles first came to San Francisco. My best friend at the time, Pam Riley, was an only child and I got the invite to go with her to see The Beatles at the Cow Palace. We got there about 2.30pm and the show started at 8. As we entered, we saw the stage and the famous drum with The Beatles logo. The place filled up fast once the doors opened and I felt sorry for the acts that opened before them as the crowd chanted 'We want The Beatles!' and nothing would satisfy them until The Beatles were on stage. Once they entered the arena, the loudest, most piercing screams assaulted your ears. I had to cover mine because of the shrillness of the screams. As the show went on, I would get pelted by thrown jelly babies – and they hurt! All around me the girls were screaming. I wasn't one of them because I wanted to hear The Beatles but that was just about impossible. After they left the stage, I walked up and collected a couple of the jelly beans from the stage and a flash cube from a camera and saved them as a souvenir. I have them to this day, except the beans kind of disintegrated. Once I got home, my ears were still ringing and I got a bloody nose from all the excitement. But it was all worth it because I actually saw The Beatles!

In 1965, they returned to the Cow Palace and this time I was able to have a ride since my sister Mary Ann drove and was available to take us. She brought her best friend, Joanne Mahoney. Tickets cost $7.50 a person and our assigned seats were way in the back. The Beatles looked so small, unlike my experience of the year before. I don't remember the selling of T-shirts or any kind of souvenirs. If there was, I would have wanted some for sure. There was the deafening screaming once again and a too short concert. I could hardly see them or hear them but I was there.

In 1966, Candlestick Park hosted The Beatles. My sister's boyfriend's sister Diane was a big Beatles fan, like me, and drove us to the South San Francisco location for what was a night-time concert. We had tickets around the home plate, lower level, and there was a fence obstructing our view. In those days, I didn't have a camera with me to get any photos, unfortunately. I remember them running on the field in khaki-colored outfits way out in the center outfield. There was a breeze and the temperature was cool for an August night. There were the screaming girls again but I never would have dreamed it was to be The Beatles' last concert.

When I hear their music, it brings be to another place and time when life was innocent and the music made me happy. To this day, when I play their music, it brings happiness to my soul. They were a big, big, part of my teen years and way beyond. It is so hard to explain to people the craziness of the Beatles era. The whole British Invasion was the best thing that came along in the Sixties. I am so happy to have been a young teenage girl with a first crush on a band that would take the world by storm. They grew up with me and I am forever grateful for the music and happiness they brought to my life.

The show at Candlestick Park in San Francisco was to be the final concert by The Beatles.

POSTSCRIPT

Recollections, sightings and chance
encounters with The Beatles, after
they ceased playing live

I WAS THERE: CHRISTINE TOMS

The only memory I have of The Beatles was meeting John Lennon and
Yoko on the Brecon Beacons many years ago. They were in a Mini.
They stopped the car and chatted to us for some time. Julian Lennon was
with them, although very young at the time. We did get some photos but
unfortunately I did not keep them.

I WAS THERE: NORMAN SCOTT

I got to know a singer called Bobby Shafto, who was a Sixties singer.
He actually started off as Lionel Bart's tea boy. He was a good-
looking lad and he had a voice. Through him I met this guy called
Terry Doran. The Beatles do that track about a man in the motor
trade? 'She's Leaving Home'. Terry Doran is the man in the motor
trade. He was very good friends with Brian Epstein. Apart from
managing The Beatles, Brian Epstein had a car showroom and Terry
Doran's first job with Brian Epstein was running Bridor Motors. It
was called Bridor because of Bri, after Brian, and Dor after Doran.
And they only dealt in secondhand posh cars – Rolls-Royces and
Bentleys and Jags and things like that. I was only about 19, 20 at the
time and I still lived at home.

Terry Doran would borrow cars out of his showroom, and they
were all posh cars, and we'd got out for the night for a drink or a
meal or to go and see a show. And he came round to my parents
house and he'd come in and wait for me, so whenever he came round
we'd have a posh car parked outside. I always had to laugh because
obviously my neighbours never knew it was the same guy borrowing
different cars from the showroom. Terry Doran went on to become
the managing director of Apple. I have got his business card.

I did actually go to a party at Brian Epstein's house. Terry Doran invited me to that. That was rather strange. He was a strange man. I didn't get to know him at all really. There must have been about 15 people there. It was only a little gathering. I seem to recall drinking vodka and lime. And I'd never drunk vodka in my life. It was either vodka and lime or gin and lime. Whatever it was I'd never touched shorts. The glasses seemed to be like buckets. They just seemed like huge glasses.

But Brian sat on his own all night, just telling people to enjoy themselves, which I thought was rather strange. That was his London flat. I went to Terry Doran's house and he used to get the promos of Beatles pre-releases. Which was great when I was a DJ because I could play a Beatles record before it was out. I've got a few advanced copies of singles. I kept all those.

I WAS THERE: ALBERT HERNANDEZ DE LEON

I remember girls in school crying when Ringo got married, furious when John started hanging out with Yoko, and simply hysterical when rumours of a break-up started circulating. By the summer of 1967, flower power had hit and The Beatles were in India with the Maharishi. Then 'Revolution 9' was released. To me that was a total turn-off, although looking back on it I did not really listen to the lyrics attentively. But Yoko "coming between John and Paul" was something I would not soon forgive, or forget.

I WAS THERE: GRAHAM COATES

SOHO

SEPTEMBER/OCTOBER 1967, LONDON

I was 12 when I got a bike for Christmas in 1962. I couldn't ride it until late February due to the snow. But when I did finally go cycling with a friend around Hainault and Epping, wherever we stopped 'Please Please Me' was being played. After Christmas 1963 the family parties constantly played 'She Loves You' and 'I Want to Hold Your Hand' and that's what got me liking The Beatles. I eagerly waited for each release after that. I first saw John, Paul and Ringo when they were editing *Magical Mystery Tour* in Old Compton Street, Soho, in September and October 1967.

I was working for FD&H Music Publishers at the time and used to walk over to where they were working with my friend Colin and stare up at them bobbing about on the first floor and they would be occasionally stare back. Paul would be his usual self and John on one occasion put his thumb on the end of his nose and waved his fingers at us. But on one occasion John came out and walked directly towards us. We both froze, and as he brushed past us we looked round and he was gone. There was a door that he could have gone into, but we didn't hear it open or close. Wherever he went, it was a complete mystery to us.